FERRIES AND FERRYMEN

Also by G. Bernard Wood

YORKSHIRE TRIBUTE (Methuen)
HISTORIC HOMES OF YORKSHIRE (Oliver & Boyd)
WHAT TO DO FROM SCARBOROUGH (Oliver & Boyd)
NORTH COUNTRY PROFILE (Country Life)
YORKSHIRE (Batsford)
SMUGGLERS' BRITAIN (Cassell)
SECRET BRITAIN (Cassell)

In preparation

COUNTRYSIDE BRIDGES

G. Bernard Wood

FERRIES and FERRYMEN

CASSELL · LONDON

CASSELL & COMPANY LTD
35 Red Lion Square, London WC1
Melbourne, Sydney, Toronto
Johannesburg, Auckland

© *G. Bernard Wood 1969*
First published 1969

S.B.N. 304 93402 X

Printed in Great Britain
by Ebenezer Baylis and Son, Ltd.
The Trinity Press, Worcester, and London
F.569

To

Michael and Margaret

CONTENTS

Acknowledgements xi

Introduction xv

1. Monastic Heritage 1

2. Ferry Battles and Fen Strategy 22

3. Elephants, Live Carp, and *Scandal* 31

4. Water Music on London River 41

5. Hazards on the Solent 51

6. By Ferry Stages into Cornwall 63

7. Around the Severn Sea 83

8. The Welsh Story 94

9. Merseyside Memories 107

10. Lakeland Ghost and Solway Smuggler 118

11. Prince Bishops and their Ferries 130

12. Scottish Waters 140

Index 157

ILLUSTRATIONS

Photographs are by the author unless otherwise stated

after page 14
The fair ford which gave its name to the beautiful Cotswold village of Fairford
The old ferry-house still stands by Lendal Bridge which occupies the site of the Lendal Ferry over the Ouse at York
St. Christopher carrying the Christ-child, from a fifteenth-century woodcut
Winter silhouette of the ferry at Naburn, near York, in 1936
Thomas Ferres, the ferryman who eventually became Lord Mayor of Hull
The eighteenth-century wooden toll-bridge which replaced the ferry at Selby, Yorks
The Holderness hunt using the ferry at Wawne, Yorks, about 1905 (*R.A. Alec-Smith, Winestead*)
The *Tattershall Castle* crossing the Humber in a February haze
The steam ferry between Southwold and Walberswick, Suffolk, in 1900 (*Norman Parker, Southwold*)
St. Jude presents a boat to the parish church of Wiggenhall St. Germans, Norfolk
The ferry quay at Woodbridge, Suffolk, with its tide-mill
Ferry-boats on the Thames, from the bird's-eye-view map of Surrey in George Bickham's *British Monarchy* (1751)

after page 62
The coat-of-arms of the Company of Watermen and Lightermen
The Fowey–Bodinnick Ferry, Cornwall, immortalized by Sir Arthur Quiller-Couch in *Shining Ferry*
The floating bridge crossing Poole Harbour, Dorset
This sea-horse ferry takes visitors from Bigbury, Devon, to Burgh Island (right) at high tide
A carving in Zennor Church, Cornwall, represents the mermaid who fell in love with the squire's son
A hand-pulled ferry crossing the Wye below Symonds Yat

The ancient Britons probably used coracles like this one, made by Will Jones of Cenarth, Cardiganshire

The Conway Ferry in 1795. The coach is ready to take the passengers further on their journey through North Wales (*National Library of Wales, Aberystwyth*)

The Woodside Ferry, Birkenhead, in 1814

Arctic conditions on the Mersey in February 1895. A paddle ferry-boat pushes its way through blocks of ice

The *Duke of Lancaster* in dock at Heysham, Lancs

One of the milestones at Cartmel, Lancs, for travellers crossing Morecambe Bay over the sands

after page 110

The Sandside Ferry was operated over part of the Kent estuary for the owners of Dallam Tower nearby

The Windermere Ferry leaving the Claife shore where the ghostly crier used to summon the ferryman after dark

Motor-launch landings at Keswick, Cumberland

The ferry jetty on Roa Island near Barrow-in-Furness. The tiny row-boat serves Piel Island in the distance

Around 1900 Messrs Vickers of Barrow-in-Furness operated this steam ferry for their workmen living on Walney Island

Sunderland Ferry over the River Wear, Co. Durham

This pony-trap took the author to Holy Island (seen in distance) in 1935; the poles mark the safe route and the box-like refuge is for pedestrians who may be trapped by the rising tide

An enamelled glass window at Low Hall, Yeadon, Yorks, shows Mary, Queen of Scots, landing at Leith

David MacBrayne—the man to whose ferry services the Western Highlands and Islands owe so much (*David MacBrayne Ltd., Glasgow*)

Ballachulish Ferry, Argyll, in its grand mountain setting (*Laird Parker, Oban*)

R.M.S. *Columbia*, one of the MacBrayne fleet serving the Western Isles from Oban, Argyll (*Laird Parker, Oban*)

The short sea ferry route to Ireland formerly began at this harbour at Port Patrick, Wigtownshire

ACKNOWLEDGEMENTS

An author's indebtedness to other people for information, suggestions and practical help can never be sufficiently acknowledged. Below, however, I gladly make known a few of those whose help has been outstanding in the preparation of some part of this book.

Colonel Rupert Alec-Smith, Winestead; Miss G. Redstone, Woodbridge; Alan Jobson, Felixstowe; Thomas Bell, Gravesend; Bernard C. Short, Poole; Miss Foy Quiller-Couch, Helston; Brigadier C. E. Tryon-Wilson, Dallam Tower, Westmorland; Richard Gill, Portinscale. Librarians all over the country have scoured their files for my benefit, and, as always, I am particularly grateful to my friend, J. B. Shackleton, M.A., A.L.A., head of the Aireborough Public Libraries, for so assiduously rounding up certain 'off-beat' references. Museum curators have also come to my aid, where necessary, as did the Keeper of the Scottish Record Office, Edinburgh. Then, various ferry owners and ferrymen have chatted to me with such evident satisfaction to themselves, conveying so much out-of-the-way knowledge in the process, as to suggest that their calling is about the happiest in Britain.

I am most grateful to the following for allowing me to photograph or use material in their possession:

The Keeper of the Rylands Library, Manchester
Colonel Rupert Alec-Smith
The Company of Watermen and Lightermen
The National Library of Wales
Brigadier C. E. Tryon-Wilson
The Sunderland Library
Mr. and Mrs. H. M. Pickard
The Trinity House, Hull

In the extensive 'voyage' which this book offers, my wife and one or two others have been willing companions—if occasionally requisitioned for the purpose. I hope the final result, between these covers, will soothe them into acquiescence with any further exploratory venture of mine!

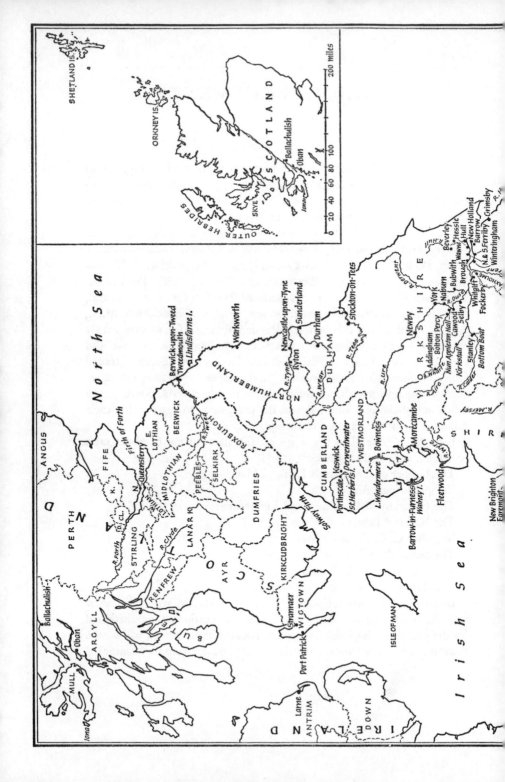

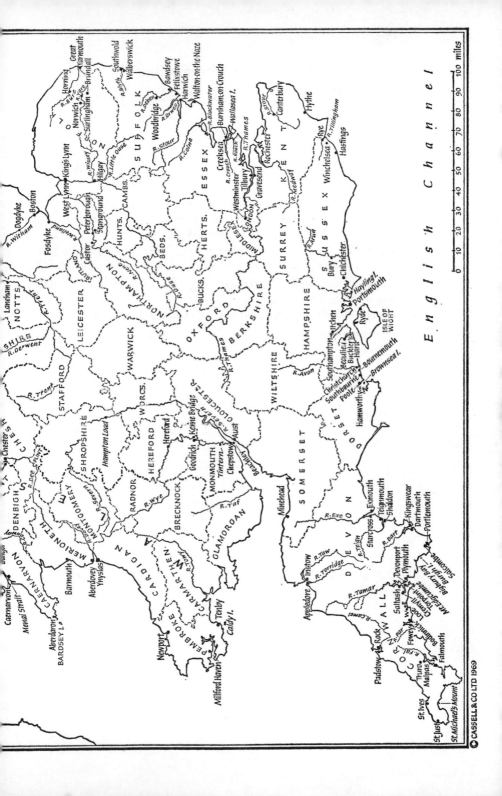

English Channel

0 10 20 30 40 50 60 70 80 90 100 miles

© CASSELL & CO LTD 1969

SOME BOOKS CONSULTED

The History of Kirkstall Forge, Rodney Butler, 1945 (private publication).
Story of Southwold, F. Jenkins; Cowell, 1949.
Essays in Cornish History, Charles Henderson; Barton, 1963.
Shining Ferry, Sir Arthur Quiller-Couch; Dent, 1905. (Quotations used are by the kind permission of the publishers.)
A Review of the Records of the Conway and the Menai Ferries, Henry Rees Davies; University of Wales Press, 1942.
Birkenhead Priory and the Mersey Ferry, R. Stewart-Brown; State Assurance Co. Ltd., Liverpool, 1925.
Wanderings and Excursions, J. Ramsay MacDonald; Cape, 1925.

INTRODUCTION

'Ferry me over the water, do boatman do.'
'If you've a penny in your purse, I'll ferry you.'

One of my earliest memories is that of clambering down some rickety old stairs which the sea covered at every flowing tide and stepping into a nut-shell of a boat. Bigger vessels were moored nearby; fishing smacks, yachts, and maybe one or two passenger steamers. Yet for me, at that moment, all the spell of maritime adventure was in the small, bobbing vessel below and the grizzled boatman waiting there to collect our fares. My aunt had got me out of bed early that summer morning and we were to cross the harbour, before breakfast, by *ferry*. I can still recapture the thrill which then elevated my young soul!

Other people have felt the same way about ferries. Robert Louis Stevenson always had the right attitude to wayfaring; amongst his delights were 'the mills and the ruins, the ponds and the *ferries* . . . here is an inexhaustible fund of interest for any man with eyes to see or twopence-worth of imagination to understand with!' In 'The Joys of the Road' Bliss Carman adds a feminine demand, which I'm sure R.L.S. would gallantly have conceded, namely, 'A scrap of gossip at the ferry'.

In this book of mine there will be gossipings at many wayside ferries, and abundant evidence of that kind of interest which Stevenson promised.

Britain had its ferries in Roman times, and probably before. As part of their public welfare work, the monasteries sponsored innumerable ferries throughout the land. Ferries have been used by kings and queens, lords and ladies, prelates—and poltroons. They have served both romance and treachery. Around them has drifted all the flotsam and jetsam of human life. Poets have sung their praises. Travellers have groaned over their shortcomings.

And all the time, through fair weather and foul, and through national perils too, the immemorial ferrymen has gone to and fro, justifying his existence by just plying his oars and telling his tale. This book is in part a tribute to him.

Here I must interpose a word or two about fords. Fords and ferries have often been near cousins; sometimes even twins. A stream that might be waded over, or crossed on horseback in normal conditions, might demand the services of a ferryman when spring rains lifted the water level.

One of the most attractive fords known to me is that at Fairford, in the Cotswold country. With the old mill at one side and the Gothic church at the other, the 'fair ford' of history makes a lovely picture. And if there are no written records of a ferry service here, it is at any rate good to find some of the church's famous windows enlivening their Biblical scenes by occasionally portraying the much-ferried upper Thames, not far away.

St. Christopher carrying the Christ-child over the river also shares the ethos of our main subject. As we shall see, giving pick-a-backs to way-farers has often been part of a ferryman's task. St. Christopher, now generally regarded as patron saint of wayfarers, might well be acclaimed in particular by ferrymen the world over. A fine, early fifteenth-century woodcut preserved at the Rylands Library, Manchester, shows the traditional scene with all its appeal: the ferryman's thatched hut, the water-mill, wild creatures of earth and stream—and the hermit shining a lantern as St. Christopher, holding the miraculously flowered staff, brings his holy burden safely to shore.

Ferries help to preserve the character of any given area, especially islands. A bridge is something of an intrusion; however much of a boon to motorists, a bridge means that all sense of reaching an island may be lost. The island's mystique has gone. Achill Island in County Mayo is no longer the other-worldly place it was when a boat was needed for the cross-ing. Garnish Island in Bantry Bay is truer to itself; different ferrymen may pester you for your custom, even as you arrive at Glengariff, but that is small price to pay for genuine seclusion. I devoutly hope that no apostle of so-called Progress ever builds a bridge over to the Isle of Skye. The various car ferries that serve Skye from the Scottish mainland provide all necessary links, without disturbing the island's integrity. The essential way to Skye is still 'over the sea'.

During the last century or so, improved roads and bridges have put hundreds of small ferries out of business. Whether one regrets this change or not, many of the older ferries make a fascinating study. Even when a ferry has vanished, it has often bequeathed a tell-tale name, or a tradition worth investigating. Many a bygone ferry, therefore, is still 'serviceable'— by offering the traveller something instructive and pleasant to remember.

In view of so many ferry closures, one poet's lines—suggesting that the louder one calls for the ferryman the sounder he sleeps—take on a new significance! Yet readers may be astonished to hear that so many ferries do persist, all over Britain. Not only car ferries, of which the R.A.C. Handbook lists over forty, but literally scores provided as of old for foot passengers.

In ancient legend Charon* is for ever ferrying his shadowy passengers over the Styx. A vessel on the lake-moat that surrounds Walton Hall, near Wakefield in West Yorkshire, was long used as a goods ferry to the Waterton's island home and came to be known as Charon's Barge, perhaps because it later accompanied the mortal remains of Charles Waterton, the nineteenth-century naturalist, to his grave at the far end of the lake.

We shall hear many other strange episodes on our ferry tour of Britain. Floating bridges, cross-Channel steamers and hovercraft may have introduced a new era, but while ferries of the older sort† remain let us too, like well-seasoned travellers, hail the ferryman and hear his manifold tale to the music of rippling water.

---

* Excavations of ancient sites have frequently revealed human skeletons with an obol in the mouth, in readiness for Charon's fare.

† These include pontoon ferries, and chain-ferries. The first was a bridge-of-boats, provided during some temporary emergency. With local variations the chain-ferry worked on a principle neatly described by William Camidge, in 1890, when dealing with the Naburn Ferry, near York. He wrote: 'They fixed a chain from bank to bank, which lays on the bed of the river; this chain is drawn up by a wheel or drum fixed on the centre of the boat; when the boat is travelling, the chain works over the drum, which is provided with spikes on its surface, and every fifth link of the chain falls on to one of the spikes . . . and by that means the propelling power is obtained. At each end of the boat pulleys and rollers are fixed to guide the chain on to the drum. The wheel is fixed on the left hand . . . of the boat.'

CHAPTER ONE

MONASTIC HERITAGE

In Yorkshire the most notable ferry is that operating from Hull over the Humber. Its first known progenitor was the river passage effected by the Romans when they pushed their highway, Ermine Street, north from Lincoln. Nineteen hundred years of ferrying, within a few miles of the same spot!

Nearly all the tributary rivers of the Humber have had their ferries, too, and because Yorkshire is my native county it seems natural to hail our first ferrymen on what are, to me, home waters.

The Humber Ferry, which has outlived most of the others in the county, will be given its full due later. Meanwhile, let us run a finger along the map, westwards from Hull, and follow the River Aire. That exploratory finger will soon discover Kirkstall Abbey on the bank of the River Aire, near Leeds. Today, one of the pleasures of visiting the abbey (despite its ruined state) is being able to view the place from a boat on the river, much as the monks would have done when ferrying themselves across from the south bank.

Towards the end of the eighteenth century, the Butlers and Beecrofts who ran Kirkstall Forge created a ferry service, barely half a mile up-river from the abbey. There was an historic echo, here, for it is claimed that Kirkstall Forge, now a world-famous industrial concern, originated from a small forge nearby with which the Cistercian lay fraternity produced their own tools and utensils. What of the eighteenth-century ferry? This crossed the River Aire, thus providing a vital link with the Leeds and Liverpool Canal (opened in 1771) which then carried most of the firm's goods. In *The History of Kirkstall Forge*, privately published in 1945 by Rodney Butler, the then Managing Director, several sketch maps show this ferry. It evidently operated from a point between the directors' gardened dwellings and the workmen's cottages.

Here, indeed, was a self-contained village, with its own brewhouse, chapel, and shop. Like any other village, this one had its farmland too, including fields known significantly as Great and Little Vesper Close. When work stopped for the day, and the ferry was stilled, workmen 'used to net salmon by the tail races from the water wheels'.

In October 1792 a ferry-boat christened the *Royal George* was launched, amid suitable rejoicings. It was large enough to take a horse and cart, and as the firm's output then included such items as shovels, spades, and patten rings (worn on boot soles to keep them clear of mud), clock faces and spitoons, frying pans, pudding dishes and anvils, one can judge how their customers all over the country, and as far afield as America, were dependent upon that small ferry in a bend of the 'monastic' River Aire.

But there was a snag. The passage could be dangerous. Housewives awaiting new kitchen utensils, or Sheffield manufacturers clamouring for anvils and vices, would have no idea of the hazards entailed. In January 1798 the firm begged Lord Cardigan, through his agent, to build a bridge at this place, as 'four persons have lost their lives at different periods by crossing the Ferry; and the lives of our men and horses are continually exposed to imminent danger . . . there is not an individual about the works but who is frequently exposed to danger by the crossing of the River in our Boats.'

But the owner of the estate turned a deaf ear. The bridge remained a pipe-dream. Not until the railway appeared on the site half-way through the nineteenth century was the ferry relieved of its varied cargoes—and the river robbed of further victims.

During the eighteenth and nineteenth centuries, the wool and coal trades used two ferries which had long been in existence on the River Calder, namely, at Bottom Boat and Stanley, both near Wakefield. Even by 1640 the Bottom Boat Ferry, which could accommodate horse-drawn waggons laden with corn, had more than local importance. In that year the ferry-boat was in such poor condition, however, that ten passengers were drowned. Petitioners for a new boat stated, somewhat ungrammatically, that the old one was 'altogether useless to the country and neighbouring towns to their great damage'. Four years later a new boat was provided, at a cost of £16 4s. 6d. No fewer than twenty townships in the area were expected to pay their share—which they did, after suitable proddings and admonitions by the local constables.

I used to visit Wakefield frequently on business and the name, Bottom Boat—then brandished as a destination sign on some of the noisy old trams—always intrigued me. Not until many years later did I meet Mr. H. C. Haldane, whose father would recall the Bottom Boat and Stanley ferries. Both father and son were farmers, living at Clarke Hall, quite near the two ferries. Several subsequent visits to this lovely old house have enabled me to visualize some of the people who crossed the Calder at one or other of these places.

Before the Haldanes arrived there would be Redman Favell of Normanton, whose name and the date 1712 are scratched on an upper window-pane; and earlier still, Benjamin Clarke himself. There can be no doubt that when the Justices ordered a new boat for Stanley Ferry, in 1671, my friend's forbears at Clarke Hall, and other landowners, would pay something towards the cost—£13 6s. 8d. A Wakefield man built this boat, which had to be large and sturdy enough to convey three horses at a time, plus foot passengers. This done, the Clerk of the Peace and two Justices appointed a 'sufficient' boatman, who had to keep the vessel in good trim.

This little cameo of rural life would hardly be complete without some glimpse of the ferryman. About the time of which we speak, the ferryman was an innkeeper called Bramham. He agreed to carry the subscribers free of charge, but others were subject to the following tolls:

each foot passenger	one penny
a horse	twopence
cart or gig with one horse	fourpence
cart or gig with two horses	sixpence
cart or gig with three horses	eightpence
a waggon with four horses	one shilling
horned cattle, each	twopence
pigs, each	one penny
sheep, per score	sixpence

From the above tariff it will be seen that Bramham either overloaded the boat, when carrying a waggon-and-*four*, or had managed to coax a larger boat from the subscribers.

Stanley Ferry was still operating in the 1850s with one James Bolton as ferryman. It might have continued much longer, but for the Aire and Calder Canal which increasingly diverted traffic from the time-honoured crossing. A few years earlier, during the war with France, the outraged ferrymen and their supporters had the grim satisfaction of seeing their competitors, the canal-boat hauliers, taken off in great numbers by the Press Gang. Even in recent years there was a flashback to the old methods. Numerous barge-horse ferries would be seen at work on the canal, taking the horses from one bank to the other where the tow-path changed sides. It was a pleasant sight, and gave momentary respite to the poor animals.

The River Wharfe once had as many ferries as bridges. It was costly to build and maintain a bridge, especially as this turbulent river was liable to rise quickly and sweep aside all man-made obstacles. For centuries the dales' folk relied very largely on stepping-stones, at low water, fords or ferries.

One ferry crossed the Wharfe a mile or so below Bolton Priory. A bridge erected at this spot in 1314 by the Prior's mother must have succumbed to the temperamental river long before; the present twin-arched bridge is mainly of the seventeenth century, but at the end nearer the Priory there still stands the Ferry House, representing the in-between period. It is a charming stone cottage, and indoors, carved on a well-preserved oak wall-beam, there is this injunction:

> Thou that passys by thys way,
> One Ave Marie here thou'lt say.

A clear survival from monastic times.

This inscribed beam was shown to me quite recently by the wife of the present tenant, Donald Wood. 'This room was the chapel,' she said, 'and beneath the lettered beam there used to be a wooden screen covered with prayers'—probably Hail Marys. The monks had one or two of their fraternity always on duty here, and wayfarers using the ferry would drop in to beseech the Almighty to grant them a safe crossing, or to give thanks for a safe landing.

Though now hidden, part of the cobbled way leading down to the water still exists. When the Wharfe got up to its tricks again and flooded the premises in 1966, a bit of the old ferry landing was disturbed. On the day my son and I called, the river was quiescent and clear. Unfortunately, we were a few months too late to see the metal ring to which the ferry-boat might have been tethered, long ago, when not in use; and too late by several centuries to overhear any muttered orisons from that little chapel.

Addingham, roughly half-way between Bolton and Ilkley, kept its ferry until early this century. The path leading down to the old crossing, from the south bank, now serves a newer foot-bridge, but the ferry once came triumphantly into its own. Ilkley's sole bridge had been washed away by flood water. Having their small ferry, Addingham folk could still negotiate the Wharfe and crow over their Ilkley neighbours. A water-colour by Gilbert Foster, probably painted about 1900, shows this lovely bend of the Wharfe at Addingham, with a flat-bottomed ferry-boat holding three passengers being hauled across by a woman pulling hard on the guide-rope at waist level.

I always feel glad that it was by ferry that I first approached some well-loved spot. Going the last stage or so by boat seemed somehow fitting.

You paid your coin, and sat back while the man at the oars, or pulling on the guide-rope, chatted about this and that, giving you plenty of time to savour the surroundings and enter into the spirit of the place.

It was in such a way that I once drew near Bolton Percy, in Lower Wharfedale. The ferryman took me over the river from Ulleskelf. Here the Wharfe is quieter, deeper and full of dark shadows. I cannot now recall what we talked about, in that little swirling piece of rural England. Not fish, because I am no angler. Perhaps it was his age-old craft—practised here in medieval times by one Roger le Feryman—that loosened our tongues. Forty years are apt to dim the memory. But I do recall what followed. Had I gone round by road to the village, instead of by the Wharfe, I should have entirely missed a most picturesque trestle foot-bridge over the intervening swampy meadows. This was (and still is) a place apart; the meadows bright with kingcups and flaming osiers, and the bridge wriggling across, like a causeway purposely devised for fen country and its strange little people. It is a place reserved for those who come upon the village slowly, from the knowing, conspiratorial river.

Ryther Ferry, a mile down-river, was still active in its desultory way until a few months ago. The last crossing marked the end of an era, hereabouts, but whether the villagers realized this, I cannot say. Somebody I met, in a neighbouring village, told me that she had often ferried over, at Ryther, with Lady Dawson of Nun Appleton Hall. In 'cooeeing' for the ferryman, as she usually did, Lady Dawson was simply echoing the call made by some nuns of the Appleton convent centuries before. The ferry they chiefly used, however, was a busier one then crossing the Wharfe half a mile away.

The Appleton sisterhood consisted mainly of women of rank who had 'retired to a nunnery' for anything but the true vocation. To the repeated annoyance of their superiors, these women frequented the waterside 'where the course of strangers daily resort'. This gossiping venue was the Appleton Ferry, then so important that two alehouses stood nearby—another source of concern to the Prioress.

Today there is no sign of that ferry. But, on the north bank of the river, Nun Appleton Hall gathers to itself the few scanty remains of the old Cistercian convent. There is also a legend which tells of Sister Hylda, whose frightful apparition only ceased to haunt the nunnery after a wandering palmer was exposed as the Friar John who had wronged her. To those easy-going sisters, the Appleton Ferry and its patrons must have been a constant menace.

As the Appleton Ferry continued vigorously until the eighteenth century, it would be known and occasionally used by General Thomas Fairfax, who came to live at Nun Appleton Hall about 1637. Andrew Marvell, the poet, who was tutor to Fairfax's daughter, Mary, said that the River Wharfe here 'curls like a snake'. It does indeed, as I saw for myself, years ago, on visiting the hall. Lady Dawson took me down to the waterside where, only a few yards from the old ferry, Sir Benjamin, her husband, had created a dock for their yacht.

Nearby the Wharfe 'glides gently into the Ouse', which we must now follow in a northerly direction for a few miles before turning again towards the Humber.

In his fascinating book, *The Yorkshire Ouse*, Baron F. Duckham names seventeen different ferries on this broad river, besides a number that once served the citizens of York almost on their own doorstep. Several ferries were in the upper reaches of the river. One envies those who could ferry across the Ouse from or to the sequestered village of Nun Monkton; many folk must have reached the beautiful priory church by this route up to fairly recent years, though in the reign of Henry VIII the ferry was privately owned. Poppleton and Clifton both enjoyed a similar service which, before the advent of the motor age, must have been a great boon because no bridge spans the Ouse, even today, between York and Aldwark, about twelve miles up-river.

Until half-way through the nineteenth century the Ouse at York would be almost as busy with ferry traffic as the Thames itself. Apart from Ouse Bridge, in the town centre, the only crossings were those worked by ferrymen. These fellows must have done a roaring trade, for ever since the Romans established their headquarters here, York has been *busy*. As the first Ouse Bridge, dating from the twelfth century, was exceedingly narrow, hump-backed and bounded by houses and the loathsome town gaol, it is easy to see why the majority of folk favoured the ferries. Monks and clergy; merchants and civic dignitaries; wandering pedlars, jugglers and mountebanks; minstrels, songmen from the Minster; apothecaries; loud-mouthed soldiers; fine ladies and fishwives; pilgrims—what a motley company would fill those boats day in and day out.

The York Corporation House Books enable us to see one of the chief ferries in operation. Known as Lendal Ferry, it dated back to medieval times. In 1477 the ferry was leased by the Corporation to John Newton 'for twenty years at five marks rent per annum'. Much of Newton's patronage would come from the monks and lay-brethren of St. Mary's Abbey nearby. After the Dissolution the authorities were more cautious in their lettings, for one reads that on 19 February 1545–6 'the round tower on the west side of the Ouse forenest [facing] St. Leonard's Landing, and the common ferry were granted to Janet Collynwood, widow, until Whit Sunday next, for which she was to pay 5s. 6d. But if anyone else would offer more rent . . . after Whit Sunday, she was to be excluded.' Poor Janet!

With the next few entries the tempo quickens considerably. '18 June 1632. The ferry-boat and round tower at St. Leonard's Landing were to be taken out of Henry Wharton's possession and an honest man was to be provided to use it. Henry Wharton was to be imprisoned and have irons laid on him, for his misbehaviour.'

As to the nature of this misbehaviour—silence, but twelve days later there is a development: 'Henry Wharton, imprisoned in the low gaol, was asked if he would sell the ferry-boat. Wharton answered that before he would part with the boat he would part with his life.' One might have expected the authorities to seize the boat; instead there is this rather tepid comment: 'Enquiries were to be made for an old boat to be used as the ferry-boat.' Presumably the inquiries were fruitless, for just over a week later, according to the records, 'a ferry-boat was to be built at Selby, or York, whichever is the cheaper'.

By October of the same year Wharton is still languishing in gaol, for we read: 'Henry Wharton's wife and children were to have 2s. weekly from the poor rates, provided they did not disturb the possession of the tower and [new] ferry-boat at St. Leonard's Landing.'

Six months pass by and Wharton is still beyond the pale. By now James Best runs the St. Leonard's Ferry, 'and anyone who used the old ferry-boat belonging to Wharton . . . should be arrested.' Spring gives way to summer, but the trouble is not yet resolved. In August a harassed Corporation decide that 'Wharton's ferry-boat was to be moved to allow free passage to the city's new ferry-boat and was not to be used to the detriment of the city's boat.'

Wharton's family, however, seems to have had the last word, for only a month later William Wharton (whether Henry's brother or son we are not told) 'was to have a lease of the boat and ferry at St. Leonard's Landing for eleven years, paying £3 rent for the ferry and 6s. 8d. for the boat.' The only stipulation was that 'Henry Wharton, his wife and children would not be chargeable to the city and that they would not meddle with the ferrying of any persons whatsoever.'

Throughout the medieval period St. Leonard's Landing witnessed another kind of traffic. Magnesian limestone for building the Minster, and occasionally for other places including the Guildhall, was brought up-river from Cawood and unloaded here. This necessitated a very large staith. If only we could unravel the past and see the concourse of people at St. Leonard's and overhear their badinage! In monastic times there was much lively altercation about the fishgarths, made of timber and wicker, that were stretched across the river to the constant danger of the ferry and other water traffic. In 1484 the Abbot of St. Mary's had one fishgarth, the Archbishop of York twelve, and the fish-hungry Bishop of Durham fourteen.

But every age contributed its peculiar hubbub. In the 1720s there were frequent rows because coal boats and dung boats would obstruct passengers going to and from the ferry. The Corporation had to intervene and order such vessels to unload elsewhere. In 1862 no fewer than 293,460 foot passengers crossed over by Lendal Ferry. During the following year, however, George Hudson, the 'Railway King', got his way at last and the ancient ferry was supplanted by the present Lendal Bridge.

Fortunately, the 'small round tower'—for so long the ferryman's house —still stands, though in changed form. As it had been neglected by one tenant, the Corporation restored and enlarged the tower in 1677. It was then used as a kind of depot for supplying water (direct from the river!) to householders. Today, the ferryman's cottage accommodates the York Waterworks office. I wonder what Janet Collynwood, or that troublesome Henry Wharton, would have thought of the electric lift that once took me through their old premises to the panelled upper chamber?

Somewhere about the middle of the sixteenth century Ouse Bridge—the one solid crossing over the river—collapsed, and a new, though temporary, ferry service was hurriedly arranged. The men whom a distraught council entrusted with the service (comprising two large boats and a smaller one) were Robert Maskewe and John Wilkynson. The fares were laid down for them, viz., '1d. for a stranger and his horse, ½d. for a man without a horse, and they were to be ferried back, if they wished, at no extra charge.' York citizens were to go over for nothing, as long as this did not upset the St. Leonard's ferryman—a doubtful provision! Maskewe and Wilkynson paid ten shillings weekly as ferry rent and were subject to a month's notice from the Lord Mayor and Aldermen. Fortunately for the town's other ferrymen, the Ouse Bridge crossing was soon effected by a bridge of boats until the new structure was ready.

And so the story of the York ferries could go on. From at least 1541 the Ouse could also be crossed at Skeldergate Ferry. The city records state that 'the water bailiff was to have the profit' of this undertaking. Not for over two hundred years is there any mention of a ferryman's house here,

8

but in 1781 the Corporation acts: 'A dwelling house is to be erected without Skeldergate Postern for the ferryman, using the materials from the old barge house.'

After another century has gone by, more of the city's ferrymen have become redundant, for in 1881 Skeldergate Bridge throws its long wide arm across the river, opposite the Castle. The last York ferry to vanish was one at Clifton; a bridge took its place in 1963. For old times' sake I am glad that the city whose people have lived by and on its river for so long still has one ferry crossing—not in the city centre, alas, but opposite Rowntree Park. Silently, unobtrusively, it represents all those many forerunners, though itself dating only from 1920.

Sometimes, however, Nature takes a hand in the best regulated and modernized cities. York is subject to flooding by the Ouse and its other, though smaller, river, the Foss. As recently as March 1968, the floods were so widespread and so many people were marooned in their homes, that the police organized ferry services in different parts of the city. One television news bulletin showed a group of women and children queueing on a wall-top for the next ferry. Others were being taken by boat to do their shopping. One elderly man had to use his drawing-room chairs as stepping-stones before he could reach the outer door where the ferry-boat awaited him.

Once again, York had become water-borne!

One would need oceans of leisure (and several books) for full contemplation of the British ferry scene in all its variety, covering past times as well as present. Here we must select in such a way that motorists, walkers, or armchair travellers can read the whole from the part. So far, our titular ferry trip has enabled us to scan the centuries, briefly, from monastic times onwards. We have glimpsed something of England's bygone pageantry, and much more awaits us downstream. One aspect recurs all too frequently—loss of human life. Mostly due to some upturned ferry-boat, this was the equivalent of our tragic road toll today.

One of the worst ferry accidents known to me occurred on the River Ure. This river is virtually the headwater of the Ouse; in fact it *becomes* the Ouse, near Aldwark. About eight miles north-west of Aldwark, and roughly half-way between Boroughbridge and Ripon, Newby Hall spreads its beautiful grounds to the very banks of the Ure. Motor-launch trips on the river are one of the attractions for visitors, few of whom will realize, however, what happened on the same stretch of water one February day in 1869 . . .

9

The York and Ainsty Hunt were out that day. Their fox crossed the river near Newby Hall and in hot pursuit they went, eleven huntsmen and their horses, crowding into the raft-like ferry-boat which two of the Newby gardeners hurriedly brought over for them. The river was in spate and the horses became restless, especially when Saltfish, Sir Charles Slingsby's favourite hunter, kicked Sir George Wombwell's horse. Within a matter of seconds there was a general mêlée. Out there in mid-stream, where the depth was about sixteen feet, the ferry-boat rocked perilously. Now thoroughly alarmed, Saltfish plunged overboard, with Sir Charles clinging desperately to its bridle. The horrified onlookers on the Newby bank then saw the boat capsize, precipitating every man and horse into the water. Amongst the survivors was one man who clung to the ferry chain and pulled himself ashore. Six men and eight horses perished. One victim was Sir Charles Slingsby, whose untimely death wrote FINIS to the long line of this distinguished family. Two other victims were those ferryman-gardeners, Christopher and James Warriner, father and son.

A year later Robert Ackrill of the *Harrogate Herald* published a book about this multiple disaster; it was called *The York and Ainsty Tragedy: or The Last of the Slingsbys*. But I like to think that the glorious river garden at Newby partly commemorates those two unfortunate fellows who left spade and hoe to man the ferry which they must have known was, on its return, shockingly overloaded. I don't suppose their protests were heeded.

Until recent years the York and Ainsty Hunt ran a ferry of their own at Naburn, between York and Cawood. A photograph I once took here shows the same kind of boat, or raft, that figured in the Newby calamity. The old ferry house at Naburn is now used by the Yorkshire Ouse Yachting Club, but I believe the former device for hailing the ferryman, from the Acaster Malbis side, still exists. A square, iron plate hangs from a wooden post, waiting for somebody to set it ringing with the knocker provided. But one would knock in vain today.

The last ferryman, here, was George Atkinson. His daughter proudly told me that during all his nineteen years (1937–56) as ferryman he never once had a boat accident. Huntsmen crossed over with their hounds. Motorists and anglers were also allowed to use the ferry, and walkers too. It can be imagined, therefore, how the eccentric owner of a neighbouring hall felt one day when, after sauntering down the river-bank from York, he clattered the gong for the ferryman, then bellowed, yet nobody appeared. Not for nothing was he a commander in the Royal Navy. When his peremptory signals brought no response he stripped, left his clothes on the bank, then swam across. Soon after, the inmates of the village inn beheld a dripping, naked figure at the door, full of sound and fury. 'Where the devil's that blasted ferryman?' he demanded. General consternation ensued until the garments were retrieved and their expostulating owner pacified!

On leaving Naburn there are six pleasant riparian miles before the Ouse receives the Wharfe, near Nun Appleton. Thus fortified, the Ouse broadens its chest and surges through Cawood to Selby.

Since 1871 the Ouse has been spanned at Cawood by a swing-bridge. Though it has no beauty of line, I have always had a fondness for this bridge: it opens up such fine views, not only of the dramatically swerving river, but also of this small village on its south bank. In one place the red roofs of Cawood yield to a tallish tower of creamy magnesian limestone. This tower is practically all that remains of the York Archbishops' palace, now popularly known as Cawood Castle. That medieval palace gives us our first legendary link with the ancient ferry which the iron swing-bridge superseded.

The story goes that Cardinal Wolsey, after his disgrace, tried to leave Cawood secretly and make his way over the local ferry in an attempt to reach York. Patrons of the Ferry Inn on the near side of the bridge have for years been regaled with this story, which gets really exciting on reaching the point where Wolsey is found, hiding in the cellar of this inn, before his plan had chance to mature.

Leonard C. Wright, the present landlord, tells me that Walter Green, his predecessor, used to entertain his special friends late at night in a small room over the ancient cellar. One night the floor collapsed under him and he disappeared from view. During repairs which this mishap entailed, workmen entered the long disused cellar and uncovered a door to a passage leading in the direction of the palace, which stands not many yards away. Due to foul air, the passage was then sealed. This may lend some credence to the old story, though more orthodox accounts state that Wolsey was arrested, not in the Ferry Inn, but in the basement of the palace.

Certainly the ferry must have been in great demand when such luminaries as Neville and Wolsey reigned and held court here. The title, 'Windsor of the North', fell like borrowed miniver on the good folk of Cawood, and the river shared in the general pageantry. True, some of the Archbishop's retinue might proceed to York up-river the whole way.

This was also the route taken by the barges carrying stone from Huddle-stone quarries for the building of the Minster. But where gaily caparisoned horses and carriages were involved, the ferry offered the necessary beginning to access by road.

In Speight's *Lower Wharfedale* (1902) there is an unsigned frontispiece showing the Cawood ferry-boat about 1700. It is a rowing-boat, pure and simple. A woman sits placidly in front, the ferryman sculls from the stern, and amidships a farmer sits on the gunwale holding his horse by its bridle. As my wife would say, in her Suffolk manner, the whole thing looks extremely 'tippety', and one is not surprised to hear that occasionally the boat did turn turtle.

This happened once again soon before the swing-bridge was erected. I heard of this accident from a man who now lives in what was formerly the Ferry Boat Inn, on the north bank. He came to the subject slowly, first pointing out the old landing stage, and then showing me the little green lane (now private) which led up from the ferry and began the long, ten-mile trek to York.

I was now properly attuned for his tale. Tommy Lund and his wife, market gardeners, were returning home to Cawood from York. It was a stormy evening and while they were crossing the river the ferry-boat was caught by the wind in mid-stream and overturned. 'A rescue boat put out immediately, picking up the ferryman and a few passengers, until only Tommy and his wife remained, clinging to each other in the water. As the overladen rescue boat reached them the boatman called out, "I can only tak' one o' ye; which es it to be?" "Save poor Bessie," spluttered Tommy, and as she was lifted from his arms he floated away and was drowned.'

The next Ouse ferry was at Selby. Its site is now occupied by the quaint wooden toll bridge of 1792. On approaching from the east side one sees the towers of the Benedictine abbey just beyond. The abbey was founded in A.D. 1069 and the ferry was probably one of its first concerns, this river-crossing being then, as now, a vital link between the East and West Ridings of Yorkshire. At the dissolution of the monasteries the abbey church escaped the general pillage and became (as it remains) a place for public worship. The Crown seized the ferry, however, and then granted it, along with the ferry-boat, to Sir Ralph Sadler of Middlesex.

Sadler, and especially his successors, made a very good thing out of this ferry, for as trade expanded it became busier and busier. By the mid-eighteenth century the owners claimed that over 141,000 persons, many on horseback, were using the ferry annually, and about 29,000 beasts were also transported. These figures may have been 'cooked' somewhat, for a bridge over the Ouse was then being proposed and the ferry proprietors were not above angling for a large haul in the way of compensation.

To offset such claims those in favour of the bridge declared that 'the Passage over the said Ferry, and every other Ferry upon the Ouse, is at all times attended with Delay, in some seasons dangerous, and at other times impassable'. To put the matter to a test, a jury of three noblemen was appointed, and a census was taken of the Selby Ferry traffic during a given month. That census revealed the following varied cavalcade:

Persons on foot, 8,743; Persons with horses, 3,052; led horses, 211; oxen, 127; hogs, 66; sheep, 2,248; coaches, 1; chaises, 15; single-horse chaises, 9; waggons, 3; carts, 16.

Suitably impressed, the noble jury decided in favour of the bridge. The ferry owner was not greatly upset, however. He had a foot in both camps. Not only was he to be compensated for the loss of the ferry, but he had also acquired a goodly financial interest in the bridge undertaking!

John Smeaton, the famous engineer of the day, designed the bridge, which is now as anachronistic as the old ferry had become. I used to visit Selby every week and several times did I miss my return train because the swing portion of the old wooden bridge jammed in the open position, thus effectively sundering one half of the town from the other. If only some of us thwarted pedestrians had been 'in the know' we could have quoted the Act of 1792 which 'required the bridge company to provide a temporary ferry if ever the bridge was impassable'.

Selby Toll Bridge still occasionally proves awkward and refuses to 'close'; but, alas, never a ferry-boat do we see in readiness!*

A few miles beyond Selby the Ouse swallows the far-ranging Derwent, once crossed by an ancient ferry at Bubwith. When this village got its bridge, a year after the one at Selby, the last ferryman—Middleton, by name—was given an annuity of five pounds. After the building of Selby Toll Bridge, Booth Ferry, nearer to Goole, became the chief one remaining on the Ouse, continuing until its own bridge was erected in 1929.

Booth Ferry belonged originally to the Prince Bishops of Durham, who had a palace in the neighbouring village of Howden. One of these bishops was Walter Skirlaugh, a local man who eventually chose to decorate his episcopal shield with interlaced bars representing the osiers his father had

* In August 1968 this ancient bridge, badly damaged by a 450-ton motor vessel colliding into it, was put out of action for about three weeks. During that time no vehicles were able to cross. Pedestrians could filter past the barrier—but nobody seems to have thought of demanding that statutory ferry service. For a certain bride and her father who, as things were, had to leave one taxi and walk over the bridge to another taxi, a ferry-boat crossing would have made a unique preamble to the wedding.

gathered on the marshland between Howden and the ferry. It needs no great stretch of the imagination to see young Walter himself, helping his father to weave the osiers into baskets for the little community then so dependent on the 'Bishops' ' ferry, and on another one at Howden Dyke.

Below Goole there was yet another important ferry, at Whitgift. Hereabouts, for several miles, the river bank is higher than the road. Villagers can only see across the Ouse from their bedroom windows, or by mounting the steep bank as my wife and I did, not long ago. Standing by the roadside is the early eighteenth-century red-brick chapel; clearly, according to the map, a landmark for those using the old ferry, which linked up with the road past Yokefleet to Eastrington and beyond.

The Ouse here is almost a quarter of a mile wide. It has none of the encompassing beauty one usually associates with north-country rivers; it looks cold and severe—an obstacle to be negotiated as quickly as the ferry would allow. I wonder how often the little fourteenth-century church nearby (another landmark) witnessed travellers' prayers for a safe crossing, for certainly the Whitgift Ferry could and did take its toll in human life. One victim was Sir John Sheffield, son of the President of the Council of the North. He was drowned here on 3 December 1614. Charles I was more fortunate; he crossed over when making for Nottingham, to raise his standard there in 1642. John Wesley's journeyings to and from Epworth, in Lincolnshire, made him all too familiar with this same ferry. His *Journal* entry for 19 May 1753 tells us that he 'preached at Pocklington again, and rode on to Whitgift Ferry. It rained a great part of the way, and just as we got to the water a furious shower began, which continued above half an hour, while we were striving to get John Haime's horse into the boat; but we were forced after all to leave him behind.'

Amongst Wesley's Yorkshire supporters were Henry and Mary Bell of Portington Hall, near Eastrington. When I visited this lovely old house some years ago, the late Sir Harold Wilberforce-Bell told me many family anecdotes about Wesley, who slept here on the night of 29 June 1790. Next day, after leaving his silver-topped walking stick behind as a memento, Wesley departed in Bell's coach for Epworth. The coach must have survived the ferry crossing both ways, for at Portington I was shown one of the travelling boxes used as part of Wesley's equipage.

That trip of mine to the district around Portington Hall coincided with the eclipse of a pontoon-cum-ferry at Beverley. The River Hull gives this grand old market town its fascinating shipyard, where fishing trawlers have to be launched *sideways* because the river is narrow. To paint his picture of a typical Beverley launching ceremony the late Fred Elwell,

The fair ford which gave its name to the
beautiful Cotswold village of Fairford

The old ferry-house still stands by Lendal Bridge which occupies
the site of the Lendal Ferry over the Ouse at York

St. Christopher carrying the
Christ-child, from a
fifteenth-century woodcut

Winter silhouette of the ferry at Naburn, near York, in 1936

Thomas Ferres, the
ferryman who eventually
became Lord Mayor of Hull

The eighteenth-century wooden toll-bridge which
replaced the ferry at Selby, Yorks

The Holderness hunt using the ferry
at Wawne, Yorks, about 1905

The *Tattershall Castle* crossing the
Humber in a February haze

The steam ferry between Southwold and
Walberswick, Suffolk, in 1900

St. Jude presents a boat to the
parish church of Wiggenhall
St. Germans, Norfolk

The ferry quay at Woodbridge,
Suffolk, with its tide-mill

Ferry-boats on the Thames, from the bird's-eye-view map of
Surrey in George Bickham's *British Monarchy* (1751)

R.A. (a native of the town) must have stood on this pontoon bridge which supplemented an ancient ferry crossing.

The Town Clerk tells me that there was a legal obligation to maintain this particular passage; hence, when the old ferry pontoon seemed out-moded (it actually sank, more than once!) a bascule-bridge was erected where, for so many centuries, local people had been rowed across for shopping and other purposes. But the ferry rights still prevail, in law, preventing the erection of a *fixed* foot-bridge. The new bascule-bridge swings open, as did the curious pontoon construction, to allow the passage of river traffic. The Romans, who crossed the river hereabouts nearly 2,000 years ago, and sailed their vessels up and down unhindered, seem to have forced their way into the twentieth century to have the last word!

Although the ferry at Wawne, three miles south-east of Beverley and also on the River Hull, was of ancient lineage, there was apparently nothing to save it from ultimate extinction. It just lapsed, in the 1950s, without even a swansong. So now there is practically nothing but a few scanty ruins and quickly evaporating tradition to commemorate Meaux Abbey, which stood nearby.

In the abbey chronicles we may read that Henry Murdac, Archbishop of York (1147–53) gave to Melsa, or Meaux, by charter 'all his lands, amounting to two carucates . . . which would include proportionate pasture in Wawne; and a ferry over the River Hull'. For centuries, Wawne Ferry played a principal role in linking up this part of Yorkshire and places even farther afield.

My friend, Rupert Alec-Smith of Winestead, Hull, spent his early days at Wawne Lodge and he has kindly recalled for me what the ferry then meant to his family. 'When we first lived at Wawne,' he writes, 'it was our usual custom to take the car over the ferry for our journeys to Beverley, but later we learned that it was really quicker to go by the very twisting Meaux Lane from Wawne to Routh, and from there to Beverley. I can remember as a child being taken by car from Wawne Lodge to stay with my grandmother in Huntingdonshire, and before we even left Yorkshire we had four tolls to pay—Wawne Ferry, which was a shilling for a car; Bubwith; Selby Toll Bridge; and finally the toll bridge at Carlton, near Snaith. Nowadays this may seem a curious route to take from Wawne to the Great North Road, but in those days there was no bridge at Booth-ferry.' At least three chargeable stages of this short, devious perambula-tion, it will be noticed, had been at some time served by a ferry.

Colonel Alec-Smith has also sent me some snapshots of the Wawne Ferry, probably all taken on the same day, about 1905. In one of them the

Holderness hounds are seen crowding the flat-bottomed vessel, together with a mounted huntsman who was probably the Holderness M.F.H. One man is pulling on the chain that propels the craft, and another—the ferryman-in-chief—uses a long-handled boat-hook to guide it to a safe mooring. The rest of the hunt have presumably crossed earlier, for a further snapshot shows Alexander Alec-Smith (my friend's father) as one of several top-hatted figures, aboard, all in riding pink.

The senior ferryman looks impressive with his bushy beard and peaked cap. He was called Donald Brewer, a name which conveniently echoed his main occupation, for he kept the Windham Arms on the east bank. On a recent visit to Wawne, via the Routh detour, I noticed Brewer's old inn, but a road sign declared (rather facetiously for such a small, out-of-the-way village) 'You have been wawned!' The warning is really against careless driving, but strangers could take it to mean that the ferry still shown at the end of the lane, on some maps, no longer exists.

The River Hull needs another five serpentine miles before it finally debouches into the Humber, at Hull. Stoneferry, on the outskirts of the famous port, is eloquent of an old ferry which, up to the early nineteenth century, carried most of the traffic to and from South Holderness.

One place which benefited by the proximity of the old 'stone ferry' was the Maison Dieu, or God's House for the poor, founded in 1384 by Michael de la Pole. This establishment seems to have enjoyed a special landing stage on the River Hull; it was marked by a large stone cross. The Maison Dieu is known today as the Charterhouse and its present range of buildings bears the stamp of Georgian times. During the last war, when I went along to photograph the place for the national records, the residents had been evacuated; fortunately so, because German raiders to whom rivers and their ancient rights were no sort of barrier, had been over and dropped a stick of incendiary bombs in the Master's garden. Another casualty was part of the old stone cross (then at the Albion Street Museum) from the old ferry landing. Several bridges over the River Hull, necessitated by industrial development, have since revolutionized this area of the city.

But as yet there is no bridge across the Humber. Such a bridge is planned, however, for the (near?) future. Meanwhile this age-old barrier, here two miles wide, effectively separates Yorkshire from Lincolnshire. From either shore the view across the vast, watery expanse suggests that a different country is materializing out of the haze.

One eighth-century writer, Nennius, contemplated this great estuary, so often whipped into fury, and, for want of a better description, called it the Humbrian Sea. His 'sea' would include part of the alluvial Plain of Holderness with its bird-haunted lagoons, and its shifting streams which had to be forded or negotiated by some sort of ferry. Even before his day the Humber had been encountered and overcome by the Romans. Ermine Street, their highway from London to York, via Lincoln, crossed the estuary by a ford near Barton. In 1953, to test the feasibility of this tradition, Lord Noel-Buxton actually waded over the Humber by this route. According to most authorities the Roman ferry—as it would be, at high tide—ran from Winteringham on the Lincolnshire side to Brough on the Yorkshire side, and earned for itself the title *Transitus Maximus*, or 'very great ferry'.

Personally, I could spend days on Humberside, trying to visualize some of those who ventured over the river long ago.

In the eleventh century there was Sweine Estrithson, one of the invading Kings of Denmark, who established a ferry service by which his army in Lincolnshire could keep in contact with his Yorkshire headquarters. They crossed between the places now known as South Ferriby and North Ferriby, that is, South Ferry Town and North Ferry Town. In his *Itinerarium Curiosum* William Stukeley, the seventeenth-century antiquary, has much to say about this neighbourhood and its ferries. While staying at Winteringham he toys with the notion that the Humber takes its name from the noise it makes. 'My landlord,' he continues, 'who is a sailor, says in a high wind it [the noise] is incredibly great and terrible like the crash and dashing together of ships.'

Ferry passengers then had to be tough and inured to hardship and peril. Listen to old Stukeley as he describes North Ferriby, which has 'a stately bridge of three arches—but now broken down and lying in dismal ruins . . . travellers are obliged to pass the river in a paltry short boat, commanded by a little old deaf fellow with a long beard: into this boat you descend, by the steep of the river, through a deep mirey clay, full of stones and stakes; nor is the ascent on the other side any better . . . This, with the hideous ruins of the bridge, like the picture of hell gates in Milton, and the terrible roar of the water passing through it, fitly represented Virgil's description of Charon's ferry.'

Carried away by his classical allusions, Stukeley now pens a diatribe in Latin, here translated:

> Hence the way leads to Fereby forlorn
> Where Ankham's oozy flood with hideous roar
> Tears up the sands and sluices ruin'd vaults.

17

A squalid Charon the dread ferry plies
In leaky scull, whose furrowed cheeks lie deep
With hoary beard insconced.

Stukeley finds the Lincolnshire landfall hardly better, for 'when we had mounted . . . from the water, and paid our naul to the inexorable ferryman, we had several clayey lakes to ride over, unpassable in winter. Two roads lead you to the town [South Ferriby], a sorry rugged place, where upon the stocks is wrote, "Fear God, honour the King . . ." ' Not a very pleasant welcome for one who had just 'escaped the Stygian pool'.

Another Humber ferry operated between Barton in Lincolnshire and Hessle, the proposed line of the Humber Bridge.* In 1306 the men of the East Riding petitioned Edward I against an increase in the ferry charges here. Edward caused an inquisition to be held and matters were soon 're-established on the old footing'. The 'old footing' was still operable, one may suppose, when in 1331 the Warden and two Fellows of Merton College journeyed with four servants from Oxford to Durham, presumably by this route, and paid the ferryman eightpence, and that would cover the whole party and their baggage.

The village of Barton (which revived Stukeley's spirit somewhat, after the above-mentioned experiences) lies near South Ferriby and ran a ferry service of its own, direct to Hull, as early as 1316. Because of adverse winds and tides, this ferry, though popular, could be hazardous. Lady Margaret Hoby, well-known in Elizabethan court circles, used the Barton Ferry repeatedly on her journeyings by coach from Hackness, near Scarborough, to London. One experience prompts this entry in her diary: 'I was so ill [at Barton] that, after I had praied, I went to bed.' In short, she had been sea-sick.

Daniel Defoe chose to go the long way round the Humber, rather than over by the Barton Ferry, when on his celebrated Tour of England and Wales. On one occasion, while Sir Henry Slingsby, the royalist, was crossing with his family, the ferry-boat was rammed and damaged by another vessel. Slingsby enlarges on the incident in his entertaining diary: '. . . we unfortunately fell foul upon another ship . . . which bore us under her and broke a little of the forepart of our boat, which set my wife and her sister, my Lady Vavasour, into such a fright as they ceased not weeping and praying till we came a shoer [ashore] at Barton . . .'

* A model of one of the Hull-Barton ferry-boats, the *Patriot* (1865), exhibited in Hull's Pickering Park Museum, offsets a model of an Egyptian soul-boat which was supposed to ferry the deceased and his servants into the next world.

In 1639 the Reverend Andrew Marvell, father of the poet, was ferrying over to Barton with a wedding party when a storm blew up and he was drowned. Latterly he had held the post of Lecturer at Holy Trinity Church, Hull, and frequently complained 'against the perverse behaviour of some of the inhabitants of Kingston-upon-Hull', referring to them sadly as his 'briars and thorns'. This may lend some point to the story, probably apocryphal, that when the Humber ferry-boat's fate seemed sealed he threw his walking-stick into the water and then jumped after it, crying exultantly, 'Ho! for Heaven!'

Two hundred years later Barry Cornwall could still write with deep meaning about the same perilous crossing, which took at least an hour and a half. His short poem on the subject concludes with fine bravado:

> Though the waves all weave a shroud,
> We will dare the Humber ferry.

Perhaps Barry Cornwall [Bryan Waller Procter] was thinking ruefully, not only of the boisterous waves, but also of the ferry battle of the previous year. James Acland, a stranger to Hull, had challenged the Corporation's authority to charge one shilling per passenger on the *Royal Charter*, and he set up in opposition with another ferry-boat, *Public Opinion*, retaining the old fare of a copper or two.

During the next few months the people of Hull and of Barton became excited spectators of this aquatic struggle. The two rival ferry-boats raced over the Humber, jostling each other for landing berths, and touting outrageously for custom. Serious collision was bound to happen sooner or later, and when it did occur, on 6 November 1831, the *Royal Charter* took the worst buffeting and had to be towed away, with hundreds of excited spectators shouting and booing from the Hull pier.

Admiralty proceedings followed this deliberate collision. The *Public Opinion* was boarded at Barton, a few days later, by the Barton postmaster and his assistant, a baker of Hull. Declaring themselves authorized bailiffs, they produced a warrant and nailed it to the mast. Acland then had the chagrin of seeing his vessel commandeered and his passengers transferred to the *Royal Charter* (now repaired), which had drawn near in expectation. Worse still, the seized boat was towed behind its hated rival, but the crew of the *Public Opinion* soon took advantage of the fact that the bailiffs had unwisely transferred *themselves* to the *Royal Charter* along with the passengers. The crew cut the towing ropes and sailed back, bowed but unbeaten, to Hull.

Acland had scored again, but his token triumph was short-lived. He had been a hero to the cheering crowds, who assembled to greet him and his 'reforming' service, on both sides of the Humber. But increasing expenses—which caused his own fares to bump up to fourpence per passenger—and heavy liabilities, compelled him at last to withdraw from the contest.

Once again the *Royal Charter* reigned supreme on the Barton Ferry route, yet its own days were running out. Competition soon came from a rather different quarter. A new and more direct ferry service was started between Hull and New Holland, with the steamship, *Magna Carta*. This ferry began the present era; today Defoe would have had no qualms about tackling the Humber. By boarding the *Wingfield Castle*, the *Tattershall Castle*, or the *Lincoln Castle* one can comfortably cross over, whatever the weather, in little more than twenty minutes.

Before we descend the bridge pontoon at the Corporation Pier, and wait, say, for the *Wingfield Castle* (a name which recalls the de la Pole family), let us 'haloo' two more ferrymen from earlier days. One was John Taylor, the Water Poet, whose visit to Hull in 1602 is described in his hilarious poem, *A Very Merry Wherry Ferrey Voyage*.

He begins:

> Ev'n as the windowes of the day did shut,
> Down *Trent's* swift streame, to Gainsborough we put;
> There did we reste until the morning starre,
> The joyfull doores of dawning did un-bare:
> To *Humber's* churlish streams, our course we fram'd . . .

Taylor had been a ferryman on the River Thames, and knew the moods of a tidal river only too well. He proceeds, giving the Humber full marks:

> The waves like pirats board our boats and enter,
> But though they came in fury, and amaine,
> Like theeves we cast them over-board againe.
> This conflict lasted two houres to the full,
> Until we gate to *Kingston upon Hull* . . .

The *Wingfield Castle* draws nearer, but there is just time to salute another man from the Elizabethan age—Thomas Ferres.

I have heard it suggested that the family name refers to the occupation of ferryman followed by some of their menfolk, including Thomas himself. Ferries and their operation, up there in the Esk valley near Whitby, could not long satisfy this youth, however. The sea called him, with its larger vessels and opportunities for making a fortune.

His fortune duly made, Thomas Ferres settled in Hull, was admitted to the privileged brotherhood of Hull Trinity House, became Lord Mayor of the city, and scattered largesse. Trinity House owes its present site, and some choice pieces of silver plate to this ex-ferryman. And to this day a fine portrait of him adorns the Council Room, which—though dating from Georgian times—is carpeted with rushes renewed periodically from the banks of the Humber near that old ferry landing, North Ferriby.

CHAPTER TWO

FERRY BATTLES AND FEN
STRATEGY

The Yorkshire ferry scene has taken a long time to unfold, but of course my home county is by far the biggest in Britain and has an amazing river system.

At first it may have seemed that ferries are pretty much the same wherever one turns. A river or an estuary has to be crossed, there is a toll to pay, and that is that. But as we have already noticed, a ferry often bristles with excitement and adventure. People have fought over them, prayed over them, wept over them. It is not too much to say that ferries have occasionally *shaped* history and determined certain road communications of today. The story of ferries is, in appreciable measure, the story of humanity—and as varied.

Having now crossed over to Lincolnshire we get a rather different slant on the Humber passage; ripe comments, too.

Once, after the current Minister of Transport had visited Hull and given renewed assurances that the Humber Bridge would indeed be built (without specifying any date!), a New Holland ferryman said this to a reporter: 'Well, they was talking of it in mi Grandad's time, and they've talked a deal about it since then, but always when it's come as to who 'as to pay for it—well, they've just kept on putting up with *us*.'

'Putting up' with the ferrymen was a feature of local life in Canute's day. Then, in 1300, Edward I crossed over from Barton to Hessle Haven, thus establishing what boatmen were pleased to call the 'Royal Ferry'. In Edward III's reign one Thomas Crispin was operating a boat from Barrow Haven to Hull. This must have been a profitable venture for it was later acquired by the Constable family of Burton Constable, in Holderness, and sold by them in 1748 to the Reverend William Kirk. One supposes that the parson suitably augmented his stipend by farming out the ferry rights. Things livened up considerably in 1848 when Tommy Dent and a few associates began to work the Humber passage between a little creek near Barrow, and Hull. Originating perhaps as the Golflete, or Yellow Creek, of Domesday Book, this haven came to be known as Dent's Creek. By day, Dent and another man called Lumley were simply ferrymen; by night, they turned their coats and smuggled gin over the water. As gin was normally packed in cases called hollands, the immediate neighbourhood of Tommy Dent's Creek earned the nickname New Holland.* An alternative theory suggests that New Holland, now the Lincolnshire terminal of the Humber Ferry, was so called because the flat land hereabouts resembles the Dutch scene.

Yarborough Hotel erected nearby for the convenience of ferry passengers takes the name of a renowned Lincolnshire family. The Hull Transport Museum has custody of the Yarborough state coach, built about 1860; surrounded by cattle also in transit, the coach must have crossed the Humber Ferry many times. A perilous undertaking, for collisions with trawlers were not infrequent. Also, the boat could easily founder on one of the mud-banks and have to stay there until liberated by the tide.

Mr. E. B. Woodruffe-Peacock of Polegate, Sussex, tells me of such an incident. 'My uncle,' he says, 'was on a ferry steamer that was stuck on a mud-bank, betwixt New Holland and Hull in the 1880s. A passenger had with him a barrel of oranges—which steadily rose in price as time slowly passed!' Even today the modern car ferries can occasionally strike one of these sand-bars, which shift about so that no river chart is completely reliable. Today, however, passengers stranded in mid-stream can while the time away in the refreshment buffet which each vessel now provides.

Another Humber ferry ran from Grimsby to Hull, a lateral distance of about seventeen miles. This service was granted by charter of Henry III to the Mayor and Burgesses of Grimsby *for ever*. Henry's ministers could not have envisaged the present time when a couple of paddle steamers 'bend' the route round somewhat, in the summer period, by cruising with their passengers from Grimsby to Spurn—that long narrow headland shaped like a curlew's beak, at the Humber mouth.

Still, the Grimsby–Hull Ferry did continue unchanged for a goodly part of that eternity stipulated by royal command. Through the centuries, Grimsby Corporation kept faith and let the ferry to suitable persons. At length, in 1828, the newly-formed Pelham Steam Company was allowed to modernize the service, by providing a steam packet, the *Pelham*. But this soon led to friction. A rival concern must have won some councillor's private ear, for another steamboat, the *Sovereign*, now set out in opposition to the *Pelham*.

Instead of working alternately from the two Humber terminals—the only sensible procedure—the boats raced to reach the other side first.

* For other details see *Smugglers' Britain* by the author.

More river battles followed. For the spectators they were better than any football match, and had more repercussions. On the Lincolnshire side, touts went far up the Scartho road to meet coaches from Louth, offering prospective ferry passengers a *free* trip on the *Sovereign* to Hull and even a bottle of porter! Of course, the *Sovereign* could not long offer such inducements. Ultimately, its owners had to sink their disappointments in whatever porter remained, and withdraw their boat. The *Pelham* was left to plough its undisputed way across the Humber, solvent as well as victorious.

The seventeen-year-old John Wesley once wrote to his mother, from Oxford, 'I propose to be busy as long as I live.' His *Journal* shows abundantly how his prophecy was fulfilled. He travelled thousands of miles through eighteenth-century England, and perforce used many of its ferries. They helped to colour and vivify his busy life.

We have already seen him crossing the Ouse at Whitgift Ferry and shall meet him again later. His own native district, the Isle of Axholme, could once have been called Ferryland because of its many little unbridged waterways. The Isle of Axholme lies in the north-west of Lincolnshire and is bounded on the east by the River Trent, now moving swiftly towards its marriage with the Humber. Wesley must have known all the ferries of the neighbourhood, small ones as well as the larger ones that so often demanded a passenger's fortitude besides his fare.

A good map of this area indicates these old ferry crossings. One near Fockerby on the Trent is significantly dotted around with three inns; they and the ferry eased Lincolnshire folk into a lobe of Yorkshire centring upon Goole. A few miles up-river the West Kinnard Ferry took people to and from the Isle of Axholme by a route reputedly used by Edward the Confessor when he was seeking allies against his southern enemies. It would be difficult to authenticate this claim, but as early as the twelfth century the place was known locally as King Edward's Ferry, corrupted later to Kinnard Ferry. Its privileges included the right to exact ferry tolls, not only at this point, but at other Trent ferries bordering Epworth Manor.

In short, if you crossed over by the ferry at Butterwick, Althorpe, or Owston, you paid double fare, the extra charge being prestige money due to the Kinnard monopoly. In the reign of James I this ferry and the ferry-house, with all the ancient 'liberties, advantages, dues, customs and profits' fell to the lot of John Terry, a distinguished citizen who was already in clover as a goldsmith.

Read's *History of the Isle of Axholme* (1858) refers thus to the Kinnard

Ferry: 'Three boats are here kept constantly afloat, one for passengers exclusively, another for passengers and their horses, and a third for carriages and droves of cattle. In fine weather, during neap tides, the passage is made in a few minutes; during spring tides and heavy freshes it is much more tedious, and when the river is encumbered with ice, sometimes dangerous.' The author says nothing about passengers having to chance an encounter with the Trent Eagre, or bore. In *The Mill on the Floss* George Eliot romanticizes this phenomenon:

The broadening Floss [the Trent] hurries on between its green banks to the sea; and the loving tide rushing to meet it, checks its passage with an impetuous embrace.

The 'impetuous embrace' of a river bore—here amounting to a six or seven foot surcharge of tidal water—has sometimes upset ferry-boats and drowned all those aboard.

One of England's most important ferries lay south of Gainsborough, at Littleborough, where the Romans pushed their road from Lincoln to Doncaster across the Trent. *Segelocum*, the neighbouring Roman station, has yielded many archaeological rewards, not least the skeleton of a young woman clad in a garment secured with a Roman brooch. In life she may well have used this same river-crossing, rejoicing perhaps in the wild flowers and grasses on either bank. At times the Trent could be forded here; in 1066 Harold, hastening south to his fatal encounter with the Normans at Hastings, used this passage, and it is considered likely that two years later William the Conqueror followed suit while proceeding from York to subdue Lincoln. The stones that paved the ford became visible during the drought of 1933, but there must have been a boat service too, to cope with more normal river conditions.

I once spent a pleasant morning at Laneham Ferry, a few miles farther south. To all appearances the ferry was not simply part of an abiding place-name but a reality, like the ferries at Farndon near Newark and Stoke Bardolph near Nottingham. Several small craft were drawn up on the river strand and the Ferry Boat Inn nearby gave me refreshment. But to get across the Trent into Lincolnshire that day I should have had to swim, or make some private arrangement with a member of Laneham's flourishing boat club. I was just fifteen years too late to catch the last ferry-boat! Yet my visit was not wasted. The Trent at Laneham glistens like a river in some old fable. I sat there happily, watching the fishermen and the passing barges.

Later I walked down the river-bank as far as Dunham. The Trent is here spanned by an ugly iron bridge. Of far greater appeal to me were some waterside posts, rotting with age, such as John Constable loved to paint. A little causeway dips towards them. For those who have eyes to see, causeway and jetty posts indicate the former ferry landing.

Prior to 1831–2, when the bridge proprietors bought out the ferry, Dunham was an attractive little community, with its clog and patten maker, blacksmith, wheelwright, maltster, watchmaker, fisherman, two tailors, three inn-keepers and nine farmers. John and Joseph Clark were there to work the ferry and bring outsiders from the Lincolnshire bank to market. Thomas Roberts kept the village school and the Reverend Edward Younghusband saw that everybody went to church on Sundays.

Parson and schoolmaster were probably the only villagers who knew, however vaguely, that their own ferry had, in the dim past, once basked in splendour. This was on 30 October 1695 when William of Orange crossed the Trent, here at Dunham, during his progress through Cambridgeshire, Northamptonshire, Lincolnshire and now Nottinghamshire. How the villagers would gape as the new King of the Realm stepped into their little boat, on the far shore, accompanied by Dr. Sharp, Archbishop of York, the Dukes of Shrewsbury and St. Albans, the Earl of Portland, Lord Godolphin and Lord Wharton. One supposes that such a weight of gorgeous dignity would necessitate at least two or three trips. Certain it is that on leaving the ferry-boat, at the Dunham jetty, the King was welcomed into the fair county of Nottinghamshire by the Duke of Newcastle. The Duke then escorted William to his palatial home at Welbeck, but the good folk of Dunham needed neither stag-hunting nor venison feasts to round off the event. Their own humble ferry had received its own accolade.

I am surprised at not finding any evidence of a ferry service over the River Witham at Lincoln. Fords, yes, as perpetuated in the names of Wigford and Brayford Pool—a fascinating spot which reflects the towering cathedral in its broad, swan-rippled waters and could well do with a small pleasure-boat service for visitors. Another ford once ran beside the High Bridge; it was overlooked by a small chapel dedicated to St. Thomas of Canterbury.

After leaving the town, however, the Witham comes up to expectations. There were ferries at Washingborough, Bardney, and at Southrey, where the call 'Bo-oat!' would bring a response until a few years ago. Stixwold and Kirkstead each had a chain-ferry, also Dogdyke and Langrick. At least seven ferries on the Witham between Lincoln and Boston, with a 'special mention' for Dogdyke because it once belonged to the Duke of St. Albans and was considered so important that when Tattershall Bridge was erected about 1793, an Act stipulated that no other ferry should work within a mile of the said bridge.

Dogdyke Ferry had evidently more than earned its keep in the earlier days when Ralph Lord Cromwell, the King's Treasurer, welcomed to his castle abode some of the cream of English nobility. Today even the castle moat is permanently bridged. But Dogdyke Ferry expired in the 1920s.

The fine old port of Boston remained faithful to some of its ancient ferries until early this century. The picturesque wharves and quays along the Witham, as this snakes past Boston 'Stump' and the overhanging warehouses, still seem to demand a little ferry-boat or two, linking the two halves of the town.

A ferry crossed the river, here, long before a bridge materialized to take some share in local affairs. This original ferry seems to have graced the Witham nearly opposite the present Boys' Grammar School. Later, another ferry—St. John's—gave Boston townsfolk an alternative route.

While the town bridge was being built in 1556 the old ferry still flourished and the Corporation collected the tolls. But the Corporation's right to do this was contested, resulting in a case heard before the Duchy Court of Lancaster.

The action took an amusing turn, for onlookers at any rate. It was brought against the Mayor of Boston for having detained a mare, whose owner had refused to pay the penny toll for ferrying it across the river. The Mayor's wisdom in seizing the mare (and how the locals would play upon the punning theme!) was questionable, for he would have to pay somebody to feed and water the animal. But the court proceedings avoided that promising field and concentrated, instead, on the legal ownership of the ferry.

I can hear the Clerk's sonorous voice as he intones these words:

'. . . for the convenience of the inhabitants living on the east and west side of the river, the Dukes of Richmond, who owned the Manor of Boston, of their mean benevolence, only for the ease and relief of their servants, residents and inhabitants of Boston, did find, maintain, and keep to their great charges and expenses, within the said manor, upon the soil and ground belonging to the same manor, one ferry or passage over the said part and water, and certain watermen, boats and great bottoms or keals, called horseboats and wayne boats, only for the conveyance and transporting over the said water and part of their tenants and inhabitants and their beasts, goods, chattles, wares and merchandise.'

The voice then drones on to the effect that 'any foreign persons, who, not being inhabitants of Boston, attempted to cross by this ferry, were withstanded and resisted as trespassers'.

After this long preamble came the statement that in subsequent times the Lord of the Manor had transferred his manorial rights to the Mayor and Burgesses. So, after all, the current Mayor was legally justified in laying hold of that debateable mare.

What happened to the animal thereafter is not recorded. The Corporation had things of greater moment to bother about just then. They had taken over a hitherto private bridge which the Duke of Richmond had built nearby, but 'by the extreme rage and influence of the seas' it was suddenly 'braste and overthrown'. Until a new bridge could be erected, the old ferry came back into use, as it did repeatedly in future years whenever the bridge was closed for repairs.

I should have welcomed the little boat service, during the last war, when the town bridge often became blocked with traffic. In any case, some of Boston's historic waterside buildings which I was then recording would have photographed much more effectively from the ferryman's angle.

The history of a neighbourhood is often the history of its ferry communications. This is particularly true around Peterborough, which has always been an important transport junction. In earlier days the abbey at Peterborough could hardly have thrived as it did without the fords and ferries that brought pilgrims and others over the River Nene and the surrounding fen country.

The abbey itself established Gunwade Ferry, at Milton near Castor, roughly three miles west of Peterborough. Time has erased this ancient ferry, but it is still recalled by a couple of boundary stones on the river side of the main Peterborough–Castor road. Standing eight yards apart, the stones once marked the boundaries of St. Edmund's Balk, that is, 'a strip of land acquired by the Abbot of Bury St. Edmunds from the Abbot of Peterborough as a roadway for the carriage of stone from the Barnack Quarries, in order that it might be free of the Peterborough tolls at

Gunwade Ferry'. The stone was then conveyed by water to Bury St. Edmunds for the building of Abbot Baldwin's monastery there.

It was none other than William the Conqueror who smoothed the way for this traffic in building stone, Abbot Baldwin of Bury being William's physician and personal friend. Climb to the top of the Norman gate tower, at Bury St. Edmunds, and the guide will assuredly tell you of the Barnack stone used in its construction. The present excavation work near-by is revealing more of the original abbey structure.

But the other half of the story is embodied in those riverside stumps, five miles south-east of the famous quarries. On the one-inch Ordnance map they are named Robin Hood and Little John. Notches in the two stones are supposed to indicate that the two outlaws shot some arrows from this place to Adwalton Church, beyond the ferry. A more reliable account makes the arrow-like notches a memorial to St. Edmund, who was slain by Danish arrows. It is just possible, therefore, that the notches were cut by some stonemason while awaiting the barge near Gunwade Ferry.

Another attempt to avoid Peterborough tolls explains the former Stanground Ferry, two miles east of the town on the Huntingdonshire side of the Nene. This ferry provided access to and from Thorney causeway which, in turn, served Thorney Abbey, a Benedictine house occupying an island in the fens.

Most English people revel in the story of Hereward the Wake and his misty, treacherous fenland. Hereward's watery domain around Ely joins up with the Peterborough 'archipelago', which required yet another ferry for its monks and those who had dealings with them. This ferry was at Horsey, near Stanground. Whether it came under the jurisdiction of Thorney Abbey, or Ramsey Abbey farther south, is not now clear, but Canute the Dane (994–1035) is believed to have had a hand in constructing two local dykes still named after him. In this area, ferries would once be as invaluable as stilts. And all the way into Cambridge-shire and Norfolk the same tale is unfolded, though mostly today by place-names and a general awareness of local geography.

Dr. E. A. R. Ennion visualized Romans and others employing ferries to cross the innumerable meres and reedy waterways. And so may we, reinforced by one's own knowledge of the fens, where so many of the church towers long served as beacons for water-borne wayfarers. Indeed, the church at Terrington St. Clement, near the Wash, became a refuge during the floods of 1607 and food had to be ferried over to the inmates, from King's Lynn.

This kind of thing had been happening hereabouts for centuries, which perhaps explains why the craftsmen responsible for the splendid bench-ends at Wiggenhall St. Germans Church, near King's Lynn, should include one carving of St. Jude seemingly in the act of presenting the parish with a fine, timber boat.

CHAPTER THREE

ELEPHANTS, LIVE CARP, AND
SCANDAL

King John losing his baggage while skirting the Wash is a story that comes readily to mind anywhere between Boston in Lincolnshire and King's Lynn in Norfolk. Before 1814 wayfarers between those two places had to cross the Welland estuary, near Fosdyke, by ferry, unless they had time enough to go round via Spalding.

Amongst its splendid array of civic plate King's Lynn has several interesting mementoes of this rather intractable sovereign, who granted the town its charter. One treasure is the famous King John's Cup, which warrants this brief mention here simply because the charming enamelled figures that adorn its bowl and stem* illustrate the kind of people who would walk the streets of Lynn, and use its almost equally important ferries, in the reign of Edward III. Obviously of noble birth, the people wear strange attire, like the liripipe, the tippet, the cotehardie, and rich, flowing gowns that hide the ladies' feet.

Most of the town's life then clung to the Great Ouse, which joins the Wash not far away. All the chief buildings, whether civic premises, merchants' houses, or parish church, are still to be found hereabouts. And pushing through this waterfront, as though part of its original plan, is a narrow alley called Ferry Lane . . .

We have already visualized some of those who would patronize this ferry in early times. Add to the company such persons as the Town Cook (a very important official), Dr. Burney and his daughter Fanny, who lived here, and you get a more representative picture. When I climbed into the little motor-boat ferry, years ago, Dr. Burney was by my side, so to speak, still absent-mindedly engaged on the material for his *History of Music*.

Nobody seems to know exactly when this ferry service to West Lynn began. It is first mentioned definitely in local records in 1285–6, though ferry rights might have existed here even earlier. That first documentary

---

* As the costumes worn by these figures are a hundred and fifty years later in style than those of King John's time, this silver-gilt cup can no longer be regarded as his gift to the town, though some future merchant may have presented the cup to commemorate John's various grants to Lynn.

reference, occurring in a deed of conveyance, brings more townsfolk into the limelight. According to this deed: 'One carrying boat for the passage of the water of Lenne called the Ferrye, with all the liberty or right pertaining to the same vessel, was conveyed by Philip Peyteun and his wife Agnes of West Lenn to John Ode, a burgess of Bishop's Lenn, for forty silver marks and a yearly rent of clove.' This conveyance and later ones were solemnly drafted by the Town Clerk and witnessed by the Mayor, who ranked as High Admiral of the neighbourhood.

By 1649 cloves gave place to something tastier, as part payment for the ferry rights. In that year the Corporation acquired the ferry from the Trinity Guild and then let it to a certain John Bird, on a seven-year lease. Bird agreed to pay ten pounds yearly to the borough funds, and make an annual present to the Mayor of a brace of well-fatted swans.

As the centuries rolled by, more and yet more of the citizens evidently used this ferry, which provided a short cut, via West Lynn, to the Holbeach highway and the Wash. In 1851 the ferry was so lucrative that the annual rent had risen to four hundred pounds.

It is not always clear, however, which ferry is meant in the town records, for even in the thirteenth century, and up to recent times, the Great Ouse could be crossed by ferry-boat from at least two places. The most convenient one for Fanny Burney and her father would be that heading across from Purfleet Quay, quite near their home. Another ferry operated from Common Staithe Quay, near the Docks. Here, in 1413, Thomas, Duke of Clarence, and Margaret, daughter of the Duke of Kent, had been given a ceremonious welcome after braving the broad river. Some idea of their reception can be gained from the fact that the Duke and his suite needed three hundred horses to carry them. The ferryman would need a lot of help that day! The party were to take up temporary residence at the monastery of the Augustine Friars. How their gay outfits would overshadow the sombre garb of those friars deputed to join the 'reception committee' at the ferry landing!

As in other places, alas, the church bells of King's Lynn sometimes had to toll for those drowned while attempting the ferry passage. Perhaps the spring tides were responsible. In 1630 eighteen persons lost their lives; in 1796, twenty-two persons; in 1811, nine or ten.

The ferry route is now stabilized and the motor-boat has been in use since 1920. Nowadays, however, competition from road transport has rendered the ferry an uneconomic proposition for the private individual, so the Corporation has taken it over, paternally, as a public amenity. I wonder whether the Mayor, as city father in chief, still receives any succulent swans?

The ferries of Norfolk make map perusal quite exciting. A few miles south of King's Lynn the Little Ouse is marked with a ferry at Ten Mile Bank, near Hilgay—birthplace of William Manby who invented the rocket apparatus for saving life at sea. His early experiments took place in this part of the fen country, where, as we have seen, ferry-boats could also come to grief. Today, Stoke Ferry bestrides the River Wissey, a tributary of the Little Ouse, with a road bridge; life-saving nearer home.

Over in the east of the county, between Norwich and Yarmouth, a fine crop of ferries is shown, mostly on the River Yare. Opposite Brundall, where Roman galleys once pulled in for repairs, there is the Coldham Hall Ferry. This still functions and nobody seems to mind that the boats used may be pensioned-off sailing craft. Surlingham Ferry once provided the only crossing of the Yare between Reedham and Norwich and was always in great demand, even as recently as 1949 when fifteen daily crossings were made—'thirty times there and back in all weathers, including gales and strong running tides'.

At Surlingham you can still pack yourself and your bicycle into a small row-boat and chance what comes. Cantley Ferry, nearer Reedham, only operates today for the benefit of workers at the local sugar-beet factory, while Thurne Ferry, on the River Bure, enables a local farmer to take his cattle across to their marshland grazing.

Horning Ferry, on the Broads, began over a thousand years ago as an essential link on the main route from Norwich to St. Benet's Abbey. When my wife and I were at Horning about 1950, foot-passengers were pulling themselves across the Bure, by chain, in a small, flat-bottomed ferry-boat. To get near the abbey we had to go by motor-launch. In Canute's day St. Benet's must have resembled an island monastery. Today, in its ruined state, the place looks as though it had drifted down from some vanished world. It is thickly hemmed in by tall reeds, through which a grebe or two will warily steer its colourful way.

In 1246 Henry III granted the abbot the right to hold an annual fair at 'Grabbardes ferie', or Horning Ferry, which would be only one of several well-used passages in this water-logged region. Where the fairground was situated it is difficult to imagine. After the Dissolution a Ferry Inn which appeared on the site of the monk's eleventh-century mead house suggests the growth of a small, waterside community.

Our launch did not stop at the rebuilt Ferry Inn, but desire for refreshment was satisfied when a floating shop drew alongside and regaled us with fresh fruit, chocolate and orangeade. Horning Ferry and its environs were keeping pace with progress. I am told that, distinctly as a ferry, Horning 'gave up' early in 1967. But its ethos is ineradicable.

Norwich, distant terminal of the older Horning Ferry, has its own delightful commentary on our theme. You go down, past the cathedral, to the ancient water-gate, where stone for the building of the cathedral was delivered long ago. On my first visit to Norwich my companion took me to see this picturesque corner, but the *approach* to it was all important. We had to walk along the far bank of the Wensum, climb down some steps, and then wait with a few others for a strange-looking object to come over and fetch us. Anybody who has seen coracles pirouetting on the Welsh rivers may form some faint idea of that object, for it appeared to be an outsize coracle, shallow in draught and having neither stem nor stern. We were at the renowned Pull's Ferry and this was the ferry-boat, now being punted slowly towards our waiting group.

It was a short, though truly romantic voyage. It gave the sense of being ushered into the Elizabethan age, when Germaine Sandling held the ferry rights from the Dean and Chapter. Sandling was a chorister at the cathedral and would often have the pleasure of taking his friend, Sir Thomas Browne of *Religio Medici* fame, over the river. The charming old house adjoining was home to the chorister and to his successors, also, though the ferry retained Sandling's name until 1796, when John Pull came into possession.

An enterprising fellow, this John Pull. He used part of the Ferry House as a tavern and allowed music parties to hold concerts inside. Sometimes, for a change, the musicians took their wind instruments into the *Apollo*, a barge moored nearby, so as to give the whole neighbourhood a sample of water music.

A partner in Pull's venture was Daniel Clark, of the cathedral close, for he owned the *Apollo*. The inn licence lapsed on the death of John Pull in 1841. Mr. Feltham, the Dean's verger, who followed him, had to be satisfied with a teetotal ferry, and dry the house remained until the last ferryman, Cecil Mollett, surrendered his post in 1943. Changed social conditions, including the removal of the Norwich Football Club ground from the county side of the river (this killed a profitable Saturday afternoon ferry trade) a few years earlier, had sounded the death knell. The 'burial' followed Cecil Mollett's departure, for—whether by intention or accident—that oversize 'coracle' and other ferry-boats were then sunk in the river.

There might have been obsequies over the Ferry House too, but for a timely bequest from the late Miss Camilla Doyle. This bequest, supplemented by other monies and grants, enabled the grand old house with its leaning chimneys and pantile roofs to be rescued. In 1947-8 the premises became a suite of architects' offices, which left room for the Norwich Girl Guide Association headquarters. There are few more nostalgic spots in any English city, especially when the cathedral bells begin to chime like a voice from the past.

Artists still find Pull's Ferry worthy of their attention.

A lament for lost ferries might be raised at many other places in East Anglia—at Great Yarmouth, for example, which had several ferries, including the North Ferry over the River Bure. Robert Cory junior, Mayor of Yarmouth in 1816, was proprietor of this useful passage, but he himself gave it the *coup de grâce* by building a bridge on the same spot in 1829. Another ferry, of medieval origin, crossed the Waveney at Herringfleet, a few miles south of Yarmouth. But this beautiful village brings us into Suffolk, which still manages to keep some of its old ferries alive, if only with a shadow service.

Harbour Road at Southwold, Suffolk's select holiday resort near Lowestoft, is lined with picaresque bungalows and caravans in the gayest mood, all in striking contrast to the rest of the town, where the houses are grouped sedately around seven charming greens and a magnificent church. Up in the town there is a spacious dignity, as of old ladies forever entertaining the clergy to tea; down by the harbour Southwold relaxes a little and chats with its arty neighbour, Walberswick, across the River Blyth. A ferry of some kind has facilitated this hobnobbing since the thirteenth century.

It is not a wide crossing—about seventy-eighty feet at low tide and a hundred–a hundred and twenty feet at full tide—but fickle, like so many others. On a July evening in 1616 a party were returning home from Dunwich fair and on reaching Walberswick they all crowded into the ferry-boat. It capsized and twenty-two persons were drowned. One of the victims, according to the register at Southwold Church, was 'Elizabeth, daughter to Mr. C. Yonges, Vicar and Minister'. Her brother John was the man who later founded Southold, Long Island.

For old residents, memory has much to feed upon, down by the Southwold–Walberswick Ferry. The most humorous episode concerns some elephants.

An old fisherman recently told my son, Peter, that a travelling circus once wanted to cross over, lock, stock and barrel, by the ferry. The two circus elephants proved awkward, however; the ferryman dare not take them both together and as one elephant refused to go without the other, they had to be walked all the way round by road via Blythburgh, a distance of about seven miles. Oddly enough, Miss F. Foster of the Southwold Archaeological Society feels sure that one of these animals must have been coaxed aboard, after all, for she reports 'a childish recollection of seeing an elephant walking most astonishingly up the village street at Walberswick and having been certain that it had come over from Southwold by the ferry'.

By that time, of course, the vessel was no longer a row-boat but a steam pontoon, working on chains, and capable of carrying two or three cars. A photograph taken in 1900 is before me as I write. Straw-hatted mothers sunning their infants, and lounging gallants wearing boaters, have foregathered on the Southwold bank, as the ferryman puts off for Walberswick. Perhaps the sturdy-looking figure in the pontoon's cabin is Old Todd, a ferryman who earned the nickname, 'I know it', because this was his inevitable response to any piece of ferryside gossip.

In his *Story of Southwold* the late Frederick Jenkins recalled a ghostly anecdote from the same period:

'A visitor to Walberswick . . . requested Old Todd to row him over [in the small boat] to Southwold early one morning. Walking down to the shore he overtook and passed an old man leading a child by the hand. Thinking they too wanted to cross he told Todd to wait, but, glancing up, he saw the wide road was empty. Said the ferryman in sepulchral tones, "We never waits for *them*!" and pushed off. George Todd's usual air of omniscience had taken a creepy turn.'

I was chatting with my Suffolk sister-in-law beside this ferry not long ago and she, too, began to recall things she had heard, chiefly about an old naturalist friend, the Reverend Julian Tuck, who would come in his ancient tweeds to the ferry side, year after year, to watch the birds cross over on their annual migrations. Daniel Defoe had marvelled at the same spectacle, and hundreds of discerning ferry passengers must have done likewise.

An old ferry accumulates so many memories. How glad some of us are that although the chain-pontoon has gone from the Blyth estuary, there is still a small row-boat to keep the two riverside communities in friendly touch.

Another rewarding spot for visitors is the ferry quay at Woodbridge, on the River Deben. Here you will see a tide-mill, which has been worked by the rise and fall of the tide since about 1190. You will see yachts in gay panoply, especially during Regatta Week in August. Amid all this activity you may also hail a ferryman to take you and your bicycle over the estuary to the wooded Sutton shore, where one of England's greatest archaeological discoveries was made in 1939. I refer to the Sutton Hoo Ship Burial.

Miss G. Redstone, one of three sisters to whose historical researches Woodbridge owes such an incalculable debt, tells me that in earlier days she and her sister Mabel frequently went over by ferry to picnic beside some curious, bracken-covered mounds. Mrs. E. M. Pretty, owner of the Sutton property, had often puzzled over these mounds and wondered about their possible contents. Something of her curiosity was imparted to the Redstone sisters, and when the archaeologists eventually opened the mounds it must have seemed odd to realize that the Saxon chieftain's ship, buried there with so much treasure, had been rowed to its final bourne (probably by slaves) across the same water now traversed by this ferry.

In 1951 a case was brought before the High Court to decide whether the Woodbridge U.D.C. was obliged to maintain and operate this ancient ferry. Miss Lilian Redstone's intensive research among mounds of old documents led to a verdict which established the Council's responsibility. Times had apparently changed since 1509 when John Beale, the first recorded ferryman, himself agreed to keep the ferry-boat, or 'shipp', in repair.

A sail down the beautiful Deben now awaits us, preferably in the imagined company of Edward FitzGerald, whose chief amusement was boating along his 'Queen of Rivers' towards the sea in his little craft called the *Scandal*. As Thomas Newson was FitzGerald's skipper we must have him too. And a strange pair they make, the poet wearing his customary attire—including a feather boa and a silk hat that conceals his lunch; and Newson looking like a magpie peering into a quart pot, according to 'Fitz', and 'always smiling though the father of twins'.

The name, 'Newson' eventually appeared above the door of the Ferry Boat Inn at Bawdsey, suggesting that Tom or another of the same family became landlord. This would be quite natural as the translator of *Omar Khayyam* and his skipper had long frequented the inn, with its skittle alley and other allurements. FitzGerald's *Scandal* was so named, he tells us, because 'scandal was the chief product of Woodbridge'. The same thing might have been said, and with more reason, about Bawdsey and its ferry (sometimes called Felixstowe Ferry) for the district reeked with smugglers. Perhaps that is why the *Scandal*, on being acquired by

Sir Cuthbert Quilter after the poet's death, was renamed the *Sapphire*. It sounded better, so.

The early ferry service here, reaching back to the twelfth century, was maintained with row-boats, and any horses which travellers brought with them had to swim across. A new era dawned when, in the late nineteenth century, Sir Cuthbert Quilter introduced a steam ferry, operating on chains stretched across the bed of the River Deben. A few locals can still recall 'this old clanking, clattering contrivance with its deck house and smoking chimney, complete with warning whistle'. It was 'a great sight, especially when it had as cargo a coach-and-four, complete with top-hatted coachman and sounding horn'. What a pity that FitzGerald, that master of the bizarre, never lived to see this 'bit of theatre', though he was here by proxy, so to speak, for Sir Cuthbert was still sailing to and fro in the rechristened *Scandal*, with Ablett Passiful—who had ferryman's blood in his veins—as skipper.

There were two chain-pontoons, apparently. *Lady Beatrice* was reserved for the summer service, and *Lady Quilter*, a smaller edition, for the winter one. A gruesome element that might have appealed to 'Fitz' was that both were managed for years by 'one-armed Brinkley', victim of an accidental gun explosion.

Despite all these attractions the days of Bawdsey steam ferry were numbered. After about forty years' grinding backwards and forwards on those slimy chains, *Lady Beatrice* and *Lady Quilter* went into retirement. A sailing boat took over. Today a motor ferry-boat serves this quaint little area, which even has its Ferry Church, dedicated to St. Nicholas. During the last war, airmen stationed at Bawdsey Manor (built by Sir Cuthbert Quilter) found a less demanding means of transport in this same down-to-earth ferry.

Bawdsey Ferry figures prominently in the story of Margaret Catchpole. Anybody living in East Anglia will need no introduction to this bygone heroine. My wife's family, all Suffolk to the core, were brought up on the story, which tells of a Nacton girl who had the misfortune to fall in love with Will Laud, a smuggler; after many escapades on his unworthy account she was transported to Australia for 'borrowing' her master's grey gelding. What concerns us here, first, is that many of the smuggled cargoes were landed at the mouth of the Deben with the ready connivance of the ferry community, and to the benefit of waiting folk at Woodbridge and places farther inland. The ferry witnessed some of the desperate scuffles with Preventive men. It was from the ferry, also, that Will Laud sent his love token to Margaret Catchpole—a bulky package containing 'silks and shawls, caps and lace, ribbons and stuffs, gloves, parcels of tea, coffee, tobacco and snuff: together with curious-headed and silver-tipped pipes; in short, enough to stock a small shop'. Suspecting contraband, Margaret refused the gift and told the messenger he could take it back to Will Laud at Bawdsey. The romance is dealt with in more detail in my *Smugglers' Britain*.

Now Will Laud's father, Stephen, was a ferryman of some renown. For many years he worked the ferry service across Harwich Harbour from Landguard Fort, which occupies the narrow spit of land just south of Felixstowe. As it linked Suffolk and Essex and put people on their way to London, this ferry could be used by civilians, but its chief purpose was to convey soldiers to and from Harwich and to carry parcels and letters for the Fort.

Stephen Laud was therefore a Government servant receiving Government pay. He had a house near the barracks and breathed the same air of military prestige and discipline. Left a widower, he kept a careful eye on his boy and at length apprenticed him to a boat-builder at Aldeburgh. But he had not reckoned with unscrupulous persons like John Luff and Captain Bargood. It was they who lured Will Laud into the smuggling business. As we have seen, Margaret Catchpole was involved against her wishes. Stephen Laud was another innocent victim. Because of his son's defection from respectability, the ferry service between Landguard and Harwich was given to another man.

A third ferry in this area crossed the River Orwell from Walton, now part of Felixstowe, to Harwich. It was a happy inspiration to call it the Wagtaile Ferry, from Wagtaile House which stood near the late fifteenth-century Ferry House. As Elizabethan days were left behind, however, inspiration dwindled. By 1769 it was known simply as Johnson's Ferry and, later still, the Dooley.*

Decay followed hard upon these prosy efforts. Mr. S. D. Wall, compiler of a manuscript *History of Felixstowe*, tells me that the ferry creek on the Walton side was 'closed before the railway was built in 1877. After the jetty fell into disrepair, the passengers were brought ashore from the boat on the ferryman's back.' If romance here seems to have vanished, it would be well to explore Walton's Ferry Boat Inn. Each room is equipped with a bewilderment of doors, designed for use by the 'knowing' as quick getaways whenever the Press Gang combed the neighbourhood for likely men, and whenever Preventive officers pursued smugglers.

* Probably derived from the local term for a boundary path.

Of certain other ferries that have at various times served this fascinating corner of England, I need only mention the Harwich–Zeebrugge Train Ferry. In a booklet issued about thirty years ago by the London and North Eastern Railway Company some extraordinary ferry cargoes were recalled, among them being four elephants on their way to Olympia, and a 'consignment of live carp weighing over three tons, from Lyons'.

Elephants we have already encountered, but *live carp*! I remember reading how Marie Antoinette admired these fish so much, for their beauty, that she stocked the lake at Versailles with them. Was somebody in London trying to emulate one of the Queen's more innocent passions?

CHAPTER FOUR

WATER MUSIC ON LONDON RIVER

When, in his younger days, my father-in-law kept a grocery shop at Burnham-on-Crouch he must have been as familiar with the neighbouring Creeksea Ferry as with his own horse and cart. Alas, no anecdotes are now recoverable from that source, but two old friends of the family have gladly set their memories to work for my benefit.

With their help I can just descry the Creeksea Ferry Inn as run by a man called Amos, assisted quite fittingly by a Mr. Wiseman who also 'did the ferrying'. Prospective passengers rang a bell which hung from a post and out came the row-boat. If the horse ferry was required, there was an arm like a railway signal to be pulled down. In either case there might be a touch of adventure. At low tide the ferryman would have to put on a St. Christopher act and carry passengers over the muddy Crouch shoreline. The horse ferry was apparently a square float. I can well imagine my wife's parents using this ferry, and it must have been highly amusing if a lot of squeaking pigs were just then coming over to market (as they sometimes did) by the same strange craft; I wouldn't be surprised if some of those pigs were destined for my father-in-law's bacon counter.

All is changed now. A large timber wharf has taken the place of the Ferry Inn, and when a bell is rung it is inside the modern hotel nearby, calling for a different kind of service. Yet Burnham still has its ferry. It is operated by motor-boat from the town steps to Wallasea Bay, across the river. One of my informants admits the convenience of this ferry, but misses the 'rustic flavour' of the old one. 'My father,' she says, 'used to walk the mile from Burnham to Creeksea along the sea wall to catch the ferry, then walk from the south bank to Southend station (eight miles distant) if he wanted to catch the 7.30 a.m. train for London.' As my other correspondent expressively sums up, 'Cars were then hardly existable.'

These Essex rivers—the Stour (one bank of it) which gave John Constable so many of his waterside subjects, the Colne at Brightlingsea, the Blackwater, Crouch, and Roach—demanded ferries as by natural right. How else could Essex folk get about, even on their limited errands? The coastal marshland is riddled with waterways, large and small. As S. Baring-Gould once wrote, the sea here 'creeps in like a thief . . . and battles like a dotard over the mean shells and clots of weed on our strand'. Any detailed map shows how these sinuous waterways were—and in places, still are—crossed by ferry. A ferryman in his pride would furnish Essex with a neat historic symbol.

But we are now bound for the Thames at Tilbury, following more or less in the wake of those who once made the same journey with the aid of ferries at Burnham, Fambridge, or Hullbridge, all on the River Crouch, or by some of the older roads running west of the water-locked region.

The Gravesend–Tilbury Ferry, one of the oldest in the south-eastern area, was once known simply as the Cross Ferry. There was evidently no need to indicate *which* river it crossed or which two counties were here connected. The remark that somebody was using the Cross Ferry, or again the Long Ferry, clearly indicated that our traveller was in the one instance crossing the Thames from Essex to Kent, under the shadow of Tilbury Fort; or, in the other instance, that he was going up-river on that twenty-mile trip to London, as courtiers and merchants and pilgrims had been doing for centuries.

It was to the Cross Ferry that Charles I (when Prince of Wales) and the Duke of Buckingham came one day in 1623. They were on their way to Spain to woo the Infanta for the youthful Charles. To keep this mission secret they travelled in disguise, but when Buckingham proffered a gold piece for the ferry fare, not having any small change, the boatman's suspicions were aroused. He suspected they were spies, or gentlemen on their way to fight an illegal duel, and promptly had them arrested.

Tilbury Fort had been constructed by Henry VIII for the defence of the Thames. It was here that Queen Elizabeth I reviewed her troops before the Armada attack and delivered herself of the memorable words: 'I know I have the body of a weak, feeble woman, but I have the heart and stomach of a king, and a king of England too.'

One vulnerable feature of this defence system seems to have been over-looked; the public right-of-way to the ferry actually ran *through* the Tilbury Fort. This nice little invitation to spies and busybodies was to prove very troublesome during the Civil War. Meanwhile, trouble of another sort had occurred. The ferry was owned by the Lords of the Manors of Tilbury and Parrock. In 1694–5 Gravesend Corporation acquired the manor of Parrock and bought the Gravesend section of the ferry rights. The old order was crumbling. What was to be Tilbury's reaction? The Governor of Tilbury Fort offered to forego the back-pay owing to him if he could have the Essex end of the ferry and the right to build a public house there. He seems to have been granted this boon.

Henceforth, the Governor's livelihood was comfortably augmented by his share of the ferry proceeds and by the takings of the hostelry, known to this day as the World's End Inn.

The World's End had an opposite number on the Kent side. It was known alternately as the Three Crowns, or simply the Ferry-House. This place was equipped with a long causeway which served well enough when the ferry was maintained by wherries, but with the advent of steam it proved inadequate. Eventually, after a floating bridge had been tried and found wanting, the Town Pier was adapted for a service of ferry steamers bearing such names as *Queen Elizabeth*, the *Earl of Essex* (which rolled badly), the *Earl of Lester*, and the *Tilbury*—later renamed *Sir Walter Raleigh*.

I hope our mid-Victorian ancestors enjoyed voyaging on the Thames in the company of such eminent Elizabethans. It was certainly an honour for the paddle-ferry régime when the *Tilbury* received the accolade of Raleigh and his knighthood; but with such heady nomenclature the railway concern which by now ran the service had evidently set themselves too high a standard. Some years later, passengers (and cattle) began to make the Cross Ferry on such vessels as the *Cato*, the *Thames, Rose, Gertrude*, and *Edith*. Gloriana and her favourites had gradually melted away, like ghosts of the past. And it was left to the *Edith* to effect the transition from steam to diesel, in our day.

Regarding this transition, Mr. Thomas Bell of Gravesend kindly sends me the following notes from his personal diary:

28 February 1961. My wife and I took the 3.15 p.m. ferry from Gravesend on the *Edith*, which was her last trip as a ferry-boat.

At Tilbury the new diesel *Edith* was ready, manned, and looking very smart, to take over from old steam *Edith* and inaugurate the new service of diesel boats, *Edith* and *Catherine*, from their namesakes of the steam era. Several dignitaries were on board; the speechmaking was brief, as the service must go on. Among those present were officials from the Port of London Authority and British Railways, and the Mayors of Gravesend and Thurrock.

My wife was the first lady passenger to board the new *Edith*, and she still has a memento, a piece of the yellow ribbon which had been cut on the gangway of the new *Edith*, jointly by the two Mayors a few moments before. The return to Gravesend was done in good time. On both the last trip of the old *Edith* and the first of the new *Edith*, every ship in sight gave their farewell and welcome signal on their sirens . . .

A pretty picture! And although British Railways withdrew their *vehicle* ferry service here on 31 December 1964, owing to the construction of the Dartford Tunnel, the 'ferry of water' mentioned in 1304 as a possession of William de Tilbury still operates across Old Father Thames.

Now for the Long Ferry and its thousand years of history.

This passage seems to have been in use, on a ferry basis, even before the Norman Conquest. From Gravesend it offered the only feasible route to London, as the roads on either side of the river were few, circuitous, and in shocking condition.

Domesday Book refers to a small hithe, or haven, at Milton. This is believed to have been the Gravesend terminal of the Long Ferry. Towards the end of the thirteenth century, people stepped into the waiting barge here, surrendered the halfpenny fare, and grumbled to the authorities later if the waterman demanded anything extra. A halfpenny seems ridiculously cheap for that twenty-mile voyage, and one may sympathize with any boatman who asked for a little more, but in those days this small coin would buy two wheaten loaves, or nearly half a gallon of ale. Even by the fifteenth century, burgesses journeying by road or water to represent their town in Parliament received no more than twelve pence per day; and, as G. M. Trevelyan says, 'a country parson who had £10 a year from all sources was considered to have a tolerable income'.

However, the ferry charges were raised to twopence per passenger by royal charter of Henry IV. In 1379 the Thames estuary had been invaded by the French and the town of Gravesend was set aflame. This royal charter, confirmed by Henry V, Henry VI and Edward IV, was designed to help the survivors by granting them the privilege of transporting people profitably between Gravesend and London. The twopenny fare seems to have retained legal sanction until 1737 when there was a sudden jump to sixpence. Soon afterwards the boatmen, having made conditions rather more comfortable for their clients, required another threepence. By 1790, without any legal authority or increased facilities, the fare demanded was one shilling. All this has a similar ring, even today!

Wolsey used the Long Ferry on at least two occasions, during the twopenny period. In 1505–6 Henry VII dispatched him on a mission to the Emperor Maximilian; Stow takes up the story thus:

> . . . he [Wolsey] took his leave of the King at Richmond about noone, and so came to London aboute foure of the clocke, where the barge of

Gravesend was ready to launch forth, both with a prosperous tyde and winde; without any abode hee entered the barge, and so with such happy speede, that he arrived at Gravesend within little more than three houres . . . and then travelled so speedily [by post horse] that he came to Dover the next morning . . .

Seventeen years later, in 1522, Wolsey repeated the journey, this time 'with a numerous and brilliant train of Earls, Knights, Bishops and Abbots, and thirty Chaplains, with a hundred gentlemen, and seven hundred yeomen . . .' They were on their way to welcome the Emperor Charles V, on his arrival at Dover from the Low Countries. Henry VIII joined the party next day, and after a period of mutual felicitations and conviviality at Dover, and then again at Canterbury, '. . . the great cavalcade reached Gravesend by one o'clock Monday, 2 June where thirty ferry barges were ready to receive the Emperor and King with their respective retinues, and they embarked for Greenwich'. The ferry community at Gravesend had never seen such wonderful processions. Let us hope that it felt suitably rewarded in other ways too, as the glittering boats were cheered out of sight.

Although the Long Ferry provided a quicker route to Dover, via Gravesend, than if the whole journey were undertaken by road, it had hazards and perils of its own. There were river 'highwaymen' and thieves. Boatmen themselves had been known to slit the throats of their passengers and make off with their belongings. Boats occasionally capsized. On 25 October 1553, for example, a barge at Gravesend was overturned and fourteen passengers were drowned. In 1592 a Gravesend tilt-boat was run down by a hoy off Greenwich and between thirty and forty were drowned, in full view of Queen Elizabeth. Most of the accidents were caused by overcrowding, and despite an Act of 1737 limiting the number of passengers to forty per boat, regulations were often ignored for the sake of a few extra sixpences.

A century later Samuel Pepys ferries up and down the Thames on his various colourful occasions. Sometimes he whiles away the time on the water by reading Shakespeare, or scanning some Navy papers perhaps. On 15 July 1665 he accompanies his friend, Philip Carteret, Postmaster General, over the water to Dagenhams, priming him as they go on how to comport himself with his lady-love. Carteret was exceedingly bashful, but Pepys knew all the skills! Carteret's suit prospers and on 31 July Pepys sets off for the wedding:

Up; and very betimes by six o'clock at Deptford, and there find Sir G.
Carteret and my Lady ready to go; I being in my new coloured silk
suit, and coat trimmed with gold buttons and gold broad lace round
my hands, very rich and fine. By water to the Ferry, where, when
we come, no coach there; and tide of ebb so far spent as the horse-
boat could not get off on the other side [of] the river to bring away
the coach. So we were fain to stay there in the unlucky Isle of Doggs,
in a chill place, the morning cool, and wind fresh, above two if not
three hours to our great discontent.

Because of this three-hour hold-up, Samuel and the bridegroom's
parents have the chagrin of missing the ceremony; they arrive to find
the happy couple leaving the church already married!

On 20 August of the same year he goes by ferry to church:

where a dull sermon, and many Londoners. After church to my inn . . .
and so about seven o'clock by water, and got between nine and ten to
Queenhive, very dark.

An ominous note follows: 'And I could not get my waterman to go elsewhere for fear of the plague. Thence with a lanthorn, in great fear of
meeting dead corpses, carrying to be buried . . .'

A year later, during the Great Fire, Pepys describes how multitudes of
horrified citizens flee to the boats, taking their household treasures with
them. Often, to the momentary delight of Pepys' musical soul, somebody
steps aboard with a pair of virginals. His own treasures chosen for safe-
keeping, across the water, include 'pictures and fine things'. When
pestilence and fire die down, one sees Pepys and other householders,
now merry again, as they hire some ferryman for the recovery of the
belongings they had hidden away.

Stow, in his *Survey of London* (1598), stated that the Thames then
gave employment to forty thousand men. Many of these worked the
shorter ferries across the river. The Company of Watermen and Lightermen was formed about 1555 to exercise some degree of control and to
protect the interests of 'wherrymen and watermen exercising rowing
betwixt Gravesend and Windsor'.

Amongst the information kindly supplied to me by the present Clerk
of the Company I find references to the destruction of the Company's
first Hall in the Great Fire and to the building of the current Hall in
1780. In the Company's Court Room the Arms granted by Queen

Elizabeth I make a fine plasterwork device over the chimneypiece. The crest is a waterman's arm brandishing an oar. Two dolphins support the centre-piece which carries a pair of crossed oars and a small boat riding the water. The motto, 'At Comaunde of Our Superiore', at once calls to mind all those who have ever worked the Thames, either by carrying freight in the lighters, or passengers in the 'wherry ferries' as Taylor, the Water Poet, was pleased to call them.

We have already sampled a little of John Taylor's exuberance at Hull. Here, in the Company's headquarters, his portrait in oils graces the Court Room, for he became one of the Company's renowned Freemen. He springs to life again through his writings—prose, poetry and sheer doggerel—that illuminate a career including much ferrying on the Thames, being pressed (seven times!) into the Navy, and officiating as collector of wine dues on the river. In the interests of his fellow watermen he protested against the transference of theatres from the Surrey side of the Thames, which meant loss of fares, and poured scorn upon the introduction of sedan chairs and hackney carriages ('hackney hellcarts' he called them) to the streets of London. His fulminations were not in vain. With the Company's co-operation 'he was successful in keeping the carriages from London for thirty-five years unless the journeys ended at least two miles from the river, for so long, London's "High Street".' He seems to have argued that Nature *intended* a river people to travel by ferry.

Many other things could imperil the waterman's livelihood. At one time the Company received grants from the Government to relieve distress among their members when great frosts immobilized all traffic on the Thames. In 1814, however, when large ice-packs formed on the river, a few venturesome ferrymen made as much as ten pounds per day by taking people across to the merry-go-rounds, printing presses, and other frost-fair attractions established on these temporary shores and islands. When a bridge was built over the river, the Company received compensation for the loss of ferries. Another source of income was from the watermen themselves; the Company had the power to fine their freemen for bad behaviour and foul language.

The Thames was then notorious for its 'water language'. Ribald jokes were flung from boat to boat as the ferrymen plied their oars. Anybody might become a target for abuse and vituperation. Not even royalty escaped this fusilade. Earlier monarchs seem to have been no more offended by such scurrilous chatter than by the privileged jibes of their own court jesters. But the Hanoverian kings were different. They could

E

not understand or endure ferrymen's noisy twaddle and tried to have it suppressed. When George I made his first progress up the Thames it was suppressed for him by the *Water Music* which, so the story goes, Handel partly composed for this very reason.

George I's accession is still commemorated on the Thames by an annual sculling race organized by the Watermen's Company and open to Freemen. The founder of the event, Thomas Doggett, an Irish comedian, would have been gratified to see the orange-red coat bearing his badge which is awarded to the victor. From London Bridge to Chelsea—the course to be sculled by competitors—is a furlong short of five miles, but all that Doggett wanted, one bad night in 1714, was to be rowed a little way up-river to his home. Because tide and weather were unfavourable, most of the ferrymen refused to turn out, but a young fellow who had only just received his Freedom, and needed all the patronage he could get, obliged.

Doggett showed his gratitude by forming this contest between first-year Freemen of the Company. Once again, the ferryman's calling had been honoured. Two of those who have won Doggett's Coat and Badge in recent times are Harold Green (1924), now one of the Queen's Watermen, and Bert Barry (1925), the Queen's Bargemaster.

In his *British Monarchy* (1751) George Bickham captures the spirit of the contemporary Thames in one of his peculiar bird's-eye-view maps. The foreground near Westminster is busy with small row-boats, and ferries carrying men and women of fashion. On the Surrey bank a typical ferry-house presents its many gables to the waterside. Richmond and Kew are shown in the mid-distance, but not Twickenham, where, to this day, a fine group of Georgian buildings surrounds the ferry known to Pope and Horace Walpole, J. M. W. Turner and Charles Dickens. Whatever its deficiences, the bird's-eye-view map prompts one to borrow Bickham's fancy and see the folk in his sculling boats as so many privileged visitors on their way to Twickenham, Richmond's neighbour across the river, which had developed into an elegant suburb—whose grand villas deign to echo the adjacent ferry in their names—after George I had survived all that water-borne invective.

George Bickham, always so keen to match his little extravaganzas with fine calligraphy embodying legend, fable and tradition, somehow overlooked one of London's best stories.

One Sunday night in the reign of King Sebert a fisherman named Edric was putting his salmon nets into the Thames when a stranger in foreign attire called to him, begging to be ferried over the water. Ferrying came to Edric as easily as a bit of night fishing so he took the stranger across, landing him, as directed, on Thorney Island near a church due for consecration the next day. Suddenly the air became electrified and from his boat Edric beheld hosts of angels hovering around the new edifice. He was still sitting at his oars, dazed with the wonder of it all, when the stranger returned, saying, 'I am Peter, keeper of the keys of Heaven . . . and have consecrated my own church of St. Peter.'

Edric was rewarded for his services in curious manner. 'Pull out into the river,' said Peter, 'and you will catch a plentiful supply of fish, mostly salmon. This I have granted on two conditions—first, that you never fish again on Sundays; secondly, that you pay a tithe of them to the Abbey of Westminster.'

In this miraculous way was Westminster Abbey founded, but in the present building, unfortunately, Edric the ferry-fisherman is nowhere represented by even the simplest stained-glass panel or stone carving. I find this surprising and regrettable. Many a lesser story has been fan-fared beyond all merit. Surely one of our needlework guilds could set things right?

The ferries of the upper Thames provide much of the charm of William Morris's *News from Nowhere*. A Utopian dream, of course, but it is signi-ficant that in the lovely, blissful world here envisaged Dick the Ferryman plays a prominent part; not a subservient Dick, but one who is the equal of his neighbours; a craftsman in fine metals, too, and as fully conversant with salmon fishing as was Edric down there by Westminster.

I think often of Morris's ferryman as he puzzles over the coins which the guest from an earlier day offers as fare. Suddenly, Dick recalls hav-ing heard of this old custom and remarks, disarmingly, ' ". . . you see this ferrying is my *business*, which I would do for anybody; so to take gifts in connection with it would look very queer. Besides, if one person gave me something, then another might, and another, and so on; and I hope you won't think me rude if I say that I shouldn't know where to stow away so many mementoes of friendship." And he laughed loud and merrily, as if the idea of being paid for his work was a very funny joke.'

And to think that at Bablock Hythe Ferry, higher up the river near Oxford, monetary instincts were so prevalent—in real life—that people used to say that a coin thrown into the water from the landing-stage would return seven fold!

The names of some of these Thames ferries have a poetic quality: My Lady Ferry, near Cliveden; Spade Oak Ferry near Cookham; Sonning, near Reading; Chalmore Hole, beyond Great Missenden; and so on.

J. H. B. Peel records the following pleasant anecdote in *Portrait of the Thames*: 'One morning, when no ferryman was at hand, Bridges removed his trousers, slung them over his shoulder, and forded the stripling Thames at Hinksey Ferry; but he himself was not a stripling, for it happened when he was eighty years old.' This was Robert Bridges, Poet Laureate, who in his verse evoked some beautiful scenes beside 'the silver Thames' where

> . . . laden barges float
> By banks of myosote;
> And scented flag and golden flower-de-lys
> Delay the loitering boat.

One who earlier passed all these fair scenes, with no more than a professional glance at the different ferries, perhaps, was our ubiquitous Water Poet. Fleeing from the plague, Taylor rowed up-river to Oxford and found refuge with the Provost of Oriel. When Charles I established his headquarters at Oxford, this irrepressible ferryman-rhymester had the satisfaction of being made a Yeoman of the Guard.

CHAPTER FIVE

HAZARDS ON THE SOLENT

One hot, fretful summer's day I sought the welcome coolness of Canterbury Cathedral and tried to recapture the pilgrim spirit of the Middle Ages. Chaucer, thinking of Thomas à Becket and his shrine, tells us that

> . . . from every shires ende
> Of Engeland, to Canterbury they wende
> The Holy blisful martir for to seke.

What concerns us just now are the routes taken by the pilgrims. Those of Geoffrey Chaucer's versatile company made the journey from London by road, cutting out the Long Ferry altogether, but all the way down from Yorkshire and beyond some of the ferries noticed already carried their share of pilgrims. 'Ye go to Canterbury: God you speed.' This traditional greeting, or something like it, must have sprung to the lips of many a ferryman on the Humber, say, or the Trent, or the Thames itself.

Other pilgrims came along from the Winchester direction; these have not won the place in literature which the Wife of Bath enjoys, or Chaucer's other companions, but no doubt there were many knights and merchants, well-fed friars and monks, scriveners, hard-up scholars and gay women, in this company, too, and a motley sight they must have made as they pulled up on the bank of the River Medway and prepared to cross over (as some authorities think) by Snodland Ferry, a few miles south of Rochester. Today people visit this neighbourhood for its many associations with Dickens; the pilgrims bound for Canterbury tend to be put out of countenance by Pickwick and his coterie as they disport themselves at Cobham's Leather Bottle or at Dingley Dell.

The pilgrims come into the picture again, however, by means of a ferry service established within the city boundaries as recently as 1932. On peering down from King's Bridge one sees another motley assortment of people, holiday makers, all availing themselves of the little boats that ply up and down the River Stour, passing Blackfriars' Monastery, the Pilgrims' Hospital, the 'Weavers', and Greyfriars' Monastery. This ferry service may be comparatively new, but it takes one through the heart of old Canterbury and quite near to the Chequers of the Hope where the bygone pilgrims lodged.

Until a few years ago, when a bridge was built on the site, Grove Ferry dominated the River Stour six miles east of Canterbury. It served that part of Kent known as the Isle of Thanet, and once again the scale of charges gives a nice cross-section of the community: passengers and cycles 1d.; beasts ½d. each, sheep 6d. per score; carts and wagons 3d. per wheel. Then, to keep abreast of changing times, the ferry began to take motor-cycles over the river for 2d. each, or 3d. if there was a sidecar, while a motor-car cost 1s. 2d.

This historic bit of England is still keeping pace with progress for, as I write, one of the world's first international hoverports is being built, for Channel ferry services, at Pegwell Bay, near Ramsgate. St. Augustine —bound for Canterbury on his mission sponsored by Pope Gregory, in A.D. 597—is thought to have landed at Pegwell Bay. I expect he would have a rough boat crossing, lasting several hours. The hovercraft 'which floats on a cushion of air above the water and is driven by air-plane type propellers' will cover the twenty-eight miles from Ramsgate to Calais with a full load in about forty minutes.

It is pleasant to think that when Augustine made his landfall at Pegwell Bay there would be myriads of waders and gulls and wildfowl in evidence as there are, hereabouts, to this day. In fact, the local hovercraft plans were held up for some time because of nature-lovers' protests at the intrusion. Whether the birds themselves will protest and seek other haunts remains to be seen.

But down here along the south-east seaboard we are still in pilgrim country, for there were many who came to Becket's shrine from over-seas. The cross-Channel routes they used have since gone through the steamship-ferry era, and now come the hovercraft. One early would-be invader of England proposed to rid himself of the Channel barrier by assembling enough elephants, along the French shore, to drink up all the water. Naïve fellow! He would have been bereft of speech could he have known that a day lay in the distant future when people would be ferried over that same barrier with ease, speed and luxury, without benefit of boat *or* elephant! Personally I find it most gratifying that whether the hovercraft take-off from Ramsgate, Dover, Southampton or Portsmouth, the respective companies still apply to their services the time-honoured term *Ferry*. It seems the inescapably right thing to do.

Farther along the south coast, at Rye, a ferry once crossed the River

Tillingham to Cadborough. If you lived on the Rye side, you probably left the commercial quarter called Wish (conveniently situated near the various smuggling taverns) first, then turned down Ferry Road, passed the time of day with some of the fishermen setting out their nets to dry on Pole Marsh, made the sign of the Cross when skirting the town gibbet, and finally—after refreshing yourself at the Ferry Boat Inn— hailed the ferryman.

On returning, towards evening, you might spend a copper or two at the open-air theatre or the fair at the town end of Ferry Road. This low-lying area was subject to flooding, however. It is recorded that in 1577 the water rose 'eight or nine foot in men's houses' so 'William White having a bote fecht a great companie of them out of their windowes, and carried them to drie land as fast as he could fetch them, which were in great danger and feare'. It sounds as though the ferryman was busier than usual that day.

Rye boasted another ferry, which began near the harbour and put you on the road for Winchelsea. Indeed, you had no choice; even by Queen Elizabeth I's reign, this was the only practical route to that other member of the Cinque Ports federation. Having crossed by this ferry you climbed the hill towards Udimore, then strolled down Dumb Woman's Lane to the marshes. When these were under water another boat was kept in readiness, and yet a third ferryman had to take you— over the River Brede, this time—before you could enter Winchelsea at Pipewell or Ferry Gate.

After his great victory over the Spaniards in Winchelsea Bay, Edward III returned by this route as far as Udimore, where Queen Philippa was anxiously awaiting him and their two sons. 'Think now, your mother will be sure to ask. *How* many ships did we sink?' I can imagine Edward priming his lads on this vital point, as they were sculled across the Brede, though I expect Philippa, being wife and mother, was far more concerned for their own personal safety. What were forty enemy men-of-war by comparison?

Because of the enveloping marshes one can readily understand how John Taylor, the Water Poet, felt when he came this way. His poem entitled *The Certaine Travailes of an Uncertaine Journey, 1653* contains this diatribe:

> Near unto Rye, 2 dirty Ferrys be
> So Muddy, that they mir'd my Mare and me.
> I past them, And on Ultima Augusti

Well meated, Mounted, man and beast both lusty,
I cross'd o'er Guldeford ferry, and I went
From Rye in Sussex unto Hythe in Kent . . .

His 'Guldeford ferry' was evidently the one that crossed the River Tillingham.

Like so many other parts of Britain, the Sussex countryside has lost many of its ferries. I hope some of them survived, with their peculiar charm and 'paintability', against the time when J. M. W. Turner came along while staying as Lord Egremont's guest at Petworth. How he revelled in such waterside scenes!

As long ago as 1392–3 there was a ferry on the River Arun at Bury, and the man in charge seems to have been paid a bushel of corn when taking the Lord of the Manor's servants across this 'passagium'. As John Galsworthy lived at Bury one may assume that he would know this pretty spot, though by 1877 the boat was no better than a 'cumbrous tub'. Arundel is not far away, which explains why the Dukes of Norfolk owned the Ferry-House at Bury for many years. But its knell has been sounded. A signpost to the river is now marked 'Ferry Closed'.

In 1301–2 the Duke of Norfolk's Arundel estate included a ferry at Rustyngton, for which a rent of one shilling was due every Michaelmas. Stopham's fourteenth-century bridge over the Arun replaced an ancient ferry. Before Meeching became the busy port of Newhaven, the River Ouse was crossed hereabouts in the same manner; perhaps this ferry persisted long enough to bring ashore some of the people fleeing from France at the time of the Revolution.

And so the story of bygone Sussex ferries might continue, if only one could delve more deeply into local surveys, family deeds and other ancient documents. Many antiquaries have done their best to recover such fragments of forgotten lore. Here is one fragment, given by J. Manwaring Baines in *Historic Hastings*:

. . . a ferry across the marshes is mentioned in 1335, and the road leading from the church of 'Bolewarthethe' [Bulverhythe] to Hastings was known as the 'Chawceye' (? Causeway) in 1369.

If one is familiar with Hastings this remark can kindle one's interest until the town's modern developments recede in favour of the fisherfolk who, jabbering away in a dialect laced with French words and phrases, ferried over the water every Sabbath to Bulverhythe. Something of their religious fervour is reflected in a paraphrase of the Twenty-Third Psalm, composed in 1874 by Captain John Roberts of Hastings. Although his words refer to the sea and its perils, the opening lines would apply just as well to some of the ferries we have encountered so far:

> The Lord is my Pilot, I shall not drift,
> He lighteth me across the dark waters,
> He steereth me in deep channels,
> He keepeth my log . . .

Our leave-taking of Sussex must be from the western extremity of the county, where Chichester Harbour embraces so many little promontories that connecting ferries are, or were, as natural as the air one breathes. Pedestrians can still reach Bosham the lovely spot where Canute is supposed to have commanded the incoming tide—by one of these ferries. Another crossed over from West Wittering to Hayling Island. This ferry was actually worked by H. M. Preventive Service—all too conveniently, for the district was once a smugglers' paradise. On being signalled, the ferryman came over but his first duty was to scrutinize passenger and his belongings; only then did he collect their sixpences and hand them into the boat.

Hayling Island is an island no longer. In 1824 the Duke of Norfolk, Earl Marshal of England, opened a bridge that crossed the narrow channel formerly spanned by the Wadeway and served what locals called 'the northern ferry'. In 1857 Charles J. Longcroft wrote the following about this awkward passage, before it was 'tamed' by the bridge:

> . . . the situation of the islanders must up to this time [1824] have been pitiable indeed; . . . from the violence of the winds and sea the Wadeway was frequently covered by the tide the whole twenty-four hours together, and boats were often totally prevented from crossing the harbour, by reason whereof any communication between the mainland and Hayling Island became impracticable and great inconvenience, difficulty, and loss were thereby occasioned, and the lives of His Majesty's subjects were very much endangered.

The good people of Hayling must have thanked Heaven when the Havant Bridge materialized and their life-line was thus assured. But Hayling islanders, and trippers from Portsmouth, still enjoy one old ferry service. It is operated by launches which chug across Langstone

Harbour from Sinah Point, Hayling, to Eastney Point near Portsmouth. Yet another ferry shuttles its way through this fantastic piece of natural filigree, which must look unreal from the air. Its last reticular flourish, Portsmouth Harbour, is linked by boat with Gosport.

The Isle of Wight ferries from Portsmouth are now operated by the Southern Region of British Railways, but before they achieved such distinction there were centuries of confusion and strife. It was the drama of the Humber all over again, but with many variations.

First, the Abbess of Wherwell set her possessive foot on 'Ride' beach and controlled the boats which took passengers over the Solent to Portsmouth. That was in 1420. Soon after, to confound matters, the term 'passenger' was applied to the ferryman, not to those paying a fare. It is necessary to keep this peculiarity in mind, lest a fine of six shillings and eightpence and a period in the town stocks—imposed on some 'passengers' for refusing to tackle the crossing—be misunderstood. It was the boatman on duty who thus rendered himself liable for correction, not some hapless traveller.

Regulations were tightened as the years went by. A rota of 'passengers' was drawn up and woe betide anybody who tried to jump the queue. In 1604 at the annual Court Leet it was further enacted that there should be no Sunday ferry service, unless a fare could prove he was on King's business, or carried a special warrant from the Lord of the Manor. In 1655 the Court Leet gave instructions for the repair of the Ferry Dock at Hyde, and then examined the case of Mary Shamble. Her offence?—not attempting the four-mile passage from Ryde to Portsmouth although it was her turn to handle the boat and the weather was fair. Verdict? A fine of twenty shillings. Heavy, to be sure, but I expect she was glad to be spared that other penalty—an hour or two as anybody's Aunt Sally in the town stocks.

Under such strict rules of conduct did this ferry service continue until the reign of George III. Then, for many years, good ferry behaviour gradually went to the winds. Of this, however, there is as yet no hint in the guidebook covering Portsmouth and Southsea about 1800. Readers were told that 'Beizeley's vessel arrives from Ryde every morning and returns at two o'clock, where a coach awaits the arrival of the vessel to convey goods and passengers to Newport. The Master may be spoken with at the Quebec Tavern.' It all sounds a very gentlemanly affair and nobody could mind paying five shillings, single, for being looked after so well in this friendly sailing packet.

The event that brought about the change was the introduction of *steam* ferries. Men who remained loyal to the former sailing craft were 'on a dying horse'. But they put up a valiant fight, and had the repeated satisfaction of seeing the interlopers fail, commercially. A paddle steamer of seventy-five tons, capable of travelling at eight knots, made its maiden voyage on 9 June 1815. Despite its potential, it must have looked a squat, smoky thing against the tall masts and billowing sails that graced some of the most beautiful craft that ever crossed the Solent. One can imagine the jeering and the insults that would be flung at the horrid little newcomer as it ploughed its pioneer course.

A second challenge to the old régime appeared two years later. In May 1817 the *Hampshire Telegraph and Post* informed its readers that 'the fine new steam packet *Britannia* will sail regularly from Portsmouth every morning at half past eight and return at ten o'clock, and in the afternoon will go over at three o'clock and return at half past five o'clock. No expense has been spared to render this superior packet deserving of public patronage which the proprietors humbly solicit. The Master to be spoken with at The Fountain, Star and Garter, Isle of Wight Tavern, and the Roebuck.' Convivial occasions are thus envisaged.

Despite all these allurements, even this service failed; the sailing packets—lovelier than ever, it would seem to their devotees—resumed their old monopoly of the Solent ferry passage and retained it until 1825.

But Progress will not long be denied. Thwarted at first, the new era that was to put old John Allan of London and Whitby (and many others) out of business because he liked nothing better than a sail full of wind to bring his cargoes home, began to prove its convenience and cash value. John Allan traded with the Far East and knew many oceans, but I can hear him snorting disgustedly, along with those other diehards who simply navigated home waters, when local newspapers kept printing announcements like this: 'We find that the beautiful steamboat *Union* has been purchased by a few public-spirited individuals and is fully equipped for the passage between Portsmouth and Ryde, where she is intended to be kept going and returning all day'. And, soon joined by further steamboats, 'kept going' it was, so much so that by 1832 you could step into your carriage at one terminal and alight from it at the other, free to drive at will among the 'antique castles and towers rising from their wooden acclivities, which gave their peculiar features to the northern side of the Island'.

Thomas Roscoe, who wrote the above eulogy of Wight in the early nineteenth century matched his eloquence to the hour and further extolled the steam ferry services, which in 'double-quick time' were enabling passengers to 'set foot in the loveliest Isle of Britain's realm' and to 'take a stroll in the Garden of all England' and 'to visit the Queen of Watering Places . . . the charming and salubrious Ryde'.

Roscoe must be allowed another word before we hear the unpleasant sequel. Referring to one particular 'aquatic trip' across the Solent in a new iron steamboat, he remarks, '. . . it was delightful to feel ourselves borne, with wind and tide favouring, at from twelve to fourteen miles an hour, till we seemed to partake of its bounding elastic speed, like a thing instinct with life'.

'Instinct with life!' The phrase was truer than he intended, for when steamboat companies began to set up in opposition to each other, in the mid-Victorian period, the Solent became an *ordeal* for ferry passengers rather than the gateway to Roscoe's terrestrial paradise.

At the pierheads, boats jockeyed for the best positions.* Passengers, almost bullied aboard, became helpless victims of the battles that ensued after leaving port. Regardless of damage or public weal, the boats rammed into each other with a fervour that would almost have done justice to the Armada scrap, centuries before, in these same Channel waters. Women swooned in their crinolines. Men passengers gave loud voice to their feelings, but secretly, perhaps, took sides in the battle as the boats shuddered and rocked dangerously.

The antagonists in these engagements were the Old Company, namely, the Portsmouth and Ryde Royal Mail Steam Packet Company; and the New Company, which struck a belligerent note even while advertising itself as the Portsea, Portsmouth, Gosport and Isle of Wight Steam Packet Company. This new company had been formed in 1849 'by local inhabitants to protect the public, prevent monopoly, and give increased accommodation at reduced fares'. This may have sounded promising, but the result was disastrous, and (to us in the twentieth century) is uncomfortably reminiscent of certain pledges by Adolf Hitler.

While those two concerns were fighting for supremacy, giving their clients anything but protection, a third company slyly entered the lists, though waving a flag of peace. 'Our steamboats,' announced this upstart Southampton and Ryde Packet Company, 'are peremptorily forbidden to race with other steamers, and the attention of each Master is

---

* Human nature changes little. I vividly recall the early, privately-owned motor-buses in the 1920s, and how they often raced and overtook each other, regardless of public safety, so as to forestall a rival at the next picking-up place.

strictly called to the motions of all other steamers in their vicinity, so that no wilful collisions may ensue. Travellers are cautioned, therefore, to ship themselves direct at Southampton for Ryde *if they are not tired of this world.*' (My italics.)

Did this third conciliatory venture calm the troubled waters? Did intending ferry passengers now breathe freely again and recover their love of life? Not a bit of it! One soon hears of stormy scenes between the pacifically inclined *Princess of Wales* and the rival *Prince Albert*, with a lot of dockside ruffians hired by the latter's captain to attack the other boat's crew. If both passenger contingents were not now completely 'tired of this world' they must have been tough indeed. Such incidents put them in imminent danger of being flung overboard.

Peace was only achieved in the Solent when, a year later, the different ferry companies saw the light and wisely decided to amalgamate. The peace lasted for twenty years. And then hostilities broke out afresh, the 'evil genius' being a parvenu ferry enterprise, the Solent Steam Packet Company. By this time Queen Victoria was visiting the Isle of Wight, bestowing an aura on the place which it has never seemed to lose. Perhaps her repeated presence at Osborne, and at Ryde—where she frequently travelled on the horse-drawn tram that took intending ferry passengers along Ryde Pier*—had an admonitory effect on mischief makers. Certainly, the Solent Steam Packet Company scorned to use the old buccaneering methods; they wore kid gloves and devised new methods, equally effective.

You would be about to board one of the United Company's boats, and suddenly notice your luggage was missing. Not until the vessel steamed away did the luggage as mysteriously reappear. This sort of conjuring trick was accomplished by a number of pier porters, bribed for the purpose by the rival company, whose boat—bright as a new pin —now hove to and awaited your service. It was as simple as that. Ramming a competitive vessel was altogether too crude, too brutal. Guile was all one needed for success. And this could take other forms, too. A short-sighted passenger could easily be convinced that the Solent Company's ferry-boat was the one he wanted. Even if he had already bought a United ticket, there were ways of persuading him aboard the other vessel and then selling him a 'correct' ticket.

---

* The tram was later electrified and in 1935 it crashed into the pier buffers, thus effectively terminating its career as an adjunct of the ferry. It is now exhibited with other bygones in Hull Transport Museum.

We have travelled a long way since some genial old ferryman would touch his cap, thankfully take your fare and recount much local lore as he rowed you across his stretch of water. Something of that leisurely past was lost to Southampton when the Itchen Ferry gave place to the Floating Bridge in 1836. Only a little earlier Jane Austen had used the ferry on her way to visit friends. Earlier still Samuel Pepys had been taken across, to be greeted on the other side by the Mayor who had a sturgeon caught in Southampton Water ready for their luncheon. At one time, as part of the Beating of the Bounds ceremony, the Mayor and his party would stop at Itchen Ferry Hard to receive due homage from the ferrymen's community; they were then rowed over the water gratis. One old lady in the fifteenth century had caught a chill while waiting for the ferry, beside this little creek, and left a sum of money for the erection of a small shelter so that others should benefit.

Until the Second World War destroyed its character, Itchen Ferry was a friendly place, surrounded by fishermen's thatched cottages. No cut-throat competition here. Indeed, the Itchen ferrymen seem to have enjoyed a reputation for helpfulness which could be traced back to pre-Tudor times when their forbears earned the name Algerines because they frequently went to the rescue of youths and maidens who would otherwise have been carried off to the slave markets of Algeria. It is pleasing to think of those Barbary Rovers, who were then raiding the south coast for their human spoil, being balked to some appreciable extent by the men who normally rowed their little boats over the Itchen.

Not long ago I stood with some friends beside Southampton Water, near Hythe, in the stillness of a spring afternoon. A small back eddy, fringed with reeds, rippled at our feet. Beyond further reed banks and some tiny peninsulas which only a bird could trust for footing, the great waterway swept by, seawards, taking with it just then a steamer which for me, in my pliable mood, represented the large steam ferries that have headed for Cowes on the Isle of Wight. Our view of Itchen, over the water, was somewhat hazy, but Hythe itself, only half a mile to the south, awaited us with its own ferry lore.

Being accustomed to the West Riding hills and dales, I find this part of Hampshire amazingly flat. And yet it was another Yorkshireman, from the same hilly area, who literally first put Hythe Ferry on the county map, in 1575. Christopher Saxton was the man and Queen Elizabeth I allowed her portrait to appear as frontispiece to his famous Atlas of Great Britain. Like other cartographers of the period, Saxton was sparing in his map details. That Hythe Ferry was shown at all, points to its importance to the Elizabethans, who probably used it as a short-cut to Southampton from Christchurch, Lymington, and the New Forest.

As Hythe Ferry even today provides the quickest and best approach from Southampton to Beaulieu, there can be little doubt that, after the dissolution of Beaulieu Abbey, the ferry would be used by the Wriothesleys who then acquired this beautiful place, and by such later owners as John, Duke of Montagu, who created Buckler's Hard on the Beaulieu River. And I cannot imagine Henry Adams and his family, who made Buckler's Hard into a shipbuilding centre during the eighteenth century, travelling overland to Southampton when there was a wherry to take them more conveniently over the water from Hythe.

It is true that the wherries were but sailing boats of Scandinavian origin and could carry only twelve passengers each. Still, to a shipbuilder a boat was a boat, even though wind and weather could prolong the wherry's passage over Southampton Water from twenty minutes to a full hour.

By 1836, however, steam forced its way through; the Southampton Directory for that year referred to the introduction of 'steam communication between Southampton, Hythe, Beaulieu, Lymington and the New Forest', and that 'on and after Monday, July 25, the *Forester* will leave Hythe for Southampton every morning at seven o'clock and hourly until eight in the evening'.

The name, *Forester*, was obviously bestowed in recognition of the fact that although the god of steam was now in the ascendant, Hythe Ferry was for Southampton folk still the old, beloved gateway to the New Forest, that enormous area of ancient woodland supervised, as for centuries past, by its Court of Verderers. From Hythe Ferry, Beaulieu is reached by road in a matter of three or four miles; and Beaulieu with its ruined abbey, its palatial mansion and its charming river scenery, holds the key to this part of the Forest.

A large-scale map of Beaulieu River suggests that ferries would occasionally be required to cross its sinuous, five-mile course between Beaulieu village and Lepe, which overlooks the Solent. While still a port in its own right, Lepe ran a ferry service to Gurnard Bay, near Cowes, but according to Captain H. Widnell, Lord Montagu's archivist, there are but scanty records of ferries on this famous yachting river itself. Between Gins and Exbury, where they are said to have had a chapel, the Cistercian monks of Beaulieu crossed by stepping-stones. If they operated a ferry for themselves, either here or nearer the abbey, no record of it has yet been found to enrich local traditions.

Knowing how often monastic communities did operate ferries, in other parts of the country, I confess to being rather deflated here. A river sporting such delightful names as St. Catherine's Creek, Need's Oar, Fiddler's Reach, Factory Mead, Buckler's Hard and of course Beaulieu Quay, had sounded so promising. And then I noticed a passing reference in the account of Buckler's Hard written by the present Lord Montagu. After a short visit to Buckler's Hard in 1750 'Frederick Prince of Wales', it seems, 'was ferried over the river to Gilbury Hard', whence a lane leads circuitously to Exbury and Lepe. Taken along with other slight references eventually unearthed for me by Captain Widnell, this incident may well signify that a ferry service hereabouts was too commonplace to warrant any written record. After all, one doesn't need to write home about ordinary, everyday affairs.

Among the famous vessels built by Henry Adams at Buckler's Hard were H.M.S. *Agamemnon* (1781), Nelson's favourite ship; the *Indefatigable* (1783); the *Euryalus* (1803); and the *Hannibal III* (1810). Workmen who lived on the Exbury shore would probably be ferried over as required. The only alternative was a five-mile trudge via the bridge at Beaulieu; and I cannot visualize old Henry Adams tolerating that when a new naval vessel was in the stocks! His workmen could be fetched across the water and be vigorously at their various tasks within five minutes.

An old Mr. Hendy was known to be ferrying labourers from Buckler's Hard to Gilbury Hard each morning, and back again in the evening, as late as the 1890s. A service so obvious, so convenient, must surely have begun somewhere about the time (*c.* 1724) when John, Duke of Montagu was envisaging Buckler's Hard as a port that would some day rival Southampton and Lymington.

That hope was never realized. The nearest thing to a regular ferry service here are the pleasure boats that now run up and down the Beaulieu River, during the summer, from the Solent ports. Beauty and quietude (except during Bank Holidays!) have thus been largely preserved. Lymington also manages to retain some natural charm; its Yarmouth (Isle of Wight) ferry packets are first seen, across the wide harbour, from a fore-stage of tall, stately swans.

The coat-of-arms of the
Company of Watermen
and Lightermen

The Fowey–Bodinnick Ferry, Cornwall, immortalized
by Sir Arthur Quiller-Couch in *Shining Ferry*

The floating bridge crossing Poole Harbour, Dorset

This sea-horse ferry takes visitors from Bigbury,
Devon, to Burgh Island (right) at high tide

A carving in Zennor
Church, Cornwall, represents
the mermaid who fell in
love with the squire's son

A hand-pulled ferry crossing the
Wye below Symonds Yat

The ancient Britons probably used coracles like this
one, made by Will Jones of Cenarth, Cardiganshire

The Conway Ferry in 1795. The coach is ready to take the passengers further on their journey through North Wales

The Woodside Ferry, Birkenhead, in 1814

Arctic conditions on the Mersey in February 1895.
A paddle ferry-boat pushes its way through blocks of ice

The *Duke of Lancaster* in dock at Heysham, Lancs

One of the milestones at
Cartmel, Lancs, for
travellers crossing
Morecambe Bay over the sands

CHAPTER SIX

BY FERRY STAGES INTO CORNWALL

'. . . if all persons . . . would spend some of their tyme in Journeys to visit their native Land . . . it would form such an Idea of England, add much to its Glory and esteem in our minds and cure the evil itch of overvaluing foreign parts.'

Celia Fiennes is speaking, during that 'side-saddle' ride through the country which she undertook in the reign of William and Mary. The point of her remark is even more valid in our day, when so many English tourists know the Continent better than their own fair land. A good way of getting right to the heart of England is to discover and, if possible, use its historic ferries.

Around the Solent we have seen many modernized ferries, now supplemented by hovercraft, but viewed from Christchurch Bay the Isle of Wight is just a grey strip on the eastern horizon, too remote for excitement and therefore leaving this grand little town to its own quiet affairs. For centuries, those affairs have revolved very largely around its own three ferries.

The old name of the town, Twynham, referred to its situation 'between the waters', that is, the Avon and the Stour. Though probably as old as Christchurch Priory, Wick Ferry still provides a crossing over the Stour, from Southbourne to Christchurch. Now operated from Pontin's Holiday Camp, on the Christchurch side, it is flanked by tennis courts, a putting green and a miniature railway. Early this century, however, the great attraction here was the Ferry Tea Boat, moored beneath some willows, where you could buy 'plain teas' at sixpence per head. Tea baskets were also available for those who wished to hire their own boats: 'Ask the Ferryman', said a notice on the small thatched hut beside the jetty. About this time the ferry-boat was a punt and contemporary post-card views show crinolined dames enjoying the trip, while the pilot, looking very efficient in peaked cap and fustian jacket, yarned away— as anybody had a right to expect for his halfpenny fare.

Local inhabitants thought a lot about their ferrymen in those spacious days. They were pivotal characters, as essential to the life of the community as parson or 'bobby'.

F

63

Here is Eli Miller. He started an alternative ferry from Christchurch to Wick in 1800 and his family kept it going until 1903. The Millers were followed by a Mr. Edmund who worked the ferry daily from 5.30 a.m. to 11 p.m. and only retired from his labours in 1946. He seems to have been helped by one O'Brien, a man so huge of stature that special boots had to be made for him—by his long-suffering sister. Artists would come down to the riverside to paint his portrait; some of these studies later appeared in the Royal Academy.

When any historically minded visitors cross the River Stour at this point they have a fine view of Christchurch Priory as reward. One soon realizes that the ferry itself is liquid parochial history.

The Avon and the Stour unite at the landward end of Christchurch Harbour, which is of such a curious, pincer shape that another ferry is required at the narrow harbour mouth. This is the Mudeford Ferry, for years a perquisite of the Derham family. Visitors find this motor-boat crossing very useful after exploring Hengistbury Head, which once masked the activities of local smugglers. Today, the nearest one could approach those nocturnal adventurers—Abraham Coakes, for example, and Isaac Gulliver—is through ferryman's reminiscent chatter.

Another local ferry took its name from the village of Blackwater, just beyond the Christchurch boundary. It was one of those ferries where you were taken across by the boatman pulling on a fixed rope overhead. As part of the Heron Court Estate it had presumably known good times; by 1909 the ferryman could only pay the Right Honourable the Earl of Malmesbury a half-yearly rent of £4 1s. 3d., which covered the use of the ferry-boat, and the Old Ferry Cottage and garden.

The *Bournemouth Graphic* for 16 February 1905 was not very polite about the place: '. . . a cottage and an old punt is what you will see. It sounds uninteresting, but if you are thirsty . . . you can get, within that tiny cot, a nice tea for 4d. or 6d., or even a bottle of ginger beer'. No such luck today; the River Stour lost its Blackwater Ferry—and its 'nice teas' —during or shortly after the First World War. Some photographs kindly loaned to me by the local Librarian show what an idyllic spot this must have been, despite the *Bournemouth Graphic*'s rather grudging remarks. The Ferry Cottage (demolished over thirty years ago) was of two storeys and had a fine thatch which extended like a blanket over a stable at one end. Some of the photographs include the punt. In one picture, taken at the turn of the century, the ferryman's wife (?), wearing black bustle, is posing at the top of the ferry steps. I cannot think how anybody could allow such a lovely place to become nothing but a memory.

Redhill kept its ferry rather longer, being closed in March 1934 although fourteen thousand persons had used it during the previous year! The closure brought a storm of protest, but the 'moderns' won the day.

This ferry was for many years the only link between West Parley and Bournemouth. To be poled across the Stour here, with the prospect of a 'strawberry tea' at Marshall's Riverside Tea Gardens, must have been as delightful as one lady called Myra suggests on a postcard view of the place she sent to her Exmouth friend in 1909. I am looking at that postcard now, enjoying the scene by proxy. There, on a bend of the Stour, people are gathered on both banks waiting for the ferryman with his punt. The Tea Gardens are hidden by some trees as effectively as the old ford, which had existed for centuries. Riddlesford (Red Hill Ford) they called it; the Roman legions are believed to have crossed by this ford when on their way to attack the British at Badbury Rings, beyond Wimborne. But Myra made no mention of that on her postcard. I don't suppose she even knew.

At Poole Harbour, the so-called 'Lake of Dorset,' local history is animated by the story of its ferries. Despite Poole's overseas trade, there was no danger of its citizens 'overvaluing foreign parts' while this huge natural harbour filled the horizon. The Beating of the Bounds of Poole Harbour still demands much of the port's joint Mayor and Admiral; much deviatory rambling, eased at Wareham by a friendly pledge in wine.

Part of the official peregrination covers a little lobe of land, hatchet shaped, called Hamworthy. This is how Leland described the place in the reign of Henry VIII: 'There lyith agayn the Kay [of Poole] a point of land, as a causey, after the facion [fashion] of a brode swerd . . . the poynte is agayn towarde the town, and the broad part hangynge up to the land, and by this causey men cum from Litchet to the fery.' A map, or better still, an aerial survey, would add some clarity to Leland's quaint remarks and show how vital this ferry must have been before a bridge was erected to connect Hamworthy and Poole in 1837.

But Leland's prose could be matched, here in Poole—witness the lease granting the ferry at Hamworthy to a local man about the time when the famous antiquary visited this beautiful town.

This lease—the earliest known reference to the ferry—is dated 22 May 1541: 'Grant from John Notherell [Mayor] and all his Brethren for fifty-one years of the Passage House and Passage [that is, the Ferry] to John Henbury, merchant, to pay yearly, one couple of capons.' In simpler words, this passage-boat or ferry-boat was being leased to Henbury on condition that he provided the Mayor and Corporation with an annual tribute of two nice fat cockerels. Remembering also that wine from Wareham, it must be gratifying to be elected Mayor of Poole. As the Hamworthy Ferry was in use up to recent years I cannot help wondering whether the capons continued to appear before His Worship? One could inquire, of course, but that would be to risk spoiling a choice little cameo from the picturesque past!

Let us be content to visualize Henbury earning his cock rent while collecting the penny fares from passengers on his raft-like vessel. This he hauled from one side of the quay to the other by rope; an arduous if sometimes entertaining task, especially should his full quota of seventy passengers be aboard, all talking away in the tongue of Thomas Hardy's rustics.

Henbury and his successors would have been astonished could they have known that a time would come when the harbour mouth, about a quarter of a mile wide, would have its mechanically operated ferry. This gap, between South Haven Point and Studland Bay corresponds to the neck of a Bellarmine jug, for the harbour swells out to a width of seven miles and a breadth of almost five miles.

Across the mouth of Poole Harbour a ferry service of sorts had long been inevitable. At first it was run as a side-line by the fishermen. All went smoothly until Admiral Sir Christopher Hatton—appointed Governor of Brownsea, or Branksea, Island by Elizabeth I—began to meddle. He argued that as the boats plied across his 'private' water, the profits should all come to him. The fishermen took a dim view of this private logic, but had to look out for themselves and their livelihood when Hatton's officers were deflected from their normal duties to raid the ferry-boats, and appropriate the fares!

The outrage reached such a pitch that Poole Corporation brought the matter up before the Court of Admiralty on 25 August 1581. The charge ran thus: 'That the gooner [Governor] of Brankseye Castell doth moleste the inhabitants of the towne and will not suffer them to passe any persons from northhaven pointe to southaven pointe butt doth threaten them to shoote att them and vyolentlye doth take their monye from them, wh' is not onlye a greatt hinderaunce to poore men [the ferrymen] that were woonte to gayne monye that wayes butt also an infrynginge of our lyberties, wher-fore we thincke ytt verye necessarye to be remedyd.'

The 'remedye' is not recorded but one hopes that the Admiral was commanded to leave the small fry alone and concentrate on 'bigger fish', for the Armada threat was already heating things up along the English Channel.

In 1898 a Mr. Harvey started a regular row-boat ferry service across this gap, which can be quite stormy, though the views are excellent. As an additional attraction the ferrymen altered the name Studland Bay to Shell Bay on account of the rich variety of sea shells that visitors could find there. Harvey's men had a keen eye for business!

Leaving the Sandbanks shore, at South Haven, one faces the Purbeck cliffs and hills; to the right is Brownsea Island—a fabulous green 'cushion' which looks as though it could easily float across and fill the gap, like a bottle-stopper. Smaller islands lie beyond, though still within the harbour, so that one's crossing takes on the character of a voyage devised by Robert Louis Stevenson. The sea is on the left, and so many are the tidal fluctuations that a ferryman must always have his wits about him. Today, Harvey's grandson operates this adventurous ferry service with motor-boats.

In 1923 the Bournemouth–Swanage Motor Road and Ferry Company was incorporated by Act of Parliament. The eyes of its shareholders were naturally focused on that same quarter-mile gap, Poole Harbour being a sprawling obstacle roughly mid-way between fashionable Bournemouth, and the Swanage which Charles Kingsley had extolled by saying that all this 'quaint old-world village' required 'to make it famous is houses into which visitors can put their heads at night'. The new company splashed out on 15 July 1926 with a ferry service for vehicles. An attempt to stop Harvey's older service aroused fierce opposition and a mass meeting held in Parkstone Grammar School resulted in a local barrister fighting Harvey's case in the courts until the attempted monopoly was defeated. My friend, Bernard C. Short of Parkstone, Poole, remembers that meeting and some of the salty language it drew forth.

Live and let live seems to be the policy here today. You either cross by motor-boat and savour the full romance of the passage with a running tide; or drive your car on to the floating pontoon, sharing the experience with Jaguars and trade vans, and up to three hundred passengers who occupy side galleries, like spectators. But, whichever ferry you patronize, you will be crossing one of the loveliest waterways in all Britain.

No doubt the people of Devon would make a similar claim for the Dartmouth–Kingswear Ferry. This is indeed a memorable passage. The setting is one of great natural charm and, to me, there is always an awareness of earlier days, when William Rufus, Sir Humphrey Gilbert, John

Davis the Arctic explorer, Chaucer's 'shipman', and so many others of greater or lesser renown were afloat on the River Dart. A boat trip hereabouts, whether by ferry or motor-launch, gives one sufficient leisure to ruminate, historically; two ancient castles frown across at each other, from either bank, and St. Petrox Church seems to be where it is— perched on the rock, beside Dartmouth Castle—to keep the peace.

Apparently nobody felt it necessary to record the existence of this ferry when Dartmouth was in its formative years as a port, witnessing the departure of Crusaders to the Holy Land, for example, and supporting other national causes. The ferry is first heard of in 1365. After another long silence it crops up again in the Mayor of Dartmouth's accounts for 1531–3, where it is recorded that as payment for the ferry-boat Master Korn paid 'at dyvers tymys 4s.'. Nearly three hundred years later monetary values had changed so much, and the ferry had become so profitable (although passengers still paid only one halfpenny) that it could be let to the ferryman for £120 per annum. A statement to this effect occurs in the Farington Diary under the date 6 October 1809. The writer goes on to say that 'the ferry is private property and belongs to Mr. Luttrell of Dunster Castle in Somersetshire'.

Important ferry rights were often owned by landed gentry, or sometimes by peers of the realm, as we have already noticed. On discovering that the Dartmouth–Kingswear Ferry had once belonged to the Dunster estate I wrote to Lt.-Col. Walter Luttrell, the present owner, hoping for a few family sidelights on the subject. The prospect of elaborating Dartmouth's connection with Dunster Castle, which overlooks the Bristol Channel, was alluring. I remembered looking round this castle, a few months before, and being awed by some of the family portraits. How amusing to think of some of those richly bedizened knights and ladies drawing a little of their revenue from that ferry on the River Dart, sixty miles away, across the 'boot' of England.

But it was not to be. In his reply to my query Colonel Luttrell said he had no idea that the ferry had ever been 'in the family'. Major events get their chroniclers, but homely affairs, like ferries, are apt to be completely forgotten, or 'buried' amongst a pile of fusty old documents. I still nurture the fond hope (shared by Colonel Luttrell himself) that some day the Somerset Archivist at Taunton will unearth from the Dunster Castle estate papers a few pertinent references to this delightful, halfpenny ferry which was the precursor of the present car ferry.

Higher up-river, two or three other ferries come into view. One of them takes passengers and their cars from a point near Greenway House to Dittisham, on the left bank. Here one can more readily visualize Sir Humphrey Gilbert, colonizer of Newfoundland, because he was born in the old Greenway mansion. His half-brother, Sir Walter Raleigh, came along frequently to smoke a quiet pipe as he gazed across the river. The fact that other places claim to have been first in the field, for Raleigh's pioneer tobacco adventures, need not cause any wonder. On the Dittisham Ferry there is plenty of time to discuss such pros and cons.

Arguing over some local tradition or social habit seems natural to certain ferries. We have noticed the tendency in many places and shall do so again, as we continue our ferry passage of British waters.

Fanny Burney, that most observant of travellers, provided a good example when in 1791 she made her last crossing from Exmouth, in East Devon, to Starcross. But what she commits to her Diary is not the interesting fact that this ferry service was initiated by the monks of Sherborne Abbey, a few miles away in Dorset, or that you could here take your carriage over the Exe estuary, thus avoiding a twenty-mile detour via Exeter. What *does* concern her, even to the extent of feeling quite shocked, was the sight that greeted her on stepping ashore at Starcross: the sight of some women 'with feet and legs entirely naked, straw-bonnets of uncouth shapes tied on their heads . . . strolling along with wide mannish strides to the borders of the river, gathering cockles . . .'

Sherborne Abbey's one-time ownership of the Exmouth-Starcross Ferry must have been common knowledge to Sir Walter Raleigh, for he lived in this beautiful town and worshipped with his family in the abbey. At the Dissolution, some years earlier, the abbey had been spared destruction and became the parish church. What happened to the ferry rights, exercised for so long by the Sherborne monks? They were acquired at once by Exeter!

The town's loss of tolls, because of the ferry ten miles down-river, had early been a bone of contention with the Abbot of Sherborne. Now, with the monastery closed, the townsfolk seized their chance and gained control of this former source of annoyance and competition. The Chamber of Exeter soon had the service in hand; on 28 April 1542 it leased 'all that our Ferry and passage at Exmouth and our boat called "le passage bote" . . . together with a piece of land next the sea at Exmouth called Prattishedd . . . to John Drake for twenty-nine years at an annual rent of 26s. 8d.' Foreshadowing the illustrious Francis of that ilk, over at Plymouth, another Drake christened Gilbert took over this same ferry in 1558. Today, only a small passenger ferry negotiates the mouth of the

Exe, but the route taken is that first charted, and for the same purpose, by the monks of Sherborne eight hundred years ago.

Importance followed by decline is the common lot of many things, besides ferries. But ferries show a pertinacity also. Try to close some old ferry service, perhaps because it no longer pays, and see what legal hounds are unleashed, to chase each other, expensively, through the courts! One country gentleman told me not long ago about the fury he aroused on attempting to close a ferry on his property which was proving uneconomic. After much litigation, the matter was finally resolved by the substitution of a special bus service for the 'dispossessed'.

Devon and Cornwall can provide many examples of pertinacious ferry services. Every time holiday-makers are ferried over the River Teign from Teignmouth to Shaldon they should raise a cheer. The boat may be small for these days (the neighbouring bridge precludes anything bigger), yet the service began in the thirteenth century, when the Earl of Cornwall was in proud possession. It became one of an important chain of ferry services on the road to Dartmouth and beyond.

On my last visit to Salcombe, twelve miles west of Dartmouth, I could not see the ferry-boat for schooners and yachts and dinghies and motor-vessels whose owners were most pressing in their offers to take me out fishing for shark. The harbour was full of boats, all gleaming in the sunshine and suggesting that everybody for miles around lived on or by the water. Somewhere amongst that variegated squadron a small motor-boat was ferrying people over to Salcombe from Portlemouth or back again. Each trip, I thought, must afford a wonderful object lesson in lesser nautical affairs. I expect the shark were farther off, beyond the huge bulk of Bolt Head.

There are other rewarding ferries in this splendid area of tangled estuaries and mysterious creeks; one would have to go that way often to find them all. But at Bigbury Bay one crosses over to Burgh Island, at high water, in neither boat nor glorified raft. A sea-horse is brought into service, and an elevated platform on the beach enables passengers to mount this strange amphibian. Actually, this sea-horse ferry—to use the proprietor's excusable name for it—resembles a huge skeleton; the skeleton of an old-time wagonette, though with an amazing undercarriage of metal stays and ribs. Passengers occupy the upper deck, provided with a tent-like awning, some eight or ten feet clear of the water. A petrol engine propels the 'beast' forward on its caterpillar wheels. When the tide goes out a curious, tell-tale track is seen imprinted on the wet sands.

On each of my visits the tide was low, revealing a glorious expanse of these golden sands. It was a pleasure to *walk* over to the island with its fourteenth-century Pilchard Inn, but how I should relish the experience of roaming over this small rocky island—once made his refuge by Tom Crocker, pirate and smuggler—after *riding* there on the back of the sea-horse.

The River Tamar, whose ramifications make the map of the Plymouth area like a crazy piece of fretwork, has necessitated several ferries from time immemorial. We are now on the brink of Cornwall, in which county —according to the late Charles Henderson—seventeen different ferries were still operating about 1934. Three of these brought travellers over the Tamar and two still do so, at Cremyll and Torpoint. The river lost its old Saltash Ferry fairly recently, being superseded by the Tamar Bridge.

Perhaps Daniel Defoe would have applauded this innovation at Saltash, for when he came along, early in the eighteenth century, he found 'the ferry-boats bad; so that I thought myself well escaped when I got safe on shore in Cornwall'. Defoe's *Tour Through Great Britain* was a vast under-taking, allowing little scope for the intensive local research which had made the name of Charles Henderson, for example, a byword down here in Cornwall. Henderson's zeal caused him to listen and look *everywhere*. Once, outside a little house, he heard Bach being played with uncommon feeling. At once aware of a kindred soul, he knocked at the door and made the acquaintance of the player—'an old lady of great wit and culture [who] became a life-long friend'. This story is not as irrelevant here as it may seem; it illustrates exactly how cultural alliances are sometimes formed and knowledge acquired. It also illustrates how many of my own stories, 'locked' away in somebody's memory, have been indirectly obtained.

Henderson's chief source of material, however, was probably the bundles of old documents entrusted to his care by so many friends and acquaintances. His monograph on Cornish Ferries gives us the fruit of prolonged research in such neglected byways. Here is one example: '. . . the Burgesses of Saltash held the ferry on lease from the Duchy at a rent of £10. The Duke himself provided the boat at his own cost. In 1355 a complaint reached him that his passage boat of Saltash was being repaired, and that his officers *had commandeered the Cremyll boat from down the river*.' (My italics.)

How the Cremyll ferrymen reacted to this piece of impertinence has yet to be unravelled, but one can imagine their feelings!

Here is another of Henderson's gleanings:

71

On October 1st, 1356, not long after his great victory at Poitiers, the [Black] Prince [Duke of Cornwall] gave to his 'Porter', William Lenche, for life, the Passage of Saltash, with all profits and issues of the same. Lenche had done good service to his master in England and Gascony, but notably at the Battle of Poitiers, wherein he lost an eye 'to the great emblemishing of his person', as the Black Prince expressed it when conferring the ferry upon him.

Had the record ended there we should probably have sympathized with the unfortunate fellow and tried to imagine some of the stirring tales of battle and seige he would recount as he rowed his fares over the Tamar. Actually, the sequel was otherwise. Despite 'the emblemishing of his person', Lenche continued to serve the Prince in the field and ran the ferry as many an absentee parson was to run his church.

Henderson found the Cremyll Ferry—roughly four miles downstream—mentioned in documents reaching as far back as 1250; and it still operates, linking Stonehouse, Plymouth, with the Mount Edgcumbe estate at Cremyll in Cornwall. Right up to the coaching days Cremyll Ferry was a vital nexus in that long alignment of river-passages which could be joined in Devon and followed, with all kinds of contributory hazards, via Bodinnick (Fowey), the Par and Fal estuaries, and Helford River.

Here at Cremyll the researches of Peter Hull, present archivist at Truro, focus attention on many strange happenings. Out of the haze of time there emerges, by about Armada year, a ferry service so well entrenched in Mount Edgcumbe ownership that Peter Edgcumbe could allow his lessee 'the passage house in Maker, the cottage called Shillhall to the west side of Mount Edgcumbe deer park, and herbage and pasture for one cow in the deer park until Peter Blake could lease another pasture . . .' All this, mark you, in addition to the use of the 'great passage boat' and all the fees and profits that accrued.

Blake, of course, had to agree to ferry his landlord, his landlord's family, his landlord's servants, and any of their goods, chattels and beasts free of charge. Perhaps one of the Blakes traded too much on Lord Edgcumbe's good nature, for a renewal of the lease contained this further clause: the lessees 'were not to kill, embezzle, or take deer from the park at Mount Edgcumbe, and if they took any conies, "barbara hens", or pigeons from the park, or cut down oaks, ashes or elm trees there' they were to be fined forty shillings.

As the Blake family continued to work the Cremyll Ferry from Armada year (1588) to just before the Civil War in the following century, one may assume that they and their descendants behaved themselves and kept their hands off the estate game and timber.

By 1682 the long Blake regime had ended and in September of that year Sir Richard Edgcumbe leased the ferry to John Collings, a local sailor. There were now two ferry-boats and a smaller vessel. Collings agreed to keep them in repair and to 'trim and fitt them strong and stanch' and to employ enough men to carry 'the male [mail] or paquett'.

Celia Fiennes, whose heady invocation launched us on this chapter, seems to have had her enthusiasm for English travel somewhat dampened on tackling Cremyll Ferry, in the year 1694. The older route was then in use, from Devil's Point to Barn Pool, near Mount Edgcumbe House. Celia writes:

From Plymouth I went one mile to Cribly Ferry, which is a very hazardous passage, by reason of three tides meeting. Had I known the danger before, I should not have been very willing to have gone it, not but this is the constant way all people go, and saved several miles' riding. I was at least an hour going over; it was about a mile, but indeed in some places, notwithstanding . . . five men rowed and I set my own men to row also, I do believe we made not a step of way for almost a quarter of an hour, but blessed be God, I came safely over: but those ferry-boats are so wet and then the sea and wind are always cold . . . that I never fail to catch cold in a ferry-boat, as I did this day, having two more ferries to cross . . .

Although the Royal Mail was shuttling to and from Cornwall via Cremyll until 1791, when Torpoint Ferry took over, conditions were still anything but halcyon when John Wesley came along in 1768. We met him earlier, floundering among some north-country ferries and trying to exercise a divine patience with their short-comings. He has now arrived at 'Crimble-passage', where drownings were all too frequent. His journal remarks are pithy and to the point: '. . . we were at a full stop. The boatmen told us the storm was too high, that it was not possible to pass . . .' But Wesley—by now inured to unkind weather as well as hostile mobs— is undaunted: '. . . at length we persuaded them to venture out, and we did not ship one sea till we got over'.

Part of Wesley's mission in Cornwall was to denounce the evil of smuggling, then rife in the neighbourhood. A clause in the ferry contract, at Cremyll, expressly forbade the handling of contraband, but the women

73

of Cawsand, who were notorious for concealing bladders of smuggled spirit beneath their clothing, would sometimes offer a tempting two-pence to be ferried over, secretly, to Mutton Cove, so as to be nicely clear of Plymouth and its customs men.

I don't suppose Wesley would be troubled by the sight of any of these bold Cawsand women on that wild, tempestuous day. And certainly none are in evidence on Gibbon's painting of Cremyll Ferry, viewed from Admiral's Hard, Plymouth. The time has here advanced to 1864, and the long promenade jetty is peopled with crinolined ladies and top-hatted men; the very essence of Victorian respectability, leavened by a few children. It is reminiscent of a busy hour at Paddington Station or Waterloo, though here the family groups are either awaiting friends from one of the ferry-boats, berthed with furled sails at the landing pier, or are preparing to embark.

It must again be said that of certain ferries, as of certain towns, when one begins to flourish another may decline. The ancient borough of Hedon, in East Yorkshire, for example, was eventually eclipsed by the neigh-bouring 'ferry' port of Hull. In the case of Cremyll Ferry (and of Saltash) the usurping influence came from Torpoint, barely two miles up-river. The Mount Edgcumbe family had a share in this enterprise also; George, the current Earl, along with Reginald Pole-Carew, (and the St. Aubyn family 'as a sort of concealed partner'), launched the venture by Act of Parliament in 1791. Torpoint, then little more than a place-name, rocketed into favour when in 1836 a new road (A.389) was built to provide ferry connections.

Torpoint Ferry was running a steamboat, the *Jemima*, by 1829. Saltash Ferry experimented with one soon after but its old horse boat came back into use again later. Steamboats did not begin to serve the Cremyll Ferry until 1885, and they must have been a boon to the public who were even then allowed to visit Mount Edgcumbe, though only on Mondays. Although Torpoint was now in the ascendant, Cremyll was still a very good 'second fiddle'; early in the present century it could boast three steamboats—the *Carrier*, the *Armadillo*, and the *Shuttlecock*. The *Carrier* was the largest, with accommodation for a hundred and fifty passengers, not counting the Earl and any of his company, who had a private apart-ment on board—a comfortable retreat where, as the winds blew and the boat rocked, the Earl could sit back and rejoice over his two profitable passages over the Tamar.

The Torpoint–Devonport Ferry is now the busiest and most lucrative in the area, and perhaps the noisiest too, because of its diesel-driven turbines. Today, of course, the crew handle vehicles of every description, but one night about ten years ago there was a pleasant, if rather puzzling, diversion. A young lady arrived on *horseback*. This would have created no problem or surprise in the early days, when there were set charges even for a horse-drawn hearse—ten shillings and sixpence, which covered the outward journey, and the return journey *without* the corpse. A horse alone then cost its owner twopence. But by the middle of the twentieth century winds of change had made a horse and a rider a rare phenomenon, at such a place. One of the ferry crew then on duty declared, 'I don't think the ticket collector knew what to charge her!'

'She was a very educated young lady, too,' the man continued, 'and she was worried about where to put her horse for the night. So when we got to Torpoint, I fixed her up with some relatives of mine, and we took the horse up to the playing fields and let him loose for the night.' For one ferryman, at least, that girl's appearance meant a welcome relief from the boredom of continually putting cycles and motor-cycles and cars on their hurried way to Cornwall.

In one book it would be impossible to mention, let alone do justice, to every ferry that has graced these Isles. Around the Tamar they talk of the recently deceased Hooe Ferry; of one at Halton, which belonged to the Valletort family; and another at Calstock which the Valletorts sold as long ago as 1270 to Richard, Earl of Cornwall. Who would not be intrigued, also, by the small, obscure passages across the Lynher River, a tributary of the Tamar, at Antony, and at St. Germans? Or the ferry that still carries a handful of people over the harbour at Looe, although a perfectly substantial bridge is available nearby?

This harbour ferry deserves more than a cursory glance. It connects East and West Looe without involving passengers in the high jinks once prompted by that long bridge. Men from the two rival townships would gather on the bridge for a tug-of-war, and the losers were apt to be pitched over the parapet into the water. A silver cup, now at Looe Town Hall, commemorates this event; it was awarded to the winning team and must have recalled some of the aquatic battles once fought out by ferrymen themselves.

That long alignment of ferries carrying the main, south-coast road through Devon and Cornwall, cited earlier, had no better exponent in fiction than the late Sir Arthur Quiller-Couch. In his short story, *Frenchman's Creek*, Mrs. Polwhele—wife of the Vicar of Manaccan, on the

75

Lizard peninsula—follows the traditional homeward route, after a shopping expedition to Plymouth, by crossing the Tamar at Torpoint and proceeding adventurously with her coach-load of purchases until at length, terrified by the 'spies' amongst her fellow passengers, and deflated by the wreckage of her new Moldavia Cap *en route*, she and her waiting husband cross over to their parish by the lovely Helford Ferry. Intermediate ferries, on that long journey of some sixty miles, included those at Bodinnick-by-Fowey, Par, and King Harry above Falmouth.

If any traveller can use the Bodinnick Ferry without feeling that he has caught a bit of Elizabethan England by surprise, he must be dull-witted indeed, and should be outlawed from the Duchy.

Coming from the direction of Looe and Polperro, you drop sharply down to the Old Ferry Inn, which sports a galleon on its sign, hydrangeas below, and a sun-terrace overlooking the harbour. Although the ferry-boat waiting down there at the slip is as modern as you could expect, and ready to take you and your car over to Fowey in 'double-quick' time, the ferry *setting* is all of the past; here I always think it is the cars that seem anachronous.

Mr. T. J. Cole, Manager of the Bodinnick Ferry, has come under this ancient spell, for in addition to his normal duties he delves into old records trying to knit together the tale of a river-passage which began somewhere about the fourteenth century, when it was part of the Manor of Bodinnick. Ships were sailing in and out of the harbour, then as now, creating a more or less continuous regatta and smiled upon by terraces of cottages that have since grown in size without any loss of charm.

When Mr. Cole tells me that a certain John Davey, 'Yeoman of the King's Chambers and Valet to the King's Crown', was granted custody of the Bodinnick Ferry in 1478; that the ferry and all its rights were purchased about 1720 by Governor Pitt; and that Mrs. Blanche Clapham, the present owner, succeeded after her father acquired the property in 1934; I can only admire their combined good taste and try to stifle a feeling of envy. Such good taste was surely stimulated, at least in part, by aesthetic considerations. If anybody is curmudgeon enough to doubt it, let him come and see for himself! The view towards Bodinnick, from the Fowey side, is only one of many which caused Quiller-Couch to settle here and write his delightful stories of Troy Town.

Quiller-Couch lived at The Haven, a house that commands a fine view over the harbour and its two ferries; one operating from Fowey to Bodinnick, and the other a smaller concern—later beloved and extolled by Leo Walmsley—running across from below the small Haven garden to Polruan.

This prospect over the harbour

> Where vessels picturesquely rigg'd
> Obligingly repair

once prompted 'Q' to pen a few verses for a lady friend, concluding thus:

> And when some day you deign to pay
> The call that's overdue,
> I'll wave a landlord's easy hand
> And say, 'Admire *my* view!'

It is not long since my wife and I, too—having just patronized the Bodinnick Ferry—stopped to admire that same incomparable view. Sensing that the late Sir Arthur would have collated much lore about this ferry, I got into touch with his daughter and soon the floodgates were open. Miss Foy Quiller-Couch writes:

I clearly remember my Father telling me of a lawsuit which boiled up between his Father and the then landlord of the Bodinnick [Ferry] Inn. My grandfather was then a Doctor at Bodmin and one night he was summoned to a patient at Bodinnick. The case was urgent and my grandfather deemed that it would be quicker to ride to Fowey and cross by the Ferry rather than negotiate the narrow lanes on the Bodinnick side. When he arrived at the [Fowey] Passage Slip he was told the Ferryman had refused to turn out on the grounds that the Ferry closed at 10 p.m.

After some delay, the Doctor was rowed over in a private boat and completed his errand of mercy. Later, 'he brought an action against the lessee—his argument being that the Ferry was part of the King's Highway and as such it must operate on request at any hour of the day or night. The case was settled handsomely, in my grandfather's favour.'

This episode, along with much else concerning the Bodinnick Ferry, comes into one of 'Q's' romantic novels, *Shining Ferry*. The horse boat operated by long oars known as sweeps, and the rowing boat for pedestrians, both of which Miss Quiller-Couch remembers from her childhood, also figure in this delightful tale. And prominent amongst its characters is Nicholas Vro, the ferryman.

'Q's' portrait of Nicky Vro is based on one who actually worked this ferry when the author first settled here. In *Shining Ferry*, therefore, we see how the Bodinnick passage becomes the hub of Troy Town (Fowey), for everything spins around it and the grand old fellow who spent most of his life allowing for tide and current as he rows his fellow 'Trojans', usually full of quaint gossip, to and fro.

After lending me her own copy of *Shining Ferry* (1905), Miss Quiller-Couch added grace to kindness by saying that it would make her happy to see the following sketches of 'Uncle Nicky Vro' revived in my own book.

A friend asks Nicky what it feels like to be growing so old.

'I don't feel it at all,' Nicky answered cheerfully. 'Folks tell me from time to time that I'm getting past. My own opinion is, they're in a greater hurry to get to market than of yore. "Competition"—that's a cry sprung up since my young days; it used to be "Religion", and "Nicholas Vro, be you a saved man?" The ferry must ply, week-day or Sabbath: I put it to you. What time have I got to be a saved man? "The Lord is good," says I. Now I'll tell you a fancy of mine about Him. One day He'll come down to the slip calling "Over!" and whiles I put Him across—scores of times I've a-seen myself doing it, and 'tis always in the cool of the evening after a spell of summer weather—He'll speak up like a gentleman, and ask, "Nicholas Vro, how long have you been a-working this here boat?" "Lord," I'll answer, "for maybe a matter of fifty year, calm or blow, week-days and Sabbaths alike; and that's the reason your Honour has missed me up to church, as you may have noticed." "You must be middlin' tired of it," He'll say: and I shall answer up, "Lord, if you say so, I don't contradict 'ee; but 'tis no bad billet for a man given to chat with his neybours and talk over the latest news and be sociable, and warning to leave don't come from me." "You'd best give me over they oars, all the same," He'll say; and with that I shall hand 'em over and be rowed across to a better world.'

Later, another 'neybour' steps into his boat and, harping on the same theme of old age, asks Vro 'how many times we two have crossed this ferry together'.

Nicky Vro pondered. 'Now that's the sort of question I leave alone o' set purpose, and I'll tell 'ee for why. One night, years ago, and just as we was off to bed, my poor wife says to me, "I wonder how many

78

times you've crossed the ferry, first and last." "Hundreds and thousands," I says, just like *so*. She'd a-put the question in idleness, an' in idleness I answered it. Will you believe it?—between twelve and one in the morning I woke up with my head full o' figgers. Not another wink o' sleep could I get, neither. Soon as ever I shook up the bolster an' settled down for another try, I see'd myself whiskin' back and forth over this here piece o' water like a piston-rod in a steamship, and off I started countin' for dear life. Count? I tell you it lasted for nights, and by the end o' the week I had to see the doctor about it. I was losin' flesh.'

In point of fact, he was soon to meet his Celestial Ferryman.

The next ferry on the westward route disappeared, not through any legal hocus pocus, or neglect, but in part by what one loosely calls an Act of God. At Par the sea once ran inland as far as St. Blazey, creating a beautiful estuary—which necessitated a ferry. In 1732, according to Henderson, ownership of this passage and ferry-boat 'was being hotly disputed between the lords of Tywardreath on one side and Mr. Scobell of Roselyon on the other'. Gradually, the sea withdrew, the estuary silted up, and the ferry was no more. Nature had stepped in and settled the argument. In these days to talk of a ferry at Par, where the beach is everything, would seem ridiculous.

But there is no danger of the Fal estuary ever drying up! It is like an inland sea, with creeks and tributaries in abundance. And King Harry's Ferry still holds its own. Even during the last thirty years it has developed from a glorified raft, fitted with a hut at one side in which the ferryman ate his lunch, to a floating bridge capable of carrying ten or a dozen cars.

In this part of Cornwall the manner in which King Harry's Passage got its name is a good talking point. Some people declare that the King in question was Henry VIII of marital fame; I have heard it contended that he and Anne Boleyn used the ferry while honeymooning on this peninsula called Roseland. But Henderson, though a romantic at heart, would have none of this. 'The real origin of the name,' he stated, 'is to be sought in the dedication of a little chapel that stood at the Philleigh [Roseland] end of the passage. In 1528 this chapel was described as of St. Mary and King Harry. Clearly, Henry VI was intended'—that gentle, culture-loving Lancastrian whose short-lived escape from Waddington Hall, in my own county, had been facilitated, not by ferry, but a set of equally convenient stepping-stones over the River Ribble.* It is good to know that although he was treated so shabbily by his Queen, and others, Henry VI has this attractive and useful memorial on the friendlier waters of the Cornish Fal.

On our very first initiation to the magic that is Cornwall, over thirty years ago, my wife and I spent much of our time using the different ferries around the Fal estuary. We bought a one-inch Ordnance map, which shows them all, even the small ones that take pedestrians only. First, that water passage from Falmouth to Flushing, followed by a walk past Mylor to Restronguet Creek. Here, from the Pandora Inn, another ferry took us over to the Feock shore; anybody going in the opposite direction hailed the ferryman by clanging on a home-made gong. Forward again (though on another day) to King Harry's Ferry, and then a walk down the lovely Roseland bank of the Fal to St. Just and St. Mawes.

The enchantment (for it was nothing less) here began anew, with several Nicholas Vros waiting to ferry us across the Porthcuel tributary to St. Anthony, then to Place, and again to Percuil where there were oyster beds and the waterside café was part of the dream. From St. Mawes the steam ferry took us homewards across Carrick Roads, as this part of the river is called, to Falmouth; but on other days we often returned by this same ferry direct to Roseland, for—as around Fowey—there is so much to explore, especially by water. And the tales we heard!

At St. Just a few worshippers were still coming to church in their boats, which they moored in the very creek where Christ himself was ferried ashore during his supposed visit to Cornwall during the 'hidden years' of his life. After recounting this beautiful old story afresh, with a mystical look in his eyes, the Rector of St. Just took us to the apex of his riverside garden so that we could look right into this steep-sided creek. Almost any legend could thrive there, amongst its trees and the silent waters of its tiny, interlocked bays.

In much later times, however, Bar Creek became something of a jousting place. Truro and Falmouth were never sure of the exact limits of their respective jurisdiction over the River Fal with its network of ferries. Two obelisks situated a few yards apart, on the north shore of Bar Creek, represent the two claims, but before that compromise was reached the annual Beating of the Bounds ceremony caused a mock battle in these side waters, between the two Mayors and their supporters. After a hilarious scuffle, the Mayors 'arrested' each other for trespass

* The full story is given in my book, *Yorkshire*.

and then sailed away together to Falmouth, where a specially prepared feast enabled both parties to sink their differences.

The Truro contingent then sailed jovially for home, up that magnificent river which narrows and twists and cavorts so much during the last five miles that more ferries come into play. Not far beyond King Harry there is the Tolverne Ferry. This passage must have been a prize worth having, in the seventeenth century, for with it went 'half the fish taken in Tolverne Weir, the passage house and cellars, three fields, a mowhay, and the right to land sand and dry nets, pasture for a horse and mare in Chaple Wood, the right to take water from the spring there, and fuel of thorns, broom and furze from Polgurran Wood and Lower Burlase'. All that, and the boat too—for an annual rent of only 26s. 8d.!

One more ferry crosses the Fal before Truro comes into view; a very beautiful ferry on a sharp S-bend where the Tressilian River flows down from the north. For the villagers around Old Kea it affords an almost direct route to Truro, via Malpas. Local people call this place 'Mopus', but the word is derived from the French mal-pas, meaning bad passage. 'Bad' or not, this ferry has been in use for centuries and had the honour—in the sunglow of early saga—of taking Queen Iseult over the water when she was on her way from 'the Forest of Morrois (now Moresk, or St. Clements) to the Palace of King Mark at Blanche-Lande (in Kea)'.

Because of this association, Henderson goes on to make Malpas 'the most romantic of all [ferry] passages in Britain'. But he had to reckon without one other Cornish ferry—a much newer service which now takes visitors from Marazion, near Penzance, to the fascinating island rock known for centuries as St. Michael's Mount.

On my latest visit to this region the tide was full and the breakers were rolling in, much as they do on a glorious needlework picture sewn by the late Lady Mary Trevelyan for her home at Wallington, Northumberland. This enormous picture—'twenty-three years in the making', so Lady Trevelyan once told me—shows Sir Trevelyan, one of King Arthur's knights, astride the horse on which he has ridden and swum across the narrow channel from the monastery-crowned Mount.

To conquer this passage today, one needs neither gaily caparisoned steed, nor legendary prowess. A causeway will keep pedestrians' feet dry all the way, at low water; at other times there are ferry-boats to carry you over to this strangely magnetic spot. The National Trust handbook catches the spirit of the place. So do the island seneschals. Wearing a colourful livery that would have done justice to the Court of King Arthur, these men hand you off the ferry-boats as if you had, indeed, reached some fabled shore.

CHAPTER SEVEN

AROUND THE SEVERN SEA

Someday I should like to cross over to Padstow, on Cornwall's Atlantic seaboard, by the Rock Ferry. Many tourists must know about Padstow, if only because of the Hobby Horse joyously paraded here each May Day to commemorate its progenitor; when perched on Stepper Point this terrifying creature was once mistaken by the French for the Devil. Very wisely and quickly the enemy withdrew. The River Camel flows out to sea between Stepper and Pentire Head after splashing around a rocky outcrop, two miles up-stream. This outcrop gives its name to the ferry, which was flourishing at a time when local people could still half believe that St. Petroc, a royal Welsh saint, sailed on from here to Rome and back again in a *silver bowl*.

The vessel which the Manor of Penmayne rented to its ferry tenants was more substantial, if of less intrinsic worth; along with the passage over the Camel estuary it was valued at thirteen shillings in 1337.

But it was not only St. Petroc and his wonderful feat of navigation that bemused these good fishing folk of Padstow; there were mermaids, also, who—if angered in any way—could throw sufficient sand about to block the estuary, and then where would Rock Ferry be! It was best to take an example from Zennor (near St. Ives), where the squire's son sang so divinely in the church choir that one of the local mermaids fell in love with him, and even joined him in the sanctuary! She is still there—carved on a bench-end, true, but as vain with her mirror as any Padstow girl.

If the mermaids have enticed us away from our ferries, for a moment, who could object, or be at all surprised, here in Cornwall where facts mingle so often with old fancies, as when a Welshman's coracle turns impossibly, though rather beautifully, into that silver bowl?

At St. Ives, where a row-boat still keeps the Hayle Ferry alive, the early inhabitants seem to have lacked such parabolic imagination, for their own saint, Ia by name, is credited with a coracle, plain and simple, for his passage here from Ireland.

But, while we are on the theme, let us accord full marks to yet another saint, Decuman, for having ferried himself across the Bristol Channel in a coracle, with his pet cow as companion. To this day the Aran islanders of Western Ireland use a larger variant of the coracle, which they call a curragh. The light framework of laths covered with tarred canvas looks so fragile, and yet the men of Aran commonly ferry their pigs and donkeys to and fro in these slender craft and declare that, until the voyage is over, each oarsman must 'keep his tongue in the centre of his mouth'. I expect St. Decuman had to observe similar niceties of balance before making that landfall in Somerset long ago. A head carving on a medieval piscina at Oare Church may represent Decuman. A curious way of preserving his aqueous association, but on a recent visit to this lovely old church in the Lorna Doone country I was amused to find that he had been given a wreath of spring flowers, for it was Easter.

On all that long, jagged coastline between Padstow and Minehead, the map shows only one other likely place for an estuarine ferry; this is where the Taw and the Torridge rivers combine near Appledore, to seaward of Barnstaple and Bideford. When the Grenvilles were making history from this area, as reflected by Charles Kingsley in *Westward Ho*, great, high-pooped ships were riding these waters, and little ferry-boats too. The big events that made Barnstaple and Bideford so important in those days have tended to obscure the small, everyday things as effectively as those great men-of-war would dwarf the tiny craft peacefully carrying three or four persons to or from market. And yet there is just that wisp of a tradition about an old ferry from Appledore.

This place, as anybody can see, really demands a ferry across the estuary to Instow. In winter, only imagination can now supply that service, but during the summer months a Mr. Johns assumes the role of his Elizabethan predecessors and speeds you across by motor-boat. There can be few more satisfying trips in North Devon, for Appledore is still, in essence, the queer little spot that Raleigh would know, threaded by a narrow street leading to a pocket-size quay; while Instow has its eyes focused on the Bristol Channel, through the Bar opening. It must be grand to be ferried across such historic waters when evening sunlight is gilding the sandbars, and the sea-fowl that rest upon them gaze at you with timeless curiosity.

The scantiness of available information about the Appledore–Instow Ferry is fortunately offset by a superabundance of matter concerning our next place of call. All the way up the Bristol Channel shore old-time travellers, if bound for Wales, must have wondered, with great longing, just how and where they would be able to cross this huge barrier—this enormous wedge of water for which the alternative name, Severn Sea, seems splendidly appropriate. Of course, previous experience of the Channel crossing, when this did materialize, might dispose many a traveller to press on to Gloucester, fifty miles ahead, where the Severn offered no serious obstacle. When Daniel Defoe arrived at Aust Ferry, he soon turned tail, grumbling about the 'dirty little village, and the boats to carry over man and beast so mean that we did not venture the passage'. Another deterrent, evidently, was a recent accident in which four men were drowned while trying to save a rickety boat and its crew trapped in a dangerous spot known as the Benches. And the ferry was old, then, as old as the Roman occupation, some say, when passengers could have been ferried across by galley slaves. The very name, Aust, has by some authorities been derived from Ostorius Scapula who took his legions over the Severn by this or some neighbouring route. Another possible origin is rooted in the tradition that Augustine held a conference here with leaders of the British church, Augustine being later shortened to Aust.

The actual ferry routes varied slightly, so that at one time people were crossing at peril of their lives, and at another, able to make the passage in comparative ease. At first this ferry, like so many others, was regarded as one of the natural hazards of life in this part of England, as natural as the weather, to be taken with as much philosophy as one could muster. Perhaps that is how Edward the Elder faced the Severn crossing, when Llewellyn was waiting on the other side to parley with him. Or did political urgency make Edward ignore the ferry risks?

But other dangers awaited those who might hope to cross between Aust on the one shore and Beachley, or Chepstow, on the other. Well into Tudor times 'merthers [murders] and felonies' were occurring daily within the orbit of the south-bound ferries from Wales and the Forest of Dean. The menace got so bad that in Henry VIII's reign these ferries were forbidden to operate from sunset to sunrise. Henry passed an Act which imposed these regulations, with fines for infringement. Moreover, even in daylight hours, the ferrymen were enjoined to transport only those passengers they knew and could vouch for. Rather a blow to trade, but strong measures had to be applied in a district where even the Lord of the Manor, although financially interested in the ferry, dare not live at Aust itself but went with his family to the fortified seclusion of Olveston Court, three miles off.

Even the alternative New Passage witnessed some violence, a century later, though it was now more likely to wear patriotic rather than blackguardly colours, as the following incident shows. Charles I, closely pursued by Roundheads, once crossed safely over here with his followers, but the ferry-boats had barely time to return to the Black Rock terminal, near Portskewett, before the Roundheads swooped down, demanding to be taken over immediately, before the Royalist party could gain much advantage. It says a lot for the ferrymen that at first they refused. The King's 'sacred person' had just been in their care for a few precious moments; they were quite out of tune with any odious man-hunt. But the Roundheads made short work of such scruples. Drawing their swords they forced the ferrymen to their boats, swarmed in, and continued their threats as long as necessary . . .

They might have been wiser to sing a psalm or two, there at the Black Rock landing, and invite the boatmen to join in. As it was, truculence got its reward. With a knowing look for each other, the ferrymen plied their oars until reaching English Stones, where the awkward customers were set down. From this place at low tide the Gloucestershire shore could be gained, after a short walk. The ferrymen 'forgot' to explain, however, that the tide was already *on the turn*, leaving no time for that walk! The Roundheads—all sixty of them, burdened with their gear—were soon engulfed by the implacable Severn. When Cromwell heard the news, he had the New Passage closed, and it remained closed until 1718 when the political climate had completely changed. Meanwhile, the Old Passage, from Aust, came into prominence again, profiting from Cromwell's interdict.

Even to make a précis of all that has been written and remembered about the Severn Ferry—both the Old and New Passages—one would need the leisure of a William Gilpin, though he was primarily an artist with palette and brush. One of his ancestors had been unseated from his north-country estate by Cromwell; perhaps Gilpin gave a rueful thought to this family mishap while making for the Severn during a painting holiday hereabouts in 1770?

Soon, however, he would have to fix his mind on more pressing matters. The post-boy had already blown his horn to summon the ferry, but earlier that day the boatmen from the south side had been forced back after a three-hour tussle with the elements. Yet the boat managed to get over, eventually, and pick up the waiting passengers. But it was not child's play. Picture Gilpin the artist looking on from his carriage seat as the foot passengers and horses squelched 'through sludge and over slippery, shelving rocks' to reach the lurching boat. The carriage itself was then unceremoniously slung into the rigging, presumably for reasons of security and to make more room for the thirty passengers and eleven horses crowded on board. It is a relief to discover that after two hours the Severn and its perils were overcome. On stepping ashore, Gilpin could now thank heaven for deliverance, put Cromwell out of mind, and set up his easel again.

Pretty as Aust Cliffs were, in those days, this passage had earned for itself a bad reputation amongst travellers. Weather, one could not control, and—nearer to Newnham—this included the notorious Severn Bore. But the boatmen were often careless and callous; to them, another life or two lost by drowning seemed to be of little account—a gruesome titbit, useful to raise the hair of timorous travellers. One of our eighteenth-century diarists was never so happy as when he could record another local death, however it had happened. This was the England that Dr. Samuel Johnson knew, an England that could even gloat and make merry over a public hanging. By comparison, ferry drownings seemed mild.

At last, about 1820, the Aust Ferry came under Government scrutiny. Two famous engineers of the day, Thomas Telford and Robert Stephenson, were asked to report on the respective merits of the Old and New Passages. Although Telford was professionally daunted by the tide-lift, the currents, the hidden rocks and the shoals, and Stephenson received a drenching baptism of spray while crossing in the mail-ferry, the Committee of Enquiry still favoured the Old Passage for development. The ferry rights were therefore purchased by a new association that included some Welsh M.P.s and businessmen. They spent oceans of money repairing road-approaches and building long stone piers at Aust and at Beachley. To supplement the sail ferry-boats still in vogue, they introduced a steam packet—one of the first in the West of England. They were entrusted with the London Royal Mail, which arrived daily at 11 a.m. But in spite of every advantage and increasing custom, they also piled up debts.

Eventually, the ferry changed hands again, but the newcomers—two Monmouthshire gentlemen—were soon in mourning for the loss of the sailing packet, *Jane*, which had been hammered by a gale on to the Benches. The crew perished along with the boat.

The toll of disaster was not yet complete. One fine April day in 1855 the sailing vessel, *Despatch*, was returning a load of passengers from Chepstow market, along with twenty sheep, thirty-six pigs, five oxen and one horse. Contentedly chatting over their bargains, perhaps, the passengers were making for home at such places as Aust, Littleton and Olveston. Aust pier was within hailing distance, when the unexpected happened. A sudden swell; a sideways lurch into some stout wooden piles; a gaping hole amidships; a terrifying inrush of water, so that nothing could prevent the vessel from sinking and taking some of the passengers down with her. Out of the screaming confusion only seven passengers emerged alive; they held on to the cattle from Chepstow market as these swam ashore, and were saved.

A new era dawned with the opening of the Severn Tunnel in 1887. The days of sail and steam ferries were drawing to a close, though the diesel-engined Aust–Beachley ferry-boat, launched in 1931 with Charlie Savage as Captain, continued until 1966. Savage took great pride in the fact that this particular service never had a single accident. Times had certainly improved, on the lovely if treacherous Severn waters. Some of the old ferry landmarks are still to be seen, notably, English Stones, where those over-zealous Roundheads came to grief. From a point quite near, the railway tunnel dips beneath the Severn, impervious to tide, squall, reef—or men-at-arms. And the new road bridge spanning the age-old barrier emphasizes the modern way of life.

A few miles nearer to Gloucester the Severn becomes narrow and curvaceous, with ferries at Newnham and Framilode, while half-way up the tributary Avon towards Bristol there is a ferry at Pill (which, of course, means a creek, not medicine), for long the home of Bristol pilots. But for our purpose I am inclined to put the clock back and hail Charlie Savage, so that he may ferry us across the broader Severn and point the way to Chepstow, for the Wye Valley.

And along the River Wye anybody blessed with what Coleridge called 'the shaping spirit of the imagination' must halt and pay some sort of homage to Tintern Abbey. Before this became the fashionable thing to do—preferably by moonlight—William Wordsworth crossed the Wye here and started writing his famous 'lines composed a few miles above Tintern Abbey'. The Severn Ferry (New Passage) had brought William and his sister Dorothy over to Chepstow, without any poetic rumblings, as far as I can recall, but Tintern was ripe for Wordsworth's muse, prompting some of the finest thoughts ever expressed in the English language.

J. M. W. Turner came also, to paint for posterity his lovely water-colour (now in the Ashmolean Museum) of the ruined nave. By 1828 visitors were making the excursion by water from Monmouth or Chepstow, passing several ferries on the way.

One ancient ferry served Tintern itself; the medieval stone arch adjoining the Anchor Hotel spans what remains of the flagged slipway, making an attractive picture. An old anchor has now come to rest in part of a cider press, nearby, and only a few yards away a complete cider press fills in the picture with visions of copious draughts of home-made cider for both ferryman and his fares in hot weather. Perhaps, when they came, the Wordsworths ferried across, stirring the 'sylvan Wye's' own sombre reflections of this great Cistercian pile. I can just see Dorothy letting her fingers ripple the water as the boatman bent over his oars.

A bridge has replaced the ancient ferry, not only here, beside the abbey, but also a mile or so up-stream at Brockweir, a curious little spot which only recently ushered our little party down to the riverside. Here we stayed for the night, giving ourselves time to think back to the days when Brockweir Ferry demanded a coin from anybody wishing to reach Tintern from St. Briavel's and the Forest of Dean. The bridge is ugly; I would much rather have paid ferriage.

Redbrook has a ferry, too, and how thankful some of us were for its quiet charm and usefulness on returning, one hot day, from Newland towards our guest house at Llandogo. And you can still enjoy the majesty of Symonds Yat—that five hundred-foot limestone crag festooned with trees—from one of the little ferry-boats and the motor-launches which (from the crag summit) look like toys, as they cross the Wye.

I don't know how long these two sightseers' services have operated, but one of the neighbouring hotels—its upper storey bellied out like a boat—has a clear right to be called Ye Olde Ferrie Inn, and it is possible, I suppose, that Robert Symonds, a seventeenth-century High Sheriff of Herefordshire whose name the lofty crag commemorates, could have required ferries at or near this point. Charles Heath who in 1799 referred to the Saracen's Head Ferry as operating 'while the rapidity of the stream continues' would have been pleased to know that Symonds Yat can still look down upon this other boat service, working from the opposite shore.

The Ordnance Survey map shows several others in the neighbourhood, and one at least had a link with far-off times. Two miles across country (six miles by river) the Wye, still writhing as madly as a Severn eel, is spanned by Kerne Bridge. Goodrich Castle stands nearby. During the Wordsworths' Tintern excursion they came here too, sleeping at Goodrich Castle and quite likely using the ferry that was later replaced by Kerne toll-bridge. It is recorded that on 9 August 1387, when Henry IV, then Earl of Derby, was about to cross over by this ferry, news reached him that his son (later Henry V, of Agincourt fame) had just been born at Monmouth Castle. A tankard of ale for the messenger and another for the ferryman would have been natural, in the circumstances, but Henry was so delighted at becoming the proud father of a son and heir that he at once bestowed the ferry and all its earnings upon the astonished boatman. His largesse did not end there. It reached far into the future, for the ferry continued to profit the same family for generations.

Bredwardine had its Trap House Ferry, and below Hereford a ferry served the farming folk of Fownhope and Bolstone. Clifford, Whitney, Clock Mill, Byford, Holme Lacy; each had its ferry, and the Towing Path Act of 1809 made provision for ferry-boats to convey tow horses over the Wye at several places. In the summer months Hunderton, south of Hereford, still maintains the old ferrying tradition.

And so we might proceed, taking deep draughts of history as we are ferried among the enchanting loops and tall, wooded cliffs of the Wye. Richard de Haldingham, who about the year 1300 drew up that amazing Mappa Mundi, or Map of the World, now in Hereford Cathedral, would know the Wye at a time when bridges were few and ferries plentiful. It is quite possible that he knew the Goodrich–Kerne Ferry, and just as possible that of the twenty rivers shown in the curious portion of his map devoted to the British Isles, one is meant for the Wye, on whose banks he lived for some twenty years.

A copy of Mappa Mundi is before me as I write. In one corner the author is shown setting off on his travels; he rides horseback and is accompanied by his hounds and a page-boy. Nothing of historic or legendary importance seems to escape his notice. The Garden of Eden is there, Noah's Ark, the Pyramids, and innumerable rivers with fabulous creatures waiting to ford them. Jerusalem takes its accredited place in the map centre. The Mediterranean Sea has its mermaid and the Nile its satyr. Richard de Haldingham was certainly river conscious, in his survey. Amongst its tightly-packed wonders I cannot locate old Charon ferrying souls over the Styx, but two Welsh ferry-towns emerge—Caernarvon and Conway. And Hereford, marked as 'H'ford', is there too, so that after journeying with this naïve map-maker all over the 'known' world and through much of its entertaining lore, one is again reminded of this lovely town where de Haldingham had his cathedral stall; the town whose very name signifies an ancient method of crossing the Wye at this spot.

It may be of small consequence to others, but many years ago I had the pleasure of concluding a fortnight's tour of the Wye and its surviving ferries by staying for a few days in a house previously occupied by another Canon of this fine cathedral. A copy of the book, *Reality*, which this Canon Streeter wrote is still on my shelves. I find it amusing that from the same cathedral should come two such dissimilar works: one a landmark in Christian apologetics; the other, six centuries earlier, a map which takes such a large piece of vellum (54 inches by 63 inches) to sprinkle the world of men and women with so much *un*reality.

Our Hereford cartographer certainly peopled his foreign rivers with strange, mythical beings, yet had he ridden no farther afield than South Wales one genuine species of wonder might have met his eye. Of course, most of his map extravagances were derived from travellers' tales, but here in Wales the rivers then had their coracle-men, hundreds of them, as opposed to the few who now fish the Teifi around Cenarth and Cilgerran in Cardiganshire. After a day's salmon fishing, these men sling their coracles across their shoulders and walk home, giving the appearance of so many outsize beetles. The sight is both weird and comical.

I mention coracles again because the Towy estuary, near Carmarthen, once swarmed with these strange-looking craft. Giraldus Cambrensis says that the early British coracles were used, not only for fishing—as here—but also for river transport. If so, they were surely larger than the one-man coracles we know today. However, over this coracle-manned river there was until recently a fully-fledged ferry service, for pedestrians. It operated from Ferryside to Llanstephan. Two miles farther on, another ferry—which still does duty—crossed the River Taf to Laugharne. Brian Waters tells the story of a man who once arrived at Ferryside but, finding no boat in sight, swam across so as to keep tryst with his sweetheart on the opposite shore. Before setting off he must have been rather dubious about the ferry service, for—unlike others we have met in somewhat similar predicament—he equipped himself with a bathing costume.

Laugharne (which one learns to pronounce Larne) is the fascinating little spot where Dylan Thomas lived, from 1937 to 1953. It is the Llareggub of his *Under Milk Wood*. The ferries, providing a short cut to Kidwelly and beyond, linked up with his own threshold, for his home was the old Boat House, on the water's edge. Nearby is the self-styled Town Hall, picturesquely provided with portreeve, bailiff, halberdiers and constables, so I am told. The ferryman, equally important to this community, puts the twelfth-century castle behind him as he rows across the narrow estuary, and there is little doubt that if my friends and I had patronized him, during our brief visit, the tale of his ghostly predecessor would have come to us in nice, racy speech.

Had Laugharne Castle been English, it would probably be haunted by some diaphanous Blue or Grey Lady. But this is Wales, where even the ghosts respect national tradition. And so it is that when General Laugharne ferries his spectral self over the Taf, once every year, he does so in a *coracle*. I suspect that he never really mastered the technique, however, for he has to bale it out continually, with his cocked hat.

As in this legend, ferrying terms are often loosely applied, though quite excuseably. Chambers' Dictionary says, without qualification, that 'to ferry' means 'to carry or convey over water in a boat'. If that can apply to flimsy tradition, how much more so to the motor-launches which in summer take visitors across from Tenby to Caldy Island? The Cistercian monks of Caldy have a ferry-boat of their own, handled by one of their own brotherhood. Much of the island monastery is also exclusive, but it would be worth going over in one of those launches, if only to wander among the rocks of Priory Bay and through the monks' exotic gardens.

Before breakfast one Easter morning my wife saw one of the island monks—as fat and rosy and jovial as Friar Tuck—land on Tenby beach and make for the town. Otherwise, just then, Caldy Sound was quite bare of craft; a strip of grey creamed with low breakers, reminding one of the line from Euripides taken by Tenby for its motto: 'The sea washes away all the ills of men'. That strip of water and its guardian island looked so tempting. I really must go down to Tenby at *ferry* time!

Another morning our party headed for St. David's, though calling first at Lydstep, Manorbier, and Stackpole, all on the rocky cirque of Carmarthen Bay. On the beach at Manorbier an Ancient-Mariner-in-the-making told us where to find the best remaining bits of Pembrokeshire, linking them in his remarks with the various ferries that cross that astonishing coastal arabesque known as Milford Haven. The ferry we used necessitated a rather close acquaintance with the gloomy, though very fine Pembroke Castle which Cromwell battered with his guns for six weeks. Low tide made the neighbouring river rather insignificant as we drove by, but a few moments later the *Cleddau King* took us aboard, on the shore of Milford Haven, and Neyland was reached in grand style, with enough ships and shipyards and docks in evidence as would satisfy the most nautically minded person.

The oracle whom we met on Manorbier beach had bemoaned to us the loss of many well-loved spots, including his own childhood home —a monastic building at Flimston which had been turned into a gunnery target during the Second World War. He could also have bewailed the passing of numerous old-world ferries, delightful ones in the same area, like those at Landshipping, Llangwm, Lawrenny, Bentlass, etc., and one over the River Nevern as it runs to sea at Newport, on Pembrokeshire's north coast.

In some correspondence on the subject in *Country Life* in 1947 a writer described the Newport Ferry in these nostalgic words:

> At low tide a ferry-boat used to take us across the river to a big stretch of sands called Traeth Mawr (Big Shore). Cows always roamed about Traeth Mawr. We never thought it strange until, thirty years later, when on holiday at Newport, we were waiting for the ferry-boat to take us across from the Newport side of the river, and saw several cows alongside us looking as if they also were waiting for the ferry.
>
> When we got into the ferry-boat the cows got into the water. At first they walked, then suddenly only their heads were in sight— they were swimming across. I did not know until then that cows could swim.
>
> When they reached Traeth Mawr they emerged from the water, shook themselves, and complacently walked across the sands and the sandhills to their farm.

It sounds as though the cattle *desired* human company while fording the Nevern. Somewhat similar was the experience, also recorded in *Country Life*, relating to the Hampton Load Ferry on the Severn in Shropshire. Here, in 1892, a team of horses was photographed while pulling a timber-wagon across the river, within a few feet of the ferry slipway. The cabined ferry-boat is moored, empty, in the background. The two men who normally ran the boat seem to be helping to get the horses safely across—a pleasant change, no doubt, from level-headed 'regulars'.

CHAPTER EIGHT

THE WELSH STORY

Many of the Welsh rivers are too turbulent to encourage any kind of ferry service. In all Cardiganshire, for example, my map shows only one —that crossing the Dovey estuary to Aberdovey in Merionethshire.

Small concessions to local need there may have been, but nothing to make a stir; just the knowledge that Will Jones or John Davies would occasionally take you across the water with his fishing tackle, and expect nothing but a 'Thank You' in return. I fancy George Borrow got many a lift of this desultory nature while touring Wales.

But in history and folklore the Dovey estuary amply makes up for any lack elsewhere. Here is a beautiful estuary, backed by some of the finest mountains in Wales. In the mouth of the estuary, quite near the ferry landing at Aberdovey, Outward Bound sea cadets are put through their paces. The parent ship which I once saw there was rigged in splendid sailing tradition and, recovering this in memory, I cannot help comparing it with the Spanish caravel that boldly entered these waters at the time of the Spanish Armada. And the ferry was ancient, even then.

By the year 1566 Aberdovey was described as 'a small ferry hamlet'. But four hundred years earlier this river crossing was sufficiently recognized to be entrusted with a grand cavalcade. Giraldus Cambrensis helps us to picture the scene.

The company had set off from Hereford on the eve of Ash Wednesday 1188 and reached Chester in time to keep Easter. Then, by circuitous routes through the hills, they eventually dropped down to the Dovey at Penrhyn Point. Who 'they' were is best seen at the water's edge as the boat draws nigh. There is His Grace the Archbishop of Canterbury, attended by two archdeacons, two Cistercian Abbots, and a couple of Princes. When one adds the inevitable retinue including pages, escorts armed against robbers, the baggage men and the packhorses, the Dovey can be imagined to have reflected a lot of fuss and finery that day, as the ferry-boat went back and forth until the last man and the last bundle was safely over. The Dovey seems to have behaved during this protracted passage, for the record states, rather bluntly, 'Having crossed the river in a boat we entered the lands of the sons of Conan. We slept that night at Towyn.'

94

I wonder by how much the ferryman was enriched, that memorable day? A lawsuit during the ensuing reign of Richard II was to fix the fares here as follows:

> ¼d. per single person,
> ½d. per man and his horse,
> 1d. man and his horse and its load.

But surely the Primate and his glittering entourage warranted greater expectations in the ferryman's breast? I hope that by the time the illustrious ones were all comfortably abed at neighbouring Towyn, this unnamed fellow in his humble cottage beside the Dovey could gloat over a heap of bright coins, and perhaps promise his wife a new kirtle.

There must always have been a goodly flow of traffic by this route, from the Roman period onward. What we now call the Furnace Falls and the Bearded Lake were as much a feature of the surrounding land-scape formerly, as today, though to old-time travellers natural beauty had little or no appeal. When they arrived footsore (or saddle-sore) on either bank of the estuary their one thought was to get safely across. They might well have wondered, for the hundredth time, why a bene-ficent Creator should place such formidable obstacles in their path. A ferryman could have told them; it was to provide a living, however meagre, for those who kept a boat!

By the eighteenth and early nineteenth century, however, the local ferrymen would appear to have been 'on a good thing'. The scale of charges had arisen to the following level:

> 2d. each foot passenger
> 6d. horse and rider
> 2/6d. wheeled carriage
> 4/0d. one-horse phaeton
> 4/6d. two-horse phaeton
> 7/6d. carriage and pair.

And on Sundays the fares were doubled.

A phaeton was an open, four-wheeled pleasure carriage named, facetiously, after Phaethon, son of Helios the sun god. Phaethon was supposed to have been as careless a driver as some who drove the carriages he unwittingly sponsored. Down by the Dovey Ferry there was no scope for irresponsible capers. What rather puzzles me is that phaetons, popular in London and Bath, had to be reckoned with at all in this then remote part of Wales.

Eventually, better roads took this wheeled traffic *round* the estuary, reducing the ferry to a small boat service once more. In *Brief Glory* the late D. W. Morgan paid a tribute to the Dovey Ferry and the different boats that have carried an archbishop and his retinue, cattle, sheep, phaetons and even stage coaches. As a schoolboy Morgan gloried in the small, bobbing craft that in his day kept tradition alive. 'I used to be Hugh Hughes' shadow,' he wrote, 'pestering him to let me keep the ferryboat (which he tended for John Bell) waterborne.' Again and again his young voice would pipe out, in Welsh, 'May I keep the boat afloat, Hugh Hughes?' And an understanding Hughes usually granted his wish.

John Bell, the most noted Dovey ferryman of recent times, was flourishing in the 1890s. A photograph in Morgan's book shows him —a sturdy figure wearing peak cap and fustian—resting in his little boat, though ready to unfurl his sail when enough passengers came aboard. In the foreground, two youths are busy periwinkling.

At that time, if you were on the Ynyslas beach (south shore) you rang a bell to call the ferryman over. It must have been rung loudly and often during the last war, when the Ministry of Supply was stationed at Ynyslas, near Borth. I cannot say whether the bell has survived that treatment, but if you prefer the water passage to the roundabout road route, or to Thomas Salvin's rail crossing up-stream, a boat will still obey your summons.

Thomas Salvin had hopes of throwing a bridge across the mouth of the estuary from Ynyslas to Aberdovey, but at this point he could find no sure foundations. The next, northward ferry crossing, over the Barmouth estuary, offered the same difficulties. Efforts to span this further gap in the coastal road system by a railway bridge failed repeatedly. One prominent Barmouth citizen greeted each failure with ill-concealed glee. I cannot help wondering whether this gentleman had any financial interest in the lucrative ferry, for everybody knew that he strongly disapproved of the bridge scheme; he kept on saying to the railway engineers, 'You'll never do it. You'll *never* do it!' After yet another failure he capped his inevitable remark by adding, 'I'll *eat* the first engine that crosses the river!'

Perseverance won, however. By 1867 the bridge was satisfactorily completed. A great opening ceremony was arranged, with a banquet to follow the triumphant entry of the first locomotive into Barmouth.

The railway company sent out their invitations—not forgetting our doubting Thomas.

My wife and I were enjoying a simple, cottage lunch while facing Cader Idris across the estuary, one day, when an old record kept by the owner gave us the above story and its amusing sequel . . .

When the old diehard entered the banquet hall at Barmouth an official of the Cambrian Railway Company politely escorted him to a table laid for one. And then, with equal courtesy, he was asked whether he would have the engine 'roasted or boiled'.

The joke, I'm sorry to say, was taken in very bad grace.

Back there in Canterbury we looked on as some of the pilgrims of old made their way, by road and ferry, to the shrine of Thomas à Becket. In North Wales another pilgrim route offers itself. This has the advantage of leading along the Lleyn peninsula to its very tip, and then over the water to Bardsey Isle.

Early pilgrims from a distance would sometimes have to ferry over the Conway River, or perhaps the Mawddach at Barmouth, before reaching Lleyn, but modern pilgrimages, organized by local church authorities, have started at the lovely old fane of St. Beuno, at Clynnog Fawr, and called at many sacred spots *en route* until, at length, they attained Aberdaron and there faced the temperamental Bardsey Sound.

It is a fascinating route to follow. I remember going that way myself, some years ago, and having a meal at a curious hospice (*c.* 1300) known as Y Gegin Fawr, just as the old-time pilgrims did before venturing upon that two-mile test of endurance. It was then customary to offer a prayer for a safe voyage at the church above the beach. I do not know whether Thomas Kelli took this wise precaution; he certainly experienced a severe buffeting while crossing to the isle, though, being a poet, he was content to say, 'I set out from Port Y Meudwy [the creek at Aberdaron] to the great estuary, on a cold winged wave'.

Today, the hazards are considerably less, as the ferry-boat is a motor-launch. Only limited time prevented my using this service, for who would not take any possible opportunity of visiting this lonely monastic island which—because twenty thousand saints are reputedly buried there—goes by the name 'Gate of Heaven'? In Tudor times, however, the position was reversed. Bardsey's very seclusion made it the refuge of pirates and buccaneers.

In North Wales ferries again bring sharply into focus a number of contradictory situations. Beauty of surroundings, yet perilous waters;

97

public service, private greed; peaceful mission, warring campaign; *affaires de coeur*, plot, intrigue and cunning. The story of human life with all its tragedy, pathos, high purpose, and humour, unfolds afresh as we hail the different ferrymen—either in retrospect or reality—who await us beside the Menai Strait or on the River Conway.

The person who has facilitated this part of our survey was Henry Rees Davies. He wrote a fine book on the subject for students of local history. Actually, it is a saga, compounded of strands that might have come from the *Thieves' Litany*, *Pilgrim's Progress*, and *Pickwick Papers*. In this area alone Davies names six or seven ferries, all medieval in origin. If we project ourselves back to the early fifteenth century, however, it is more than likely that we shall shout and bawl in vain for the ferrymen; Owen Glendower's rebellion has put several ferries out of commission. Later, in the reigns of Henry V and Henry VI, these same ferries were handed over to the care of Englishmen, who were forbidden to take any Welshmen over—unless they could produce a 'special mandate'. Fortunately, London was a great way off, far enough for the men of Cymru to steer their own course in such matters. It was discovered in 1414, for example, that despite the interdict, one Meredith ap Ken operated the Llanidan Ferry and was able—just as quietly—to pay twenty shillings' rent for it. According to official records in London the ferry was still unlet, part of the ridiculous system of reprisals.

Again, in an attempt to prevent Welshmen going across to Anglesey the ferry service over Menai Strait to Beaumaris was closed to them. If a so-called trouble-maker managed to deceive the ferryman and get himself rowed over, another trap awaited him at Beaumaris, for we read that 'under the very walls of the castle, stringent restrictions were imposed' against such 'interlopers'. Whether the 'interlopers' were shot, thrown in gaol, or just sent back on the next boat, we are not told. Even without these restrictions this particular service could be awkward. The boat was repeatedly described as 'rotten' and had to be withdrawn until somebody provided a better one. Sympathy for the town sheriff, whose duty it was to control the ferry on busy fair days, would not be misplaced.

At this time the service ran from 'feryman Warth', now marked by the Green which stretches between the castle and the water. Amongst the well-known travellers who used it—with trepidation—was the Hon. John Byng. Let us follow in his wake.

In the summer of 1784 he was touring North Wales on horseback with a friend; the various ferries they encountered provided much excitement. First, they 'came to Bangor Ferry; where we were vex'd to see the inconvenience of the passage, and to be crowded in the ferry-boats with post horses, etc. Our horses being unaccustomed to leap in and out of ferry-boats, were very difficult to manage, and I was glad to alight in the Isle of Anglesey without damage.'

Their eventual recrossing of the Menai Strait, from Beaumaris, was no whit better. The beauty of the Lavan Sands, framed by water and mountain, was largely lost upon them because of the same precarious conditions: '. . . when the boat came over and disembogued it's cargo, consisting of thirty people and fifteen horses, ours were with much difficulty forc'd in . . .' It was necessary to keep the animals under constant vigil. Moreover, Beaumaris Corporation was then having to pay the ferrymen an extra fee to place poles and faggots on Lavan Sands to mark the safe route.

Travellers had to be made of stern stuff in those days. And Byng was not yet finished with vexacious matters. After Beaumaris he had to face Conway. We shall have to return to the Menai neighbourhood again, but John Byng's experiences at Conway will give us a foretaste of what then lay ahead.

Listen to the diatribe which he later put into one of the Torrington Diaries:

Conway is a poor mean place and only subsists on the travell thro' the town. There is near our inn (the Bull's Head) a very ancient large mansion now let out in poor tenements, containing nothing of curiosity but some old ceilings, numberless grotesque figures on the walls, and chimney pieces with the arms of Queen Elizabeth.

This mansion was Plas Mawr, now the headquarters of the Royal Cambrian Academy of Art and open to public view. It is a pity that Byng and his friend got such a bad impression of a very fine building, one of whose owners had presented Catherine of Braganza, queen of Charles II, with a huge pearl taken from the River Conway near the spot where the ferry service began.

Perhaps our two travellers were in no mood for such titbits of information. The ferry loomed large in their thoughts and apprehensions, and well it might, for everybody knew its evil reputation. The Hon. John Byng survived the impending experience, as this rather fuzzy comment in the diary testifies:

At the verge of the town we had the misery of embarking on board another ferry-boat, to the danger and destruction of horses; and hereabouts they [the ferry-boats] are all ill-contriv'd and dirty, and to strange horses a service of great hazard, for they are oblig'd to leap out of, and into, deep water. My horse performs these operations but awkwardly, and Mr. P's wou'd not enter for ten minutes. This bad boatage, over a stream one mile broad, is one of the causes of a new London road being open'd thro' Llanrwst, which in a short time will eclipse the old Chester road . . .

How much safer it would have been, but far less adventurous, for Byng and his companion, to take a holiday in the Cotswold country, say, where the rivers offered nothing worse than a shallow ford.

The road toll of life, today, had its counterpart on some of the ferry crossings. And had casualty records then been kept, the Menai ferries must have topped the list.

One disaster occurred on 5 December 1785, only a year after John Byng came this way. Fifty-five passengers had joined the Caernarvon–Abermenai Ferry, but only Hugh Williams of Aberffraw survived. This is how he afterwards described the tragedy:

The Abermenai ferry-boat usually leaves Caernarvon on the return of the tide, but the 5th of December being the fair-day, and there being much difficulty on that account of collecting the passengers, the boat did not leave Caernarvon that evening till near four o'clock, though it was low water at five, and the wind, which blew strong from the south-east, was right upon our larboard bow. It was necessary that the boat should be kept in pretty close to the Caernarvonshire side, not only that we might have the benefit of the channel, which runs near the shore, but also that we might be sheltered from the wind, which blew directly towards two sandbanks, at that time divided by a channel . . . These lay somewhat more than half-way betwixt the Caernarvonshire and the Anglesea coasts.

Such precautions proved in vain. The boat made for the sandbanks as though drawn there by magnetic force. It heeled over, water rushed in, and the hapless passengers—men, women and children—had no alternative but to take refuge on that dubious footing in mid-stream. There they were, said Hugh Williams, 'exposed on a quick-sand, in a cold dark night, to all the horrors of a premature death, which, without assistance from Caernarvon we knew must be certain on the return of the tide.'

In response to their united cries for help, a few boats put out but 'not one of them on discovering our situation, dared to approach us, lest a similar [fate] should also involve them'. Anybody who has sailed across this channel can fill in the scene for himself. Nature, at times so sublime, so inviting, was now apparently bent on human destruction. It was at this point that Hugh Williams determined to make a bid for his own life. Seizing a mast and an oar from the foundered boat, he lashed them together and then launched himself on the flood tide . . .

Two hours later a very bedraggled figure turned up at the Tal-y-foel ferry-house, on the Anglesey shore. Hugh Williams had won through. The rest paid the full penalty.

Perhaps this was the ferry which John Wesley had used, in March 1750, while on his way to Ireland. He tells us that he had to pace about for three or four hours on the edge of the sands for the tide to ebb sufficiently and the wind to drop, though he suspected that the ferrymen were really waiting for more passengers.

Boatmen were wily enough to make any excuse of this sort, and they could always pass the time away—for impatient would-be passengers as well as themselves—by recounting bygone disasters in heavy, lugubrious detail. One story that would loose nothing in the telling concerned an episode in 1723 when a ferry-boat had capsized and thirty people perished. The only ones to escape were a man who floated ashore on the keel of the boat, and a boy who clung to the tail of a horse that managed to swim ashore. Practically the sole survivor of another disaster—on the Porthaethwy (Bangor) Ferry—was a woman who floated in her ballooned skirt until picked up by another boat.

Such cautionary tales, told there on the beach, would presumably counsel further patience among waiting folk—and give time for others to step up and fill the boat to a ferryman's estimate of its remunerative capacity. Little wonder that when one traveller came to Lavan Sands he found 'a group of fishwomen, asleep'. They must have heard all those tales before, and decided to await the ferrymen's convenience in peace and comfort.

Yet there was a much brighter side to the picture. What about the colourful characters associated with the different Menai ferries? There were Welsh princes, for example, successive Bishops of Bangor, and various landed gentry—all very jealous of their ownership, especially the bishops, who seem to have been as keen on their ferry rights and tolls as on their stipends.

We must spare a thought, also, for those who operated the ferries. In the late eighteenth century the Bishop's Ferry, or Garth Passage, near Bangor, was worked by Grace Parry, affectionately known as Gras-y-Garth, a woman of about sixty years who signalled her times of departure by blowing on a conch shell, which brought resounding echoes from the mountains. She was followed by John Jones, or Jack-y-Garth —a big fellow who would carry passengers ashore on his broad back. He lived on the other side of the water, at Llandegfan; his ferry house was probably the one from which my own family once embarked for Bangor; a memorable occasion, for the motor ferry-boat throws up cascades of water, as a speed boat does. I wonder what Jack-y-Garth would have thought of such amenities? He must have been a grand character and known to everybody, for at his death in 1837 no fewer than fifteen boats escorted his remains across to Bangor, and between four hundred and five hundred mourners attended his funeral service at the cathedral beyond. Jack-y-Garth's ferrying career was done, but many present that day would have reason to recall his cheerful St. Christopher role down there in the Strait's ferry shallows.

Another favourite was 'Old Shon'. If he wasn't ferrying people across to Abermenai Point, the southern tip of Anglesey, he would be selling mats at his waterside cottage. A Caernarvon man who often went over by this route recalled that 'Old Shon' employed 'twelve to eighteen young women knotting mats'. I expect many a ferry passenger felt obliged to buy one or two for home use.

A touch of the macabre that Dickens would have relished gave abounding scope for gossip on the Aber Ferry. Passengers had the blood-curdling satisfaction of landing on Anglesey at a point first known as Penrhyn Safnes, and rechristened Osmund's Air because of a certain malefactor called Osmund. After crossing the ferry as a prisoner on his way to the gallows, he blithely announced that he was 'going to take the air'. Just beyond the Beaumaris golf course a small headland is named Gallows Point. Perhaps this was where Osmund took his last breath.

By the time Thomas Butler of Kirkstall Forge, near Leeds (where this book began) came down this way, in 1818, respectability had taken hold of the Menai ferries. In Butler's personal diary there is no talk of avaricious ferrymen, or of malefactors; even the stormy Straits, though still looked at askance, are shown in better light.

After feeding well, though rather expensively, at Ferry House, Bangor, and seeing the Bishop of Bangor ride past with some ladies (evidently a great treat for the observer), Butler and his companion turn their attention to the Bangor Ferry, which cost '5/od. for horse and gig'. The Yorkshireman then adds:

> They are beginning to build a bridge over the Strait. Nature has placed several rocks in the Strait . . . as if she intended to assist art in the erection of the Bridge. Over this ferry is the direct way from London via Holyhead to Ireland, and it is one of the Articles in the Union* that a bridge should be built over this Strait—it will greatly facilitate and add very much to the pleasure of Travelling . . .

He and his friend then go over to Holyhead, and return by ferry on the same day. As a fellow Yorkshireman—though separated by a century and a half of progress—I find it amusing to follow as much as possible in Butler's tracks. The Bangor Ferry has vanished, of course, but others still ply across the Straits, from Garth and Port Dinorwic. We today have this advantage over the Kirkstall ironmaster; Telford's suspension bridge (completed in 1826) takes us in fine style across the water from Bangor. The chair in which the famous engineer was accustomed to sit and ponder during its erection now enjoys its retirement in the local museum. I ferried over from Llandegfan, once, to see this and other Telford mementoes, returning 'chronologically' by his bridge which had given the main ferry its *coup de grâce*.

But the Bishop of Bangor I did not see. Nor any adoring bevy of ladies. And my lunch, that day, was hardly such as to bring that glow of ambrosial content which Thomas Butler had so evidently felt. One must need the old scenes spiced with a little of their danger, to give the authenic thrill. By comparison, bridges are so tame!

It is now time to wander up the coast to Conway. Once again, modernity —in the shape of cars, scenic-tour coaches, ice-cream vans, lollipops —robs the highway of its romance. One should be able to gear down to the pace of a few bygone travellers and pilgrims, to whom every bend of the tortuous road spelt possible ambush and the ferries ahead were so many nightmares . . .

Let us join one group now jogging up the Conway road. From here, Mona, or the Isle of Anglesey, is retreating upon itself, over the silvery Straits, and the mountains of Cambria tower up to heaven on the right.

* The Act of Union between England and Ireland was passed on 1 January 1806.

What will these approaching travellers think of it all? They make a sizeable company—but surely we have met them before, down by the Dovey estuary? Yes, it is Archbishop Baldwin's cavalcade, making a little more ground on their tour of Wales.

What the princes and the prelates are saying to each other, as they pass along, would require a Chaucer to relate. Giraldus Cambrensis, though helpful in other ways, is no Chaucer. The benefit we get by attaching ourselves to them is that of sampling one of the Conway ferries. Here, however, Giraldus has us guessing again. Was the ferry used that day by this august company the one which crosses Conway Morfa to Deganwy, where Maelgwyn Gwynedd, a sixth-century King of Britain and the Outer Isles had established his court? Or was it the ferry slightly up-stream over which the monks of Aberconway had free passage? Whichever it was, the crossing seems to have been completed without any mishap worth recording.

Perhaps the Deganwy Ferry was the more probable route for the Archbishop's party, being the older one. Some friends and I had the pleasure of using it as late as 1924. A row-boat landed us on the shingle and, looking back in retrospect, I find myself picturing those illustrious ones and their horses crunching and slithering over the same pebbly shore.

If, however, the up-stream ferry had the honour that day of carrying such a concentration of the élite, we can get a clearer picture, for the story of *this* ferry has been recorded in tears and groans and heart-burnings for centuries.

Edward I is credited with the creation, or perhaps the consolidation, of this other ferry service; it was more conveniently sited for his new borough of Conway. The present castle was also founded by him. He and his Eleanor spent one Christmas here, and in summer-time Eleanor tended a small flower-garden near her castle apartment. But whatever the season, monks and merchants, farmers and housewives, vagrants and vagabonds were soon using this ferry beneath the shadow of Edward's castle. How insignificant they would appear, they and the boats that carried them, can be judged by climbing to the castle parapets. I would not be surprised to learn that some of Conway's notorious ferry disasters had been witnessed from these same heights: puny man struggling with the forces of Nature.

In the mid-seventeenth century, for example, the ferry-boat turned turtle and more than eighty people were drowned. The only survivor was Anne Thomas of Creuddyn. Fate had been kind to her. She could still keep tryst with the lover awaiting her at Conway fair. But what a harrowing story she would have to tell, between her sobs. In August 1774 Dr. Samuel Johnson travelled this way by coach with Mr. and Mrs. Thrale and their daughter. They found the ferry arrangements rather clumsy but had no real cause for complaint except the cold dinner that awaited their arrival at Conway.

Shelley's friend, T. J. Hogg, was less fortunate. On a bitter March day in 1813, he wrote afterwards, '. . . The Cambrian coachman pulled up short at the mouth of a wide river, wild, rough and stormy as the sea itself . . . we got into a boat . . . [and] had a rude and tedious passage across. When we were midway, they spoke of a fatal accident that had occurred there just a month before; that the ferry-boat was upset and the mail-guard drowned . . .' And so, following a poor breakfast at Conway, Hogg proceeded to Bangor Ferry, but fared no better. The Bangor ferrymen bundled him 'into a large boat, with the accustomed delicacy and attention of mail-coach travelling, of which the leading principle always was—so that the letter bags and guard are safe, the passengers and their effects may go to the devil'.

The sorry tale of the Conway Ferry, and its connecting services, could be continued *ad nauseam*. I will mention just one more incident, recounted by a traveller called Richard Warner. The date is August 1798. He and some friends try to cross the River Conway late in the evening, when the tide is out. A few locals tell them that three-quarters of a mile away, beyond the wet sands, a boat would be waiting for them. This piece of news made them hesitate, but they were further told, for their encouragement, that 'if they hastened they would overtake three old women who were crossing to Conway with butter and eggs'. When these old dears came at last into view they were already 'wading through a stream with their shoes and stockings off'. At length, after making several watery detours and dodging several patches of quick-sand, all the waders reach the boat safely—and reckon that the worst is over!

Once again, Telford was to resolve the situation by building one of his glorious suspension bridges. Starting near the castle, and the former seed-pearl fishery, it pursues the line of the ferry to Ir Ynys-Tuor-Y-Castell, a one-time island noted for its wild fowl, and then joins up with the Llandudno headland. As two other bridges have since followed suit hereabouts, the river is at last harnessed. The ghosts of those who perished by ferry can take their peace.

When Telford's bridge was opened to traffic, on 1 July 1826, there were five men who did not rejoice with the rest. They were the ferry-men, who had been put out of their job. A claim for compensation was made but the result is not recorded. I should like to think that one or two of these men found employment at the Tal-y-Cafn Ferry, about six miles up-river. Some travellers already preferred this ferry to the notorious one at Conway. True, the Tal-y-Cafn route meant a long forward journey through 'horrid' mountains, via Capel Curig and the Nant Ffrancon Pass, but the risks of a watery grave were less.

Yet when Tal-y-Cafn Ferry, in its turn, was closed, there were few mourners. The ferrymen and his family, no doubt, but who else? When the supplanting bridge was opened on 9 October 1897, Dr. Arthur Pritchard, Mayor of Conway, came up-river for the ceremony. He might well have spoken kindly about the lovely scenery at this bend of the river; he certainly gave the old ferry the order of the boot! How many were the times, he took pains to recall in his speech, when his practice had required him to use this ferry—to be met, if it were night-time, by grumblings and crusty epithets from the ferryman's bed-chamber. And once, wrathfully added the doctor, he was refused altogether, so that his patient on the other side of the river had to suffer needlessly for several hours.

Other people present at the ceremony echoed these sentiments. With great glee, therefore, and a sense of mounting justice, the good doctor first had the old ferry-boat strung up to the bridge, like a felon, and then—having delivered himself of his grievances—caused it to be cut down and cast adrift.

Not long ago my wife and I went up-river to Tal-y-Cafn by motor-boat. It was the nearest thing to a ferry service we could find. The scenery is as enchanting as ever, but—I wish that doctor had not been quite so ruthless. The Tal-y-Cafn ferry-boat could at least have been pensioned-off, and given a chance to create nostalgic interest amongst onlookers, in some Welsh museum.

CHAPTER NINE

MERSEYSIDE MEMORIES

'Bring them I pray thee . . . to the common Ferrie.'
The Merchant of Venice

To pick up our story, once more, I need only recall some days spent at Chester, years ago, when the full tide of inquiry was launching me into some strange inlets of history. Sampling history at this beautiful old town is sheer joy. Stand almost anywhere—in its streets or parks, beside its old buildings or its own broad sweep of the River Dee, and your invisible companions will be Roman soldiers, Welsh raiders, kings of the realm, pilgrims to the shrine of St. Werburgh (like the one carved holding his staff, on the Dean's Stall in the Cathedral), or once-important officials like John Catherall who, because of his ferocious grin, was called 'the Cheshire Cat'.

It is such people who provide the best introduction to Chester's common ferry. But if you were to mention any of them, aloud, present-day citizens would probably think you were 'nuts'. Personally I rather like this kind of dreaming. And, while at Chester, at what pleasanter spot can one indulge the fancy than Bridgegate, or the appropriately named Wishing Steps nearby? The river is at one's feet. To the right is the Old Dee Bridge, and almost straight across, the mill recalling that famous Miller who sang, 'I care for nobody, no not I . . .' Between bridge and mill-weir was the ferrymen's domain. On the town side, it was approached through Shipgate, or Hole-in-the-Wall. This thirteenth-century arch is now set up in Grosvenor Park, but the figures who have stepped through it, on their way to or from the ferry, would make a striking pageant.

First, the Twentieth Legion and their adherents: a mixed lot including such types as a Thracian from the Sea of Marmora, and a veteran soldier from Arles in the South of France; gladiators and the women who cheered them in the ampitheatre nearby; potters like some named Albanus, Vitalis and Germanus;* craftsmen of other kinds, too; all potential customers of the ferry which was to continue long after the Romans (as it is thought) built themselves a bridge hardly a javelin's throw distant.

* Examples of their handiwork are shown in the city's Grosvenor Museum.

107

Deva, the Roman town, had become submerged in medieval Chester by the time Edward I came along, with his adored Eleanor. The royal pair probably rode into the town over the bridge, but one can be sure that the ferry-boats would be crowded with cheering spectators. And crowded boats might have been to the fore again, a hundred years or so later, when—after negotiating several outlying ferries—Richard II was led into Chester on a mean-looking nag. The River Dee has reflected few sadder sights than this deposed king, clad as a grey friar, receiving the curses and brickbats of a fickle populace.

Another busy day for the Chester ferrymen occurred in the year 1815 when a 'Glorious Pageant of the Deluge' was performed on the river by the 'Water Leaders and Drawers of the Dee'. In my self-induced dream I can see the affair, and hilarious it must have been, for the Ark itself was in great evidence and 'paper animals as large as life'.

Until a few years ago Eccleston Ferry preserved for Chester folk a charming touch of bygone England. This ferry, like that three miles away beneath the city walls, could also claim Roman lineage, but the scene familiar to so many people is of later times, centring upon the Ferry-House and a half-timbered Tudoresque dwelling which peers through banks of thick foliage to the old ferry slipway. It made a favourite outing from Chester. The boat saw you on your way to the pretty village of Eccleston, or you could just recline on the river bank in a David Cox setting and listen to children's voices and dripping oars.

Because Eaton Hall stands nearby, the spot was in earlier days often called Eaton Ferry. On Morden's map of Cheshire (*c.* 1700) it is named Eaton Boat. In his *Picturesque Cheshire* (1903) T. A. Coward could enthuse thus:

On holidays riverside Eaton is gay; below the Hall . . . is Eccleston Ferry—'Jimmy th' Boats,' the boating men call it—and opposite the Hall is the Iron Bridge. At both places tea can be obtained; they are the rendezvous of ravenous pleasure-seekers.

Where are the 'ravenous pleasure-seekers' today? Surely, between them, Chester citizens and frequent visitors could have kept this lovely place in business! Or does nobody want the ferryman's job?

Another local ferry only recently eclipsed—by a foot-bridge—is that at Saltney, where Cheshire and Flintshire meet. The Manifold family had operated this service for over a hundred and fifty years. Saltney

Ferry was one of several that could once be used between Chester and the Dee estuary. A network of roads now covers the area, but for years many motorists had reason to quail before tackling the Queensferry Bridge bottleneck. I have sometimes thought that it might have been quicker could we still have patronized one of the two ferries that conveyed eighteenth-century travellers over the Dee, in the immediate neighbourhood, or even the ferry that plied from Parkgate on the Wirral, to Bagillt between Flint and Holywell. The Sands of Dee might be treacherous at times, but they would make a pleasanter prospect than queues of impatient, hooting cars.

An amusing reference to the main ferry over the Dee estuary occurs on one of the playing-card maps issued in 1676 by Robert Morden. Each card represents a different county. This Cheshire card, allotted to the Four of Clubs, shows only two roads; one of them is the post road into North Wales. I can well imagine people of the Restoration period handling one of these playing-card packs, for instruction as well as a fireside game, and pointing out such places as they might have reason to know. Here, for example, is the post-road ferry over the Dee, near Chester. The county had other important ferries, as we shall discover, but Morden concedes nothing more on this theme. His playing-cards are of normal size and have their cartographical limits. The only indications of any kind of link between his 'Lerpoole' and 'Wallasy' are two or three tiny boats crossing the Mersey.

Most people can remember their first sight of some famous place. Wordsworth's first impressions of seeing Tintern Abbey from the River Wye were set down for posterity. Lesser men have recorded the impact made on their minds on first beholding a lovely stretch of the River Thames, say, or Old Father Humber's broad tawny carpet. My own memories of the Mersey go back to a day during the 'war to end war' when my parents took their three boys down to the riverside at Liverpool and we saw a landing-stage, actually floating, and enough boats of all shapes and sizes to keep one's mind afloat too. I had never seen the like before. It was a new world, and part of that glamorous world of ships and wailing sirens were the paddle-boats that steamed back and forth to an arpeggio of their own.

When my father jingled a few coins in his pocket and boyishly suggested a trip on one of those ferry-boats, our day was made. Had my mother realized how stormy the Mersey can be I'm sure she would have been seasick, before embarking. But all went well. The sun shone, the wind was but a zephyr, and we made an easy passage to New Brighton and back. Up till then the only paddle-steamer I had seen was the *Cambria*, which figured largely in our childhood holidays at Scarborough. Memory will not now give me the name of that Mersey vessel. It was probably named after some flower, in keeping with this ferry company's tradition. Of New Brighton itself I recall little, from that juvenile occasion. It was the ferry voyage that counted—and now, over fifty years later, that same voyage is helping to mark the course for this present ferry excursion through Britain.

Like so many other ferry services, those across the River Mersey owe much to early monastic influence. This great 'arm of the sea' makes a ferry or a series of ferries inevitable, and to meet that need a small group of boatmen were plying back and forth soon after the Norman Conquest. It would be a somewhat haphazard service at first, for the Wirral then had few inhabitants, while Liverpool, across the water, was but a small fishing village.

Gradually, as population grew, the ferrymen became more enterprising. From Birkenhead you could be taken over to Eastham, Ince and Runcorn, as well as Liverpool where a market had now been established. A probable reason for Birkenhead Priory being built on its particular site, overlooking the Mersey, back there in the twelfth century, was the proximity of the ferry landing at Woodside.

Like others, the Birkenhead monks soon needed a market for their butter, cheese and corn. Liverpool provided the answer. One annoying feature of the available boat service, however, was that the Liverpool ferrymen charged no fixed fare but according to the whim of the moment. Perhaps the monks remonstrated with the men, decorating their protests with some choice epithets in Latin. If so, the ferrymen took no heed. Protests from other ferry passengers were as disdainfully treated. If you didn't want to pay the fare demanded, you could go back home and eat your own butter!

The ferrymen should have foreseen the outcome. At that time monastic brotherhoods still endeavoured to help those in need. Hence, the Prior of Birkenhead sent a petition to the king, asking that the rights of the Mersey Ferry be invested with his monastery, for the public weal. And so it was that on 13 April 1330 a royal charter was granted which sent the former boatmen packing. Edward III granted to the Priory at Birkenhead and 'its successors for ever, Passage over the Arm of the Sea' for men, horses and goods between the Priory and Liverpool, and permission to charge reasonable tolls. 'Reasonable tolls' sounds arbitrary, but the

The Sandside Ferry was operated over part of the Kent
estuary for the owners of Dallam Tower nearby

The Windermere Ferry leaving the Claife shore where the
ghostly crier used to summon the ferryman after dark

Motor-launch landings at Keswick, Cumberland

The ferry jetty on Roa Island near Barrow-in-Furness. The tiny row-boat serves Piel Island in the distance

Around 1900 Messrs Vickers of Barrow-in-Furness operated
this steam ferry for their workmen living on Walney Island

Sunderland Ferry over the River Wear, Co. Durham

This pony-trap took the author to Holy Island (seen in
distance) in 1935; the poles mark the safe route and the box-like
refuge is for pedestrians who may be trapped by the rising tide

An enamelled glass window at Low Hall, Yeadon, Yorks,
shows Mary, Queen of Scots, landing at Leith

MARY QUEEN OF SCOTS LANDING AT LEITH

David MacBrayne—the man
to whose ferry services the
Western Highlands and
Islands owe so much

Ballachulish Ferry, Argyll, in its grand mountain setting

R.M.S. *Columba*, one of the MacBrayne fleet
serving the Western Isles from Oban, Argyll

The short sea ferry route to Ireland formerly began at this
harbour at Port Patrick, Wigtownshire

monks ran the ferry—with oar and sail—successfully for all concerned until they were turned adrift at the Dissolution, in 1536.

And then? We read that in 1544–5 Ralph Worsley, 'the King's servant', made a good bargain. He paid over to the King the sum of £568 11s. 6d.—a small fortune at that time, but consider what it put into his hands: all the property of the dissolved Priory, viz., 'The house, with a church, tower and graveyard, buildings, mills, barns, stables, dovecots and garden within the precincts', and several acres of land. But the chief plum was this: 'the ferry, ferry-house and boat, in Birkenhead, Bidston, and Kirkby Walley . . .' The ferry service was now operating, profitably, from three different places along the south bank of the Mersey.

Naturally, Liverpool—on the north bank—had been working its own ferries for a long time. The men in charge had a gala day or two in 1323 when Edward II stayed at Liverpool Castle. The royal accounts relate how local boats and ferrymen were requisitioned for the private use of King and courtiers. The keeper of these accounts was meticulous. He even named the actual ferrymen thus employed and the fare paid. Thus Hamon de Runcorn was richer by a whole shilling for ferrying the King across the River Weaver, and, another day, Richard-by-the-Wode received *two shillings* for rowing his royal client 'over the arm of the Mersey water between Wirral and Ince'.

In this same year of 1323 the Liverpool Ferry passed into the King's own possession. It had previously belonged to Edmund, Earl of Lancaster, but as Lancaster's son, Thomas, joined in a baronial conspiracy against Edward II, he forfeited his head and his family forfeited the lucrative ferry, though they regained this later.

Some idea of the altercations that unfortunately sprang up between Liverpool and Birkenhead over the respective ferry services is gained from the following item, dated December 1402: 'Lawrence de Ruthin, Henry de Hole and John de Hole came with force to the ferry of Byrkeved [Birkenhead] where Lawrence beat and wounded John de Ireland, the ferryman, and they afterwards laid in wait and maltreated so many people of Liverpool that none dared to come that way.'

The waters were still troubled in 1572, for in that year a new regulation was added to the Liverpool Town Book: 'He that hath charge of the ferie boote in yerelie rent shall not let the same ferie boote frame hensforthe [to] goo labour and carie from this towne to Chester, Eastham, Weryngton or other like creykes and landyng places wythowt the speciall licence of Mr. Maior [for the] time beying, in payne of everie tyme soe offendyng to the contrye [contrary] xx.s . . .'

It would seem as though the Mersey ferrymen about this time were as closely supervised as their opposite numbers on the Thames. Heavy fines were (quite rightly) imposed for 'extortioning', that is, over-charging and it was also laid down 'that no person using any ferry-boat was, allowed to fish therefrom but to attend to his business only, on payment of fine of 40s.' It is difficult to imagine anybody then *wanting* to fish on the Mersey, except in the calmest weather. Even when our friend Celia Fiennes came this way, over a hundred years later, the two-mile ferry passage—in 'a sort of hoy'—took up an hour and a half of her precious time.

The above are just a few dippings from the spate of literature that has accumulated about the numerous Mersey ferries. I have dipped to some purpose into records carefully compiled by R. Stewart-Brown of Liverpool, Captain J. L. Regan of Wallasey, and others. Stewart-Brown's book includes a sketch map of the different ferries that could once be encountered along the Mersey while sailing up-river from the mouth of the estuary. To anybody living on Merseyside the names must ring like so many bells: Seacombe Ferry (Wallasey), Woodside Ferry, Monks' Ferry, Birkenhead Ferry, Tranmere Ferry, Rock Ferry, New Ferry. Others could have been added, mostly plying to the same terminal, Pier Head, Liverpool, but let us now hear Captain Regan, who long ran the local ferry services for Wallasey Corporation.

He points out, first, that 'the rise and progress of Wallasey coincides almost exactly with the increasing efficiency of the Ferry Services that cross the Mersey'. A ferry existed here as early as 1515. Regan, fully conversant with modern ferry vessels on the Mersey, finds evident pleasure in recording that the earliest boats used here were single-masted, followed eventually by two-masted boats. Then again, responsible as he was for an efficient Corporation enterprise, he lingers with amusement on the old days when 'landing on the Wallasey side was achieved by passengers wading ashore, or being carried through the shallows at low tide, when the primitive gangway, consisting of a plank supported by two large wheels, could not be used'. Today, you pay a fixed price for your ferry ticket. But it was not always so. At the end of the eighteenth century the toll was usually twopence if you were a 'common passenger' just going over to market, but sixpence if you belonged to the 'upper order'. Status airs and symbols could be embarrassing and expensive. It was considered wise to have it out with the boatman and pay him *after* the return trip.

The Egremont Ferry began nearby in 1828. Its proprietor was John

Askew, the Liverpool harbour master, who named the place after his native town in Cumberland. It would have been understandable had he introduced to his ferry a horn signal that could be said to echo the traditional Horn of Egremont, but we are not told of any such device. Perhaps a replica of the horn which Sir Eustace de Lucy sounded to eject his usurper from Egremont Castle would have warded off those vessels which 'usurped' the ferry pier by crashing into it. The last time this happened was in May 1941. The steamer responsible for the damage unfortunately put the ferry out of action for good.

Another ferry which gave birth to a township operated from the north end of Wallasey borough. To set this place—New Brighton—on its feet, a certain James Atherton needed twelve thousand pounds. This was to cover the cost of building a ferry terminal and a hotel. The prospectus he issued for the benefit of investors would sound very alluring in 1832. It began:

As New Brighton is likely to become a favourite and fashionable watering place, several gentlemen have proposed to erect there a handsome hotel and a convenient dock or ferry to be called the Royal Lighthouse Hotel and Ferry, and to establish a communication by Steam Packets between that place and Liverpool. The expense of this undertaking is estimated at £12,000, and it is intended to raise this sum in shares of £100 each . . .

The practical result, as far as the ferry was concerned, throws a rather amusing light on what was then considered 'convenient'. Captain Regan relates that 'the first pier or jetty was of wood, with a small run-out stage on lines, for use at low tide, which was hauled up on the flood tide by means of a windlass worked by a horse treading in a circular track . . . On the ebb tide, each departing steamer pulled the stage out to enable the next steamer to land.' This Heath Robinson contrivance must have been diverting to watch, in action, from the windows of Atherton's 'handsome hotel'.

One would also like to have seen a device proposed at Rock Ferry, below Birkenhead. This ferry had been steadily building up its reputation since about 1660, but towards the end of the eighteenth century somebody had a bright idea. Why not *pull* the ferry-boats, to and from Toxteth, Liverpool, by endless rope? I think the plan must have miscarried, however, for only a few years later a new company took over and more normal developments, such as public baths and additional houses for a select clientele, fill the picture. The man usually credited with these improvements and their financial backing was a Nantwich tailor. As his tailoring business owed much to the patronage of George IV, when Prince Regent, people used to say that 'the King's breeches bought the Rock Ferry'.

It is rather pleasant to think of shy Nathaniel Hawthorne—while he was American consul at Liverpool—becoming a regular, daily passenger on this service. He is known, of course, for his delightful fairy tales, which seem to be echoed in the very names of the Rock Ferry vessels he would use—*Ant*, *Bee*, *Wasp*, *Star*, and *Nymph*.

A strange assortment of ferry-boats have worked from both stretches of the Wirral waterfront through the ages. In addition to some we have already signalled from the past there was the *Etna* (1817), an eruptive name for the river's first steamboat, though Captain Regan assures us that it was 'apparently nothing more than two floats decked over, with a paddle wheel between'. The *Etna* ran from Birkenhead. The earliest Wallasey steam ferries included the *Seacombe*, *Alice*, and *Sir John Moore*, followed by the *Invincible*, the *Tiger*, and the *Fairy*—a good choice. Names, however, could be misleading. In heavy weather the *Fairy* became a torment to passengers and crew alike. And if you were aboard *Thomas Wilson* when its engines were giving trouble, your help might be sought to turn the paddles round to a more favourable position.

In 1862 the *Waterlily* entered the New Brighton ferry service, offering such amenities as passengers' saloons, and illumination by coal gas, 'for which purpose a large gasometer was fitted . . . under the deck, which was refilled as required from a special main laid on to the landing stage'. No other ferry-boat was so equipped, then or later. The owners were not trying to preserve its unique character, however. Quite frankly, the boat was unsafe. *Etna*, rather than the inoffensive name *Waterlily*, would have suited its explosive potentialities better!

One Tranmere ferry-boat, *Harry Clasper*, earned the nickname *Harry Go Faster* because, being a comparative lightweight, it could travel quicker than its competitors. Maximum speed for only one penny—who could resist the lure! What a contrast these boats present to today's palatial diesel ferry-boats, guided during periods of bad visibility by radar.

And yet Merseyside folk of yesteryear loved their old 'tubs'. I have just been looking at some of the picture postcards they sent to their relations and friends. Here is one showing Woodside Ferry in 1814; a charming rural scene. A small, twin-sailed ferry-boat has just pulled up near the Ferry-House. Three ferrymen are in charge; one stands in the water to support a lady about to step out; the second splashes forward to help another bonneted client up the slipway; the third man steadies the boat for a couple of children. What a lovely, reassuring card to post to Father!

Woodside Ferry is illustrated on another card, but times have now changed. The date is 1840; the little sailing vessel has given place to a paddle steamer and the ferrymen's cottage to a few smart hotels. Other postcard views depict the old Tranmere Ferry as it was in 1815, with its wide pier; the ferry-boats toss about in front of George's Bath and Pier Head at Liverpool is seen much as it would look when Nathaniel Hawthorne stepped ashore.

One larger picture in this album of fond memories strikes an Arctic note. It transports one back vividly to a February day in 1895 when the Mersey was frozen. A paddle ferry-boat, swathed thick with ice crystals, is pushing its way through great ice floes. Men passengers are looking over the ship's rail, marvelling perhaps at their bravery in facing such odds. The women passengers are more practical. They are huddled around the funnel for a little warmth.

What a lot those commuters miss who spare no thought for the river's millennium of ferries and always cross *under*, by the Mersey Tunnel!

A trickle of water first glinting amongst the heather in the wild Trough of Bowland. A dancing stream, with sheep crossing over on fallen tree-trunks. A river that soon nourishes village life (near Abbeystead) with its Shepherds' Chapel and a small, stone bridge. An estuary, as tortuous as its sparkling progenitor amongst the hills, though much broader; in fact, a Mersey in miniature, offering timeless challenge to all who come this way. Such, briefly, is the story of Lancashire's River Wyre.

That challenge was not taken up seriously until, early in the nineteenth century, Sir Peter Hesketh Fleetwood, Bart., of Rossall Hall, conceived the idea of building a town and port at the mouth of the estuary. In 1837 Decimus Burton, an architect of adventurous ideas, marked out the first streets with a plough. The town took the baronet's name, Fleetwood, and a ferry was established to link the place with Knott End over the water. Soon, small row-boats and sailing vessels were bringing farmers and their produce from the Over Wyre district; the Croft family had begun their long period as ferrymen.

A lively picture of those early days has been reconstructed by Peter Doughty of the local public library service. We see cattle being brought over by ferry, not *in* the boats, however, but towed behind, tethered by their heads to the stern rail. We see the *Helvellyn* ferry-boat arriving daily from Piel Pier and Roa Island, adjoining Barrow-in-Furness, in an attempt to create a short-cut from Glasgow to London. We also see the colourful Zenon Vantini, a Corsican who had served Napoleon as one of his couriers, now enthroned as manager of the North Euston Notel. With this sumptuous concern as bait, Vantini kept one eye on the railway-passenger potential, and the other on the ferry traffic. An Italian operatic band added to the allure, and patrons could enjoy a private promenade and landing stage.

But at length Crofts' ferry service foundered. The Local Board declared that it was quite inadequate for a progressive place like Fleetwood and they secured powers to take the ferry in hand. This was in 1893, and loud were the lamentations of the old gang, who had the chagrin of seeing their own proud sailing vessels, *Playfair* and *Guarantee*, gradually ousted by some described as 'well-type boats with a central upright boiler and single-screw engine'. The vanguard of this new régime rang with such names as *Lune* (Lancaster's river), *Onward*, and *Progress*. Then followed *Bourne May*, *Pilling*, *Wyresdale*, *Caldervale*, and others, all preparing the way for the present *Viking 66*, which carries a hundred and forty passengers.

Fleetwood, therefore, has never outgrown its ferry service; simply modernized it. A bridge over the mouth of the Wyre would be too costly to build. Hovercraft are a possibility for the near future. Meanwhile, people of Fleetwood and Knott End use their ferry to the tune of some three hundred thousand trips per year. During the last war the annual figures soared to well over a million. This was largely due to the troops stationed in the Fylde and to the influx of refugees from blitzed areas of Britain.

Once, however, this half-mile ferry service over the Wyre estuary became Fleetwood's life-line. In late October 1927 a tidal wave pounced on the neighbourhood, causing widespread floods and devastation. It was as though Morecambe Bay—that vast basin of water fed by several rivers, including the Wyre—had risen, as so many inland lakes are said to have risen at different times in history. Fleetwood took the full brunt of the inundation. It became an island, completely cut off from the outer world —except for that ferry to Knott End.

For over two miles the railway track was obliterated by six feet of water. About five hundred families were marooned, and to rescue them a fleet of small rowing-boats was despatched from the pleasure lake in

Stanley Park, Blackpool. Boys from Rossall School, near Fleetwood, helped the Blackpool men to ferry these boats to where they were most needed, while the accredited ferry over the swollen Wyre took H.M. mails and brought back essential supplies and a few newspapers for the defenceless 'islanders'.

All that happened over forty years ago. But older folk have long memories. And floods still sweep across vulnerable areas of Britain. If I lived in Fleetwood I should nurture a friendly regard for its ferry and vigorously support the local Council in their determination to maintain the service despite some financial loss. Would it be wise to sever the town's life-line?

CHAPTER TEN

LAKELAND GHOST AND SOLWAY SMUGGLER

My own first crossing to Ireland was by steam ferry from Heysham. Dusk had fallen and all I could see were a few twinkling lights, railway lines twisting amongst the docks, a gleam of water, the ferry gangway. A quick walk around the deck as the ship drew away, and then down below to dream about the half-mythical land of St. Patrick.

I did not then realize that, centuries before, Patrick had traditionally used the same sea route, though in reverse. *His* dream, I suppose, was to convert England; a chapel dedicated to him still stands on a rock by the waterside, in Heysham village. Here you can see the wide arc of Morecambe Bay, culminating in the hazy distance at Walney Island, off Barrow-in-Furness. Almost at your feet, looking south, is Heysham harbour. But after visiting the harbour many times in recent years, by daylight—once with the majestic *Duke of Lancaster* waiting to take its ferry passengers aboard—I would say that my nocturnal experience was more genuinely romantic.

Whether the proposed Morecambe Bay barrage scheme ever materializes or not, it is at least interesting to notice how this enormous bay could be,* and already has been, traversed. The barrage would throw a ten or twelve-mile road-embankment from Heysham or Morecambe to some place along the Furness shore. Since monastic times, people have walked across the Bay sands, wading barefoot in places, but only at low tide and with the help of accredited guides. The guide service really began with the monks of Cartmel Priory, in Furness, and in Cartmel village to this day there are milestones to tell you the distance to Lancaster, or to Cark and Ulverston, over the sands. These milestones belong to the era when coaches made the crossing—and sometimes came to grief *en route*.

At half-tide and at sunset the Kent estuary—which merges with Morecambe Bay—is seen at its loveliest. But enjoy the scene as anybody must, this much seems obvious. No ordinary ferry service could ever negotiate those bird-haunted sandbars, those deceptively shallow pools and creeks

---

* In August 1968 the Morecambe Bay Hovercraft Ferry Service began to operate between Fleetwood and Barrow-in-Furness.

and shifting channels. And yet, on my last visit, a small row-boat was taking the water with apparent ease, and adding magic to the performance by catching a beam from the setting sun in its wake.

As things turned out, that fishing boat could have been mistaken for one of those small vessels which really did operate from Sandside, a little higher up-river, during the nineteenth century. Those Sandside ferry-boats were flat-bottomed, as clearly suggested in a contemporary aquatint which Brigadier Tryon-Wilson of neighbouring Dallam Tower produced for my inspection. The picture shows a ferry-boat being pushed clear of some sand; the Ferry Cottages stand on a spit of land in the mid-distance, and in the foreground a charming Gothic summer-house indicates that the whole landscape, boats and all, were part of the Dallam Tower estate.

For many generations the owners were obliged to maintain this somewhat precarious ferry service. The boat could take you at high water from the little Sandside wharf to Low Foulshaw Farm. You then walked, or thumbed a lift on the farmer's cart, reaching Grange-over-Sands, on that far shore, in less than quarter the time required by the Levens Bridge route.

But of course there were risks. At Sandside a fog horn made from a large African shell was used to guide the ferryman when visibility was poor. The tide and currents always needed careful watching. And there was a *bore*, not as mountainous as that on the River Severn, but, with a lift of three feet or so, strong enough to upset a small boat. This is what happened one day in 1905, when a ferry-boat containing ten passengers was caught. Several were drowned—and we hear no more of the Sandside ferry.

The actual date of its demise I have been unable to discover. In *The Eye of the Wind*, Peter Scott refers to his early wild-fowling adventures on the Kent estuary, about 1932, and goes on to say that the Bird Research Station since established at Slimbridge, beside the Severn, might well have grown up here, amongst the wild geese and gulls and herons of upper Morecambe Bay. I wrote to him about the Sandside Ferry but he declares that no such service was in existence during his visits. It was a little later that I approached Brigadier Tryon-Wilson on this matter. But while I talked with him, before a log fire in his beautiful Georgian home, mere dates faded in importance, for I heard that in the 1930s Peter Scott had frequently been the Brigadier's guest at Dallam. They would go punting together on the estuary, tracking wild geese.

'Oh, yes; the ferry itself had disappeared by then,' the Brigadier assured me, 'but I have often *walked* over the old ferry route at low tide, and my hounds have crossed over too.' The walking process must have been even more tricky than the ferrying, for he explained how he had to fix wide boards to his boots to prevent sinking in the treacherous mud. 'If you feel yourself sinking you have to roll over on one side, flat to the mud.' Personally, I would rather have chanced the old ferry!

The ferryman's fog horn, long kept at the Ship Inn, Sandside, seems to have disappeared. But it has a successor in an electrically operated signal which gives warning of the Kent bore. And, quite appropriately, this electrical device booms forth from the vicinity of those still-standing Ferry Cottages.

I shall often think of that afternoon with the Tryon-Wilsons, and of the family rooks that sometimes 'darken the sky'. The rookery was fairly quiescent that day, however; there was nothing to obscure our view of the estuary and the Lakeland hills beyond. Amongst those beckoning hills we shall find our next ferries, not shadowy ones, but some that are still 'at your service'.

The first of them crosses Lake Windermere from Ferry Nab at Bowness to the wooded Claife shore. Belle Isle tosses its trees on the right and, over to the left, Storrs' Temple of Heroes juts far into the water to remind those who know their local history of the old-time regattas associated with Colonel John Bolton of Storrs Hall, Sir Walter Scott, 'Christopher North', poet Wordsworth, and others. 'Christopher North' (Professor John Wilson) was as much at home on 'the Boat'—then the colloquial term for Windermere Ferry—as on the ordinary pleasure craft. Every Saturday he would row down the lake from Elleray and then help to manœuvre the ferry-boat, now piled high with market produce. Wordsworth knew one of the ferrymen here, whose daughter's voice was such that on foggy days she could guide him safely over. Whether she did this by singing, shouting, or yodelling is not clear; a bell certainly hung from a nearby tree to augment her vocal efforts.

Nobody seems able to plumb the antiquity of Windermere Ferry. 'Time out of mind'; 'Beyond the memory of man'; are the answers one is likely to get to any such query. A passage over this middle 'cubble' of Windermere's ten-mile stretch of water would have been useful at almost any period of history. It maintains the line of the Kendal-Hawkshead road. The ferry and fishing rights were granted by Charles II to his Portuguese queen, Catherine of Braganza, though I don't suppose she knew anything about the place unless, by a chance in a million, Thomas Hoggart's

'Lament', or *The Fatall Nuptiall*, fell into her hands. Both effusions refer to the tragic ferry disaster of October 1635.

A wedding party was returning from Hawkshead, on the Lancashire (west) side of the lake when, to quote 'Ald Hoggart' of Troutbeck, 'the great Boat upon Windermeer water sunck about sun setting, when was drowned fforty seaven persons and eleavan horses . . .' In 1636 a Londoner spread his wings and wrote a pamphlet on the same catastrophe, using as his title the following precis of events: *The Fatall Nuptiall: or the mournefull Marriage. Relating the heavy and lamentable Accident lately occurring by the drowning of 47 Persons, and some of these of Especiall Quality, in the water of Windermere in the North, October 19th, 1635.*

One account of the disaster states that the bridal couple, Thomas Benson and Elizabeth Sawrey, were among the victims, and were duly buried 'beneath the yews in Bowness Church'. Actually, the couple may not have been on the boat at all. Their names are not among the list of victims given in the Grasmere Parish Register.

I do not intend to trace the different ownerships of Windermere Ferry through the centuries, or to describe the various commotions when some owner tried to raise the ferriage. This aspect was sufficiently covered by H. S. Cowper in his *Hawkshead* (1899). Far more thrilling is the story of the Ghostly Crier of Claife.

Who he was, nobody knew—unless the ferryman himself got an inkling when, one stormy night, he ignored the advice of onlookers and rowed out in answer to a wild, frenzied call, 'Boat, boat!' from the opposite shore.

When at length the boat returned, those waiting for the storm to abate saw no passenger aboard; what they did see was the ferryman possessed by some nameless horror which rendered him speechless. The local people were not really surprised when he died, soon afterwards. For years, no other ferryman could be persuaded to cross over when night had put its spell upon the lake.

But the loud hallooing continued. It would always come over the water, with piteous appeal, during bad weather and after dark. The ferrymen were losing so much sleep in consequence that at last a holy man from one of the lake islands was called in, as a local rhyme so graphically relates:

They sought the good old monk of St. Mary's Holm,
With relics of saints and beads from Rome,
To row to the Nab [on the Claife shore] on Hallowmass night
And bury the Crier by morning's light.

But what that night of horror revealed,
And what that night and morrow concealed,
Of spirits so wicked and given to roam,
Lies hid with the Monk of St. Mary's Holm.

But there was no fear of ghosts or storms or sudden wreck when my family and I last used Windermere Ferry. Framed in spring foliage, the 'floating bridge' oddly named *Drake* came over for us and a large party of anglers. Most of the talk, during that brief voyage, was of the wonderful fish they were going to catch. The Ghostly Crier was not even mentioned, neither were the wrestlers who once put on an annual display for passengers' benefit on their arrival at the Ferry Inn. The thing which banished these trials of strength was the growing popularity of Grasmere Sports. What our angling companions did, on alighting, was to range themselves beside the Ferry Inn (now a freshwater research station) and prepare to wrestle, hopefully, for pike.

Derwentwater is, to the best of my knowledge, the only other lake in this glorious corner of England which ever supported any kind of ferry service. The motor launches on Derwentwater have a two-fold purpose. They provide pleasure trips, calling at various jetties around the lake so that visitors can, if they wish, step off to explore some particular part of the countryside. But because of these convenient wayside stages, local people use the launches as they would an ordinary ferry service. Indeed, my old friend, Victor Hodgson, who has been ticket-man at the Keswick landings since he and I were striplings, had every reason to look upon the *May Queen* and her sister vessels as ferry-boats. They work to a set timetable and many regular 'customers' are lake-side people coming over to market, or for an afternoon's shopping in Keswick. Hugh Walpole frequently took a seat as ferry passenger; the High Brandlehow stage is conveniently sited below Brackenburn, the novelist's home. Walpole had his own boat, true, but perhaps—being such a fine interpreter of the Lakeland scene and its characters—he sometimes needed the intimacy which is part of the charm of these Derwentwater launches.

Let us buy a ticket from Victor Hodgson and see where it will take us, and into whose company. Here is Chiang Yee, the *Silent Traveller* of so many delightful regional books, noting everything: the people at the landing stage, the boatmen and their banter, the 'white swans floating round in a circle near the island'—all reminding him of the Chinese Westlake in Hangchow. On nearing the Hawse End jetty he looks up at the Cat-bell range and says that it 'had the appearance of a camel's back with its one hump, and of the long head and neck lowered into the water to drink'. It certainly does! His impression of Skiddaw is equally discerning: '. . . saw distant Skiddaw as if she were a noble lady of Elizabethan times sitting there with her robes and draperies widely spread around her of purplish and brown colour, and shining in the [lake] reflection of the setting sun'. How true again, if, using his perception, you turn around and see Skiddaw afresh from the boat that will shortly pick up a few passengers at Hawse End.

Like all the other lakeside jetties, this one at Hawse End is a simple staging of planks bordered with tall, rough-hewn poles. So might a lake-dweller of ancient times have bridged the shallows between his log hut and his primitive, coracle-like craft.

Across Water Lily Bay, from this same jetty, a huge green hassock seems to be anchored in mid-water. It is St. Herbert's Island. We shall need to recall this island a little later. Meanwhile the launch is off once more, in itself a thing of small beauty but quite picturesque as it weaves its way amongst some of the loveliest mountain scenery in the world. Hugh Walpole thought so, anyhow, and here we may imagine him, signalling from High Brandlehow for the boat that now curves landward again in response . . .

He is his usual bland self, ready to chat with his boat neighbour about market prices, say; about Lodore Falls which appear ahead (and sometimes disappear!) beyond the reeds where the mallard nest; or on reaching Ashness Gate, the next stage, equally ready to direct somebody to Watendlath and the home of Judith Paris.

But Walpole wouldn't find any of his Herries prototypes beside him on the boat today. The men's rose-coloured coats have given place to open-neck shirts, and hoop-dresses to mini-skirts. And the ferryman would not be modelled on his grand old John Blacklock, but may appear at the helm as some youth wearing denims and a shock of unruly hair.

Hugh Walpole would also mark a few changes that have occurred in the immediate landscape since the days portrayed in *Judith Paris*. Vicar's Island, opposite the Keswick shore, no longer has its pseudo Druids' Circle, nor the little battery of guns which Joseph Pocklington, then owner of Vicar's or Paradise Island, triggered off to awaken echoes across the lake. Yet the island—now generally known as Derwent Island—was to develop a different brand of romance. When the Marshall family took possession, last century, they established their own ferry service with the Keswick shore. Victor Hodgson can remember one of those private ferrymen, William Glover. He would row family and friends over this narrow stretch of water, and a bell above the small, chapel-like building —which still stands beside the lake—was part of the daily routine. It was rung to inform Glover that mail, or newspapers, or provisions—or perhaps some belated guests were waiting to be transported to the island.

When I met Herbert Birkett, one of the proprietors of the Keswick-on-Derwentwater Launch Co. Ltd., the ferry aspect of their undertaking was amusingly ratified for me by talk of the otters and foxes and herons that reward the boats' more constant users, like those shoppers from along the west shore. I was then given a résumé of the different vessels that have plied up and down the lake since a Mr. Harker of Lodore Hotel started the service in 1905–6. Harker's route was also planned ferry-wise, though his boats *zigzagged* across the water to four different stages: Lodore, Brandlehow, Keswick, Portinscale, in that order.

I should like to have paid my shilling (one and sixpence, return) on one of Harker's boats, for Mr. Birkett tells me they were electrically driven from batteries concealed beneath the seats. 'Yes, and the batteries were recharged from Lodore Falls!' I can only suppose that when the Falls dried up completely, as frequently happens, the *Iris* or one of the other boats was temporarily out of commission.

While we were on the lake, approaching Hawse End, St. Herbert's Island (not to be confused with Derwentwater's other emerald 'holmes') took our momentary attention. It covers about four acres and is the place where Herbert dwelt alone with his God and prayed that he and his dear friend, Cuthbert of Lindisfarne, might go to Heaven together. The prayer was granted. They both died during the same hour, in the year A.D. 688.

The point of all this, for us, is that St. Herbert's Island became a place of pilgrimage. And the boats that took the pilgrims over originated the ferry service that now runs from Nichol End at Portinscale. Several times have I followed this pilgrim route from Nichol End and picnicked on the island with friends from a neighbouring guest-house, but only recently did I make the acquaintance of Dick Gill.

The present Nichol End ferry service, he informs me, was started, or more correctly resumed, in 1860 by his grandfather, Richard Mitchell. It takes people across the north end of the lake to Keswick, but St. Herbert's Island is still a 'request stop'. The Nichol End slipway is surrounded by oak, alder, chestnut and fir trees, and a cabin stands nearby for boat repairs. Red squirrels used to pop inside while Dick Gill or his father was at work here; perhaps there would be squirrels around the little shrine to St. Nicholas—patron of sailing men—which is thought to have stood here centuries ago when the pilgrims came and offered a prayer before being ferried over to the island. If the name, Nichol End, derived—as Mr. Gill thinks—from that old chapel beside the ferryman's beach, it gives us a charming link with the St. Nicholas of legend who lives on as Santa Claus.

Dick Gill—'Uncle Dick' to all the local children—retired on reaching the age of eighty. When I called to see him at his Portinscale home, soon afterwards, he looked as though he could have gone on ferrying for at least another twenty years, and kept on yarning to the youngsters as he steered course. His stories were so realistic that one day, after hearing yet again about the saintly Herbert, a wee girl passenger piped up with complete innocence, 'Uncle Dick, did you *know* that old hermit?'

One who earlier shared the Nichol End afflatus was 'grandfather' Mitchell. From 1920 onwards Dick Gill used a motor-boat for the ferry, but 'grandfather was still *rowing* people over to Keswick, or the Island, at eighty-four!' Rope-making was his sideline, and local history his constant delight. A frequent visitor was the Reverend H. D. Rawnsley, lately appointed Vicar of Crosthwaite. Many a time, on returning home at evening, Mitchell would say to his wife, 'I'd t' little parson down again. Nice little fellow, but when he comes I can't get on with my work.' If only Mitchell could have known, his chats on local lore and topography with the insatiable 'little parson' were to lead indirectly to the creation of the National Trust, and the preservation of so much surrounding scenery. For this same Rawnsley was one of the three persons who founded the Trust in 1895.

When Richard Mitchell died, on 29 November 1893, Canon Rawnsley (as he had become) mourned his friend in a rhyming Memorial. This was printed and circulated amongst the people who had known the old ferryman-ropemaker. Dick Gill showed me a copy of the Memorial and although poetry was not Rawnsley's forte, one of the five verses may here be quoted:

We shall never see him more
In his garden by the lane,
In his boat beside the shore.
He has crossed the silent flood,
He is free from care and pain,
Richard Mitchell, grave and good.

The loss of Nichol End Ferry, operating from its sylvan beach between Derwent Bank and Fawe Park, would have been a loss to local annals as well as to its regular patrons. Happily, however, 'Uncle Dick' was able to find a successor in one of his former juvenile passengers—Mr. N. M. Newby of Keswick. And having talked and ferried with Newby, too, I feel sure that the old traditions, stories and routes are in safe hands.

Some years ago, on visiting Barrow-in-Furness, my wife and I were driven across the bridge to Walney Island. It took but a moment. Once a steam ferry creaked laboriously over on its chains, but to enjoy, or endure, that kind of passage across Walney Channel I should have had to be no older than my schoolboy self, wearing sailor suit and pleasantly ridiculous beribboned hat emblazoned with some such name as H.M.S. *Dreadnought*.

A postcard view of that old steam ferry is before me now. Its tall funnel is belching smoke as the passengers alight: blousy housewives, men wearing cloth caps, several children, a horse-drawn cart and a smart landau. Newsboys stand by, hopefully, as the crowd surges forward. Over to the right a small group waits to step aboard; ladies in skirts that sweep the ground, a couple of serious, bearded men who seem to have missed a pay rise, some boys—but not one of them, alas, sporting a sailor outfit like mine.

This ferry service was established by the Furness Railway Company to replace some old fords. One ford had taken people at low tide from Cocker to North Scale; another, from Summerhill to Biggar, Walney's one-time smuggling village whose cottages still huddle together as though some conspiracy were afoot. The eclipse of these and other fords by the railway company's steam ferry slowly banished even their names from local parlance. What Barrow shipyard worker of today has ever heard of Bewley Wife's Steps, or Ashburner Wife Ford? As well ask who those two women were, to gain such distinction.

The first ferry-boat here was launched in 1878, after the railway company had dredged the channel. A larger version took its place in 1902, but even this was not commodious enough. By this time Vickerstown had taken firm root on Walney Island and at peak hours the steam ferry had to be supplemented by a number of smaller boats. These must have looked decidedly odd and primitive by comparison with the huge warships and other ocean-going vessels on which the workmen were engaged. A later supplementary service, known as the Electric Ferry, enabled another two hundred and forty men to get home for a midday meal; well worth the 1½d. per week which Vickers charged them as ferriage.

Earlier, however, the steam ferry had sometimes grounded, virtually isolating Vickerstown from the mainland, until it was refloated. As the old fords had been dredged out of existence the dwellers on Walney had an enforced holiday, among the seabirds and the spume and the lonely beaches that still lend a touch of wild nature to this place.

When Walney Bridge was opened in July 1908 there was no further need for the workmen's ferries. Trips between midnight and 5.30 a.m. which had enriched the Captain of the Ferry by ten shillings each time, also ceased, and there is no telling how much nocturnal romance went, too.

One small ferry service has survived, in this curiously fashioned corner of Furness. Not across the Duddon estuary, as the map might suggest, but between Roa Island and Piel Island. Roa is now permanently anchored to the mainland, but Piel is still aggravatingly 'at sea', in the broad mouth of Walney Channel.

The small ferry-boat was rocking in the surf, at the end of a long jetty, on the day my wife and I presented ourselves. But nobody was in sight. We have since heard that the ferryman we needed to row us over to the island of so many strange tales was also the coxswain of the lifeboat. The lifeboat-house stood conveniently within hailing distance. Next time I shall remember this and *shout*.

Farther up the coast, where the Solway Firth creates such an impressive, funnel-shaped barrier between England and Scotland, shouting would be in vain. Better road communications have somewhat tamed the area which Sir Walter Scott described with so much fervour. And yet, in a world spoon-fed with all manner of superficialities, there is gusto and a tang of adventure to be recovered by looking back to the times when raiders and smugglers and would-be conquerors alike had to measure their skill and patience against the peat mosses, the dangerous quags and creeks of the upper Solway.

Many were the recognized fords, or waths. The Peat Wath neighbourhood was guarded by Rockliffe Castle, whose governor had '100 to 200 men nightlie with him, especiallie at the ebbinges of the water, to watche the fords for the keepinge out of Scottish theves'. Stoniewath, near Burgh (later supplemented by a ferry) once witnessed the drowning of nearly two thousand Scottish reivers; they had been trapped by a tidal wave. Another Stoniewath crossed the Solway from Bowness to Annan. This was probably the ford used by some of the smugglers in Scott's *Redgauntlet*.

The ford most often negotiated by the smuggling fraternity, however, was probably Green Bed, on Rockliffe Marsh. It looked innocent enough when I drove past, but salt and whisky once flowed into England by this route almost as freely as water flows downhill. The reason for this clandestine traffic is elaborated in my *Smugglers' Britain*. What chiefly concerns us now is the alternative name given to this once lively spot. Out of deference to its resident ferryman it was called 'Willie o' the Boats'.

Perhaps this Willie was one of the men who helped to ferry some of the contraband over the River Esk. If so, he would be fully conversant with the ways and means of taking the stuff farther into English territory, where high taxation made the trade profitable. Dogs were trained to carry whisky-filled bladders across the Eden (Carlisle's river), and in various landward directions 'women of spirit' performed a similar service with the aid of canisters specially made for concealment beneath their clothing.

The signboard which once hung outside the inn at Green Bed spelt out a message of chivalry and daring. It was evidently set up soon after the erection of the Solway railway viaduct, a few miles away, and read thus:

> 'Ere Metal Brig or Rail were thowt on
> Here Honest Will the boatman wrout on
> Gentle and semple he did guide
> To either Scotch or English side.

> With them o' horseback he did ride
> An' boat the footman
> And none did ever dread the tide
> Wi' Will the boatman.

> Now tho' Will's work is done and Will himself lies quiet
> Yet lives his spirit here. Step in an' try it,
> Nor Brig nor Rail can half so pure supply it.

If Will the Boatman's spirit truly lived there, one may be sure, after all, that he did guide something else, besides 'gentle and semple' over the Solway!

There have been several versions of this rhyming inscription. One attributed to Robert Burns might have been expected to allude to the illicit traffic, for the poet was then a local Customs officer. Burns let Will 'off', however, without even the hint of a caution. A much more recent version repeats the ferryman's encomium and adds a thistle and a rose motif for good patriotic measure. At the time of writing, this board is kept inside the former inn. Perhaps, when the building finds a new tenant, Will the Boatman may turn out and sniff his native air once more.

CHAPTER ELEVEN

PRINCE BISHOPS AND THEIR FERRIES

Before entering Scotland, where ferries come so prolifically into their own, we must cross the northern Pennines to the remaining corner of England and follow a few rivers which have had to be negotiated by ford, ferry or tentative bridge from early times. It is a story, mainly, of four rivers: Tees, Wear, Tyne, and Tweed.

My own introduction to Whorlton, on the River Tees, was distinctly curious. While walking alone along the river-bank I noticed a small brown head bobbing up and down as it progressed through the water towards me. The river is fairly wide at this place and I watched, fascinated, wondering what the creature could be. On reaching dry land, the weasel—for such it was—shook itself, looked up at me rather quizzically when I whistled, and then went about its normal business.

Whorlton Ferry came into view just beyond this spot. The boat service no longer operates here but local people retain the name with affection and often direct visitors to 'The Ferry' because of the beautiful surrounding scenery. It used to be said that a Rector of Winston, the neighbouring village, 'should never propose to a lady who had first seen this enchanted place, for he could never be sure that the lady did not marry the *situation*'. It must have been sheer delight to cross over by ferry under the shadow of the coppice-grown crags that were to entrance Sir Walter Scott when he came along to write *Rokeby*.

The only other ferry I need mention, along this river, is the Bishop's Ferry at Stockton-on-Tees. It has now vanished, unfortunately, but every time you cross the town's Victoria Bridge you are in effect paying some sort of tribute to the Bishops of Durham who once drew a goodly income from that old ferry. For horses, sheep, carriages and carts the usual tolls were demanded, but foot passengers, if native to the town, enjoyed concessionary rates. Twice a year, namely, on Easter Monday and St. Stephen's Day, they simply handed over a cake valued at fourpence.

When the bridge (later named after Queen Victoria) replaced the ferry, in 1762, the See of Durham had to be indemnified for about sixty years to the lively tune of ninety pounds per annum. I was commissioned to photograph this now industrialized water-front for the national archives, during the Second World War, and the old Ferry Lane (as Castlegate) came momentarily into some prominence; but of home-made ferry cakes there was not even a lingering memory.

By force of circumstance, Durham has had to replace various fords and ferries which served this episcopal town at various points along the River Wear. The Bow Lane ford which brought the Congregation of St. Cuthbert here in A.D. 995 was also the one which saw William the Conqueror's retreat in 1070, when he thought St. Cuthbert's curse was upon him. Kingsgate foot-bridge now spans the river at this place. Framwellgate Bridge, first built by the imperious Flambard in 1128, was swept away by floodwater in 1400 and for a time a ferry service had to be restored. A similar service operated until 1574 at that delightful loop of the river now spanned by the eighteenth-century Prebends' Bridge. The ferry was maintained by the convent and gave the lay brothers access to their mill, fishponds, and orchard at Crossgate.

Prebends' Bridge provides one of the finest viewpoints for the 'grey towers of Durham', but to capture the full spirit of the Middle Ages I always walk up-stream for a few yards and then linger at the point where two old buildings that began as corn-mills stand in picturesque alignment with the great, exalted cathedral. Once named Jesus Mill and Abbey Mill, respectively, they were ritually linked with the sumptuous Jesus Altar up there in the maternal cathedral. The river flows between them, and the ferry that plied across the water nearby came under the same spiritual surveillance.

After leaving Durham City the Wear pirouettes through Chester-le-Street to Lambton, where in 1775 a certain man only escaped the fate of eight other ferry passengers by leaping out of the local ferry-boat on to a submerged rock-shelf which he knew to be there, and standing up to his neck in water until rescued by another boat.

The Bishops of Durham also had a grasping finger in the ferryman's pie at Sunderland, at the mouth of the Wear. This was due to the once-flourishing monastery of Monkwearmouth having lost its independence and become a mere cell attached to the Convent of Durham. As Counts Palatine, rich in prestige, lands, and other possessions, the Bishops of Durham claimed 'divers ferry-boats over navigable rivers within the said county'.

One might have thought that the impoverished monks of Wearmouth would at least be allowed free passage over the ferry established by their own forebears. But such thinking was foreign to Durham's 'men of God' who strutted about like peacocks and considered themselves on a par with royalty. In 1438–9 the Bishop's lessee took the Prior and Master of Wearmouth to court on this issue. Although the verdict is not clear, it would seem that episcopal influence prevailed; the Wearmouth brotherhood had to continue paying the annual rent, called Ferilaw, plus other emoluments due at Christmas and Easter.

In 1957 G. S. McIntyre, Town Clerk of Sunderland, wrote a splendid booklet on the Sunderland Ferry and I am deeply indebted to his researches on the subject. When he refers to Bishop Hatfield gaining control of Sunderland, with its fisheries and its all-important ferry, in 1345, my thoughts go back inevitably to the magnificent throne Hatfield erected for himself in the choir of Durham Cathedral. It has the distinction of being the highest bishop's throne in Christendom—but I do wish that amongst the figure carvings that decorate the masterpiece, and Hatfield's equally ornate tomb beneath, space could have been found for just one humble, god-fearing ferryman.

A later Bishop, Laurence Booth (1457–76) became so politically involved with the Wars of the Roses that Henry VI stripped the See of Durham of its lucrative temporalities, which meant that Sunderland and its ferry were handed over to a layman, Robert Bertram of Durham. The Royal Grant stipulated that 'the said Robert Bertram . . . be provided with a certain great ferry-boat for the passage aforesaid at our cost with sufficient repairs whenever and as often as shall be necessary . . .'

Later, the ferry seems to have returned to the episcopal fold, for when the Civil War broke out it again became a pawn on the chequerboard of national affairs. This time it was the Parliamentary Commissioners who played their hand; they sold the borough of Sunderland, with 'perquisites of courts' to Colonel George Fenwick of Brinkburn, Northumberland, who probably revelled in the grandiloquent language that adorns the legal conveyance. Its final flourish concerned 'the ferry and passage over the water porte or river of Sunderland aforesaid'.

At the Restoration the game warmed up once more; Sunderland was 'retaken' by the Bishops. But disputes continued, usually between lessees on the two sides of the Wear. One dispute was settled by arbitration in 1710. The Award reveals much that might otherwise have gone unrecorded. It mentions three landing places then in use, and goes on to state what was expected of tenant farmers on the north bank. They were granted 'free passage each year on payment of customary ferry dues of wheat, bunns and eggs, at the usual times, viz., at Easter yearly twenty pase [Pasch ?] eggs, at harvest yearly one thrave containing twenty-four sheafs of the best marketable wheat, and at Christmas yearly, one or more Yeoul bunn or bunns, being wheaten bread, of the value of 6d. or the respective values thereof'. So much for the '*free* passage' of the farmers' horses, cattle and goods!

When the river became thronged with keels and other laden vessels in the eighteenth century, ferry passengers became voluble. They could not get across without serious risk to life and limb. A contemporary account stated that any passenger 'coming to the riverside, and wishing to be put over immediately, must take the boat as he finds it . . .' This sounds ominous, but worse was to come: 'the [ferry] men sometimes quite drunk', and the boat so overladen 'that by the motion of one passenger the water will trickle in'. It was further reported that when horses in the boat became restless 'the foot passengers are sometimes glad to commit themselves to the water'; 'at other times the keels are so numerous that the [ferry] boat cannot get within fifty yards of the shore and the passengers have to quit the boat and step from keel to keel . . .' And so on.

Despite all these perils and humiliations, only once does the ferry seem to have taken its toll in human life. This was towards the end of the eighteenth century. One Sunday evening the boat was carrying about twenty-seven persons to the Monkwearmouth side when it capsized and only four or five survived. Many of the victims were on their way from church. Very sensibly, instead of piously attributing the accident to the Will of God, the people affected built a new church—on the opposite (north) bank.

What a panorama of dramatic history dropped its curtain when the last steamboat crossed the Wear and the Sunderland Ferry closed down, in July 1957!

Sunderland had known other ferries, too, some working the river quite near to the High Ferry just described, and one crossing over near the harbour entrance. The chief landing seems to have been that shown in a fine etching I have been allowed to copy for this book.

Overlooked by tall, irregular chimneys and a low curvilinear building with belfry, some broad, balustrated steps lead down to the waiting ferry-boat. A Dickensian scene, in effect, but this is not Wapping or Limehouse. This is a bit of the old Sunderland Lewis Carroll would see when he was in the neighbourhood writing *Jabberwocky*.* To the

---

* Lewis Carroll frequently visited his brother-in-law, the Reverend Charles S. Collingwood, Rector of Southwick, where two other ferries crossing the Wear were available to shipyard workmen. The Walrus associated with the Carpenter in the famous verses was based on a stuffed walrus now in Sunderland Museum.

town's shipwrights with their peculiar square white hats, faithfully portrayed in Tenniel's illustrations for 'The Walrus and the Carpenter', the scene would be redolent of happy days spent amongst little boats, for a change, with the kids. Three passengers are already seated in the ferry-boat; a woman approaches with a head-basket of washing for some client over the water. On the steps a youth is fumbling for his fare, perhaps one of those ferry tokens which the Corporation then issued— shiny brass tokens about the size of a shilling and stamped with the town crest.

In short, this undated etching reveals the very heart and soul of bygone Sunderland.

It would be interesting to discover how Northumberland's River Derwent was mastered by the Premonstratensian monks who founded their abbey on its banks, at Blanchland, in the twelfth century; and equally interesting to follow the Romans as they pitched some of their camps, not far away, along the North Tyne. Before bridges could be erected at any of these places, there must have been some kind of ferry service. True, Chesters—the Roman *Cilurnum*—is sited near the significantly named Chollerford. But as we have seen, a ford easily passable under normal conditions, often necessitated a boat whenever the river rose. Eventually, the Romans built a bridge to link Chesters with the opposite bank and parts of it can still be seen, at low water.

When I first began exploring this fascinating area, nearly forty years ago, I stumbled upon one ferry that is reputedly eight hundred years old. Chesters, with its modern bridge, was two or three miles behind me, and I needed to cross the river. A signpost I have now forgotten must have pointed to the old ferry, near Haughton Castle, but I do remember stepping off the road into this little backwater of civilization, frowned upon by medieval walls and surrounded by trees and shrubbery that could have been just the same when the Liddesdale raiders came this way, in 1542.

Suddenly, a small cottage materialized out of the shadows. My first thought was that the occupant must be in league with Pan, or some other musical spirit, for a row of bells hung along the cottage wall: bells of different shapes and sizes, rather like the old village handbells I used to hear in Suffolk on New Year's Eve, but these bells were on springs and connected by a cord. Did some Orpheus live here, alone with his enchanted airs?

Before fancy could go further, the door opened and a pleasant young woman appeared. She smiled her greeting, and in rich Northumbrian tongue asked if I required the ferry. 'Please,' I replied, 'I would like to see the fish hatchery over there at Barrasford.' So we got into the waiting boat, and my dark-haired companion pulled us across the broad river by means of a cable slung overhead from bank to bank. There were oars handy, in case a swollen river should deflect the boat from its wonted course, but the North Tyne held no terrors for her. She could have been—and probably was—born to the technique of ferrying at this ancient passage.

On alighting, and having paid my fare, one other thing begged to be done. I reached for a thinner rope that ran back over the water and capriciously set that carillon of silvery notes jingling. Though meant for use by anybody making for the opposite, Humshaugh bank, the signal was too tempting, even from the 'wrong' side.

That ferrywoman had understanding. She smiled indulgently, waved goodbye, and returned to her lonesome 'belfry'.

A few years ago there was some talk of closing this ferry. But local people rose in loud protest. In the original agreement drawn up eight centuries ago, between William de Swyneburn and Ranulph de Halvton, the two landowners concerned, it was categorically stated that no foot bridge should ever be allowed to replace the ferry. The agreement has been honoured, so far, and even the manner of working the ferry—by overhead cable—is the traditional one, so I was told. To me it would be a personal loss if I could never set those bells chiming again.

A few miles after the North and the South Tyne have united, near Hexham, the different ferry services begin to wear an industrial look. Ryton Ferry, six miles up-river from Newcastle-upon-Tyne, was an exception; about sixty years ago one magazine contributor could refer to Ryton and its flat-bottomed boat, and say, 'We have left behind the noise of steam hammers, engine whistles, and factory buzzers, and have arrived at a spot as sweet and as picturesque as may be found within half a dozen miles of any great manufacturing town in the kingdom . . .' Of course, he was *leaving* the place we are now approaching.

It may seem odd, but that same, busy, noisy, exciting metropolis of ships and shipping once supported far more ferry services than some large central areas of Britain have ever known. I have in front of me at this moment a sketch map showing the different Tyneside ferry stations in regular use about the beginning of this century. Between the Newcastle neighbourhood and Tynemouth there were no fewer than twenty-six, on both banks of the river, starting at Blaydon and including Bill

Quay, High and Low Walker, Hebburn, Wallsend, Jarrow, Howdon, Tyne Dock and North Shields.

The Tyne General Ferry Company operated this twenty-mile zigzag service with up to twenty-one vessels. Steam-paddle boats as a rule, they had to run the gauntlet of larger shipping, and began their busy day about 5 a.m. with the arrival of workmen, hordes of them, destined for one or other of the shipyards dotted along the riverside. Some of the men, still half asleep, had to be roused by a deck-hand who would shout out—within very close range!—the names of the different ferry stages as these were reached.

An earlier concern, the Tyne Passenger Boat Company, had originated the service with a fleet of boats known as the Red Star Line. There was also a Percy line of ferry-boats, but the Tyne General took over in 1862 and carried on until its liquidation in December 1908.

Several cross-river ferry services survive, but the Tyne has never been quite the same since passengers in their hundreds would board the Sunday morning ferries to get a good, onlookers' view of the market at Newcastle Quay; or since similar numbers crowded the vessels to witness the Christmas Boat Handicap, filling the air with their boos, cheers and laughter. One man who 'grew up' with the General Ferry Company declared that during the year in which the *Mauretania* was being fitted out, the boats carried 'over seven millions of people', a trip on the obliging ferries being ideal for viewing the famous liner. This same veteran recalled the names of the boats as though remembering sweethearts of bygone days: *Eilleen, Audrey, Phoebe, May, Isobel, Doris, Mona*; no wonder they were affectionately dubbed the 'Ladies of the Tyne'.

Where did they go, those Ladies, when the blow fell in 1908? *Eilleen* found a home in South Africa, *Phoebe* went to Bahia, and *Mona* to Constantinople. In consequence there were many heartaches among the people of Newcastle, who now had to travel to and from work by land—not half as interesting!

But there was one bright outcome. For some years Messrs. R. and W. Hawthorn Leslie, a renowned firm of shipbuilders, had run a direct cross-river service between Hebburn and Wallsend for the convenience of their own workpeople. This service began with two sculler boats and was augmented later by a couple of second-hand steam ferry-boats, each carrying 272 passengers. When the General Ferry Company closed its shutters the shipbuilding firm acquired two further steamboats and extended their service to Walker.

Looking down from that splendid viewpoint, the Tyne Bridge, a pedestrian would be lucky to pick out the ferry-boats from the general pattern of river shipping, but some of them are still weaving to and fro, thanks in part to the Mid-Tyne Ferries' concern. In 1939 four other riverside firms had collaborated with Messrs. Hawthorn Leslie to float this new ferry company.

While photographically recording Newcastle's dockside buildings during the last war I used to see these diesel vessels ploughing their way along the broad river that had witnessed the coming of the Romans, some of whose handiwork awaited my attention in the Black Gate Museum. In spare moments I would try to place these and earlier ferry-boats in the long procession of river craft which the Tyne has known and fostered through the ages. How gratifying that one can still do this, not only in retrospect, but from the deck of a new-type ferry-boat.

We could ferry up and down the Tyne for hours, listening to all the gossip or just imbibing the industrial scene, relieving this occasionally by taking a ticket for Ryton. But boat talk is really part of the trip. You may hear something of the old days, when the Red Star Line was in vogue with its four paddle steamers, *Venus*, *Mercury*, *Star* and *Planet*. You may hear about the old 8.20 a.m. ferry from Newcastle which carried fish, much to the distress of passengers in hot weather. And of course there would be juicy tales of perils and accidents.

There was one November day in 1846, for example, when the 7 p.m. ferry from South Shields was befogged on the river for seven and a half hours! Another time (5 December 1836) a gale prevented the Shields Steam Ferry from operating, which meant that on both sides of the Tyne would-be passengers were kept waiting all night. I wonder how they amused themselves? There were no transistor sets then, and perhaps no tea and sandwiches either.

But there could be excitement, as when a brewer's lorry loaded with casks of beer and spirits got out of control on the 7.30 a.m. ferry from North Shields (8 July 1875). Despite all that the drayman, crew and passengers could do, the lorry burst through the gangway and the whole outfit, including the horses *and* the casks, went into the river. I can well imagine how the incident would be bandied about by different raconteurs, especially the bit about the drayman who was rescued by a chain-hook which caught him by the trouser-leg and miraculously lifted him clear of the imbroglio. Motorists who cross the Tyne today by the Jarrow-Howdon free ferry, say, have no idea of what Time and Progress have deprived them!

137

Yet the same two depredators make it no longer possible to believe all the tales are told about Warkworth Hermitage. Luckily, however, much of its romantic atmosphere survives; in all Northumberland there are few wayfaring experiences to equal that of taking the little ferry that plies across the River Coquet, below Warkworth Castle. Its sole purpose is to leave the twentieth century where it belongs, and to introduce you to this remarkable hermitage and chapel cut out of the solid rock of the cliff face six hundred years ago.

How well do I recall my own first visit: that early evening trip across the lovely river; the mooring of the boat beneath this strange, crudely-hewn catacomb; the ferryman's explanations as the two of us stepped through low doorways and paused before the chapel altar and its amorphous effigies. A scamper up the 'breakneck stairs' which once led the hermit to his orchard, and then down again, down to the hermit's dwelling, below the chapel, and to his stretch of the river where, every Sunday, he cast a net, hoping it would yield him his 'Trinity draught of fishes'. Anything but a *little* boat, here at Warkworth, and a ferryman bred to the Coquet, would spoil the atmosphere.

Holy Island, also, has a distinctive aura, which must not be annulled by 'progress'. Lindisfarne is the better, and older name for this island cradle of Northern Christianity, which lies off the Northumbrian coast. It has certain resemblances to St. Michael's Mount in Cornwall, but at Lindisfarne a regular ferry service is impracticable. In its place there are 'fleets' of ferry-*cars* in which the islanders take you to and fro (or did until recently) at low water.

On my last visit eight of us were packed like kippers into one of those vintage vehicles. How we envied the group of nuns who were tackling the three-mile stretch of intervening water by wading over, barefoot! Many years earlier 'Booner' Cromarty took me across the old pilgrim route in his pony-trap. His tales were mainly of the pedestrians caught by the swift-rising tide. I stopped to photograph one of the box-like refuges set up at intervals for their benefit, and thanked my lucky stars that I had no need to spend a night up there, waiting for the ebb—or for a row-boat that might, or might not, come in answer to my frenzied shouts. As well hope for a division of the waters (after the style of the Red Sea miracle in the Bible) which once enabled some Lindisfarne monks to pass over, dry-shod.

A causeway now helps private cars to bridge this formidable gap, tide permitting. Fortunately it does not mar the coastline, which, from Warkworth to Berwick-upon-Tweed, is still a continual joy.

While making a few inquiries about salmon fishing at Berwick-upon-Tweed, some time ago, nothing was further from my mind than the subject of this book. Having spent several hours at Crabwater, at the pier end, watching the men casting their sweep-nets in the mouth of the river (also the rival activities of the hungry seals!) I began to delve into local records, for the historical background. Border troubles soon loomed up. At one period Berwick fishermen were forbidden to hire any Scotsmen. Earlier still, soldiers had to guard these waters, and in particular, the *ferrymen* who ran a service from Tweedmouth to Berwick.

The Old Border Bridge was swept away by floods in 1294 and there was no hurry to replace it with another structure. The south bank of the river came under the jurisdiction of the Prince Bishops and they had no desire to make things any easier for the Scots! Until about 1376, therefore, this important river passage was entrusted solely to ferrymen. Bishop Anthony Bek provided a ferry-boat to serve from Tweedmouth to Berwick, and Edward I aided and abetted the canny scheme by supplying one to work the other way, from Berwick to Tweedmouth. Six crossbowmen who stood by in case of trouble were given an allowance of 'one quarter of pease'.

Berwick's modern civic mace bears direct reference to those turbulent times. It takes the form of a battle club and one of its emblems incorporates the three historic bridges that now cross the Tweed here. No crossbows were in evidence when I was shown through the Town Hall, but this mace—along with two halberds flaunted in front of the Mayor on civic occasions—do remind everybody of the town's 'shuttlecock' history. Berwick passed between the hereditary contestants, England and Scotland, no fewer than thirteen different times. All honour to those ferrymen who caught some of the backwash. They deserved any fare they could get!

But a ferry can even register the coming of Unity and Peace.

By the end of the nineteenth century the Tweed could be crossed between Berwick Quay and Spittal Fish Quay by two small boats, *Border Pride* and *Border Chief*. The ancient hatchets had been buried for centuries. No longer did the Border spell carnage. Spittal, adjoining Tweedmouth on the south side of the estuary, could now employ four ferrymen—without having to bother about any guardian archers.

When I last stood on Spittal Quay a small ferry-boat was prancing on the wavelets, and the walled town of Berwick was sunning itself across the water. My business lay back in 'England' that day, but it is high time that we pushed on via Berwick and the Scottish lowlands to Edinburgh.

CHAPTER TWELVE

SCOTTISH WATERS

'A ferry is the most poetical of roads.'
James Ramsay MacDonald was enjoying a respite from politics by
tramping in the Highlands when he wrote those perceptive words, but
they will serve us long before we get that far. We are now at the Queensferry passage, one of the world's oldest lines of ferry communication;
one charged with enough poetry to have inspired dozens of ballads and
rousing songs.

Warlike songs, for in the seventh century A.D. the Pictish king,
Hungus, effected this passage over the River Forth after defeating Athel-
stane in East Lothian. Chants and canticles, as when pilgrims—following the example of Queen Margaret, who gave the ferry its name—
journeyed to the shrine of St. Andrew in Fife after crossing the narrows
by Inchgarvie. Dirges too, perhaps, for when Margaret died in 1093 the
Forth took the mourners and her revered body from Edinburgh to
Dunfermline, thus setting a river-course for the Abbot and monks of
Dunfermline and future generations. It was David I, Margaret's youngest
son, who instituted a regular ferry service here, granting the ferry rights
to the same monastic brotherhood.

I can imagine further lamentations at this place when the monks had
to surrender the ferry, along with their beloved abbey, at the Reforma-
tion; also a lyric or two as the bards come along, later, and frolicsome
verses from the nation's rhymesters.

But recorded history had sounded its own measures, too, as when in
1123 Alexander I was sheltered during a howling storm by the hermit
of Inchcolm, in the broader part of the estuary. Much later, James VI
of Scotland gave this ferry to his bride, Anne of Denmark, as a wedding
present. As the years went by, however, Queensferry came under the
restrictive thumb of the Kirk. Hugh Douglas in his fine book, *Crossing
the Forth*, illustrates the point with the following quotation:

In 1635 it was decreed that 'whatsoever persons shall break the Sabbath Day by sailing their great or small boats to ply this ferry from the
rising of the sun to the twelfth hour of the day, these persones shall be
fined for the first fault in twelve shillings Scots the man, and if they

shall faill in the same fault any [other?] time they shall stand at our Kirk door in sackcloth and make confession of their fault before the congregation . . .

If this ruling now seems incredible, one has only to recall the early days of this twentieth century, when many people considered it sinful to travel by tramcar on a Sunday.

But Sabbath-breaking was not the only kind of offence at bygone Queensferry. The bailies frequently had to summon ferrymen for quarrelsome conduct. In 1637, for example, George Binks and John Blair were both fined Five Pounds for 'injuring each other'. Not only that, but the two miscreants had to 'kiss and be friends', or, as the bailies more reservedly put it, 'Ye said persons [were] to end in friendshipp and to drink togedder and ye said George Binks to drink first to ye said John Blair in respect he did ye greatest violence to ye said John Blair yan ye said John Blair did to him.'

This pact having been made, the fellows went sheepishly back to their boats—to quarrel again, perhaps, over any people of rank wanting to cross the river. There was then a fare for the rich, a fare for the not so rich, and another for the poor. A duke, earl or viscount would fetch 3s. 4d., a lord 1s. 4d.; all of them worth the ferryman's forceful or obsequious attention. People of no degree, just ordinary men and women, produced only a penny per head; useful make-weight, like the horses, cows and sheep.

Generally, however, the ferrymen worked hand in glove with each other, and guarded their profession as jealously as any members of a medieval trade guild. Yet competition, thwarted in one direction, sprang up in another. The Granton–Burntisland Ferry might expose its passengers to a five-mile crossing of the quixotic Forth, against Queensferry's one mile, but both ferries had their waves of popularity.

When the Forth Bridge was erected (1883–90) many travellers still doggedly patronized one of the established ferries. To use the Forth Bridge would have been to tempt fate. Hadn't fate already destroyed the Tay Bridge, a few miles north, on the road to Dundee, hurling a train-load of passengers to their death? And the Tay Bridge, like the cantilevered monster now set up over the Forth, was also on an old ferry route!

But superstition evaporated with time. The Forth (railway) Bridge stood firm, and the ferry trade began to dwindle. And then came the motor-cars, at first a mere trickle, then in spate, demanding a way of their own across the old barrier.

The car boom had hardly begun when I spent my first few days in the area. Robert Louis Stevenson was warming my blood just then and it seemed natural to wander along to Queensferry and the Forth Bridge in his imagined company. The man who wrote *Kidnapped* and *Travels with a Donkey* was not really meant for the motoring age, and yet here were scenes known to him and some of his characters having to submit to the new craze, and doing it by means of a diesel-electric paddle ferry-boat nostalgically named *Queen Margaret*. *Robert the Bruce* soon followed. When, after the Second World War, *Mary Queen of Scots* swelled the ferry fleet, the Forth was indeed Scottish history afloat; even a fervid car-owning passenger could not escape the poetry of it all.

Ramsay MacDonald was right: '. . . the ferry is the most enchanting of all roads.'

As most tourists know by this time, the Queen's Ferry received its marching orders when the new Forth road-bridge was opened. Yet there was dignity in its going. An Edinburgh gentleman has described the occasion for me:

The bridge was formally opened by the Queen on Friday, September 4, 1964, and the last ferry sailed forty-eight hours after this ceremony. On Sunday afternoon, September 6, the *Queen Margaret* left North Queensferry for the south bank, and then made her way to mid-stream between the two great bridges. Here, some five hundred friends of the churches in North and South Queensferry took part in a service of worship to mark the closure of the centuries-old ferry.

It was a kind of requiem for Malcolm Canmore's consort, the devout Margaret.

In Edinburgh itself the closure was anticipated in the previous year by a summer exhibition devoted to 'The Queensferry Passage'. The exhibits comprised many ancient documents which lit up the one-time importance of this ferry. A volume of the Register of the Privy Council was shown, for example, which records an order issued by King James in 1602 'forbidding the ferrymen, under pain of death, to carry anyone from the south coast [of the estuary] to the north, in an effort to prevent the plague spreading from Edinburgh to Dunfermline, where the Queen and her children were then in residence'.

The ferry's former political importance emerged from such Treasury items as one 'which reveals that in 1544 the Regent, Arran, felt obliged to request the ferrymen to charge only "reasonable fares" to the lieges then hurrying to his assistance against the English, thus clearly indicating his anxiety lest the ferrymen should take advantage of the situation by demanding extortionate rates'.

By these and many other references was the ferry's long life-story unfolded. Dunfermline, birthplace of many Scottish kings, figured repeatedly in that story. So did some of the small rocky islets that mark the ferry route; also the old Hawes Inn where, in *Kidnapped*, David Balfour's abduction was plotted. To visitors who saw this display at H.M. General Register House the various documents and pictures must have seemed like an obituary to an old and valued friend.

A country house with Scottish associations, near my own home in West Yorkshire, has one of its rooms illuminated by a lovely set of enamelled glass windows. They depict eleven different scenes in the tragic life of Mary Stuart. Having long been a privileged visitor to this Tudor dwelling—Low Hall, Nether Yeadon—I have often gazed upon these colourful scenes, two of which call for particular mention here because they show Mary—the Queen who possessed 'some enchantment whereby men are bewitched'—seated in a small ferry-boat.

The first of these boats lands her beside the quay at Leith, in the August of 1561. Doubtless for artistic reasons, the window-designer has banished the mist which shrouded the port that morning, the mist which John Knox saw as an omen of disaster, boding 'sorrow, colour, darkness, and all impiety'. A ferryman steadies the little craft as Mary, wearing a crimson gown slashed with silver, is handed ashore by a worthy citizen, probably Captain Lambie. Scotland's Queen had come!

The second ferry-boat is the one that has been requisitioned to effect Mary's escape from Loch Leven Castle. The young Queen, heavily mantled, sits in the boat near Willie Douglas, the lad of eighteen who has fallen victim to her charms. To delay pursuit Willie Douglas had locked the castle doors behind him. When the boat pushes off he throws the keys overboard, and then signals with his cloak to confederates awaiting them on the lake shore. Meanwhile, the two oarsmen bend to their task. Perhaps they have been bribed. As the castle is perched on an island, half a mile from the shore, the family living there would need such regular ferrymen. Despite his grizzled mien, one of the ferrymen portrayed in the window scene, looks as though he, too, had come under Mary's spell.

How different is the word-picture given by Dorothy Wordsworth in her account of a ferryman's family she encountered in their hut beside

Loch Katrine during her *Tour Made in Scotland*. No imposing castle across the water here. No glamour; Sir Walter Scott had yet to romanticize the scene in *The Lady of the Lake*. Just a rude dwelling where the ferryman lived with his wife and child and went to bed by candlelight, as Dorothy herself did, revelling in the quaint shadows amongst the rafters and the patter of rain. 'I did not sleep much,' she wrote, 'but passed a comfortable night, for my bed, though hard, was warm and clean: the unusualness of my situation prevented me from sleeping. I could hear the waves beat against the shore of the lake . . .'

The ferryman's hut and cow-house must have disappeared by now, but his boat service lives on in some steamer trips across the lake.

There was no such immortality for the man who had worked the ferry over the River Teith, near Doune Castle, some twenty miles east of Loch Katrine. His career was terminated by spite.

Down to this old ferry, one day, came Robert Spittal, who in his capacity as 'taillyour' (tailor) to King James IV and his household was bound for Doune Castle, where the Dowager Queen Mother then resided. Spittall was evidently one of those wealthy fellows whose prestige alone could normally open all doors and remove all obstacles. But he hadn't reckoned with this canny ferryman, who always demanded his fare before pushing off. Now Spittal had forgotten his purse that morning. but promised to pay later, and handsomely. The ferryman was adamant. No spot cash, no boat! So the King's Master Tailor, his bubble pricked, was left on the river bank, breathing fire and slaughter after the receding boat and threatening to put the impudent rascal out of business by having a bridge built at that place. The bridge was duly built; a 'tailor-made' bridge as the local people are apt to call it, even today. It is inscribed with the date 1535 and a large pair of scissors. One can construe the scissors either way: as symbols of Spittal's trade, or as a token of the cutting asunder of that old ferryman's livelihood.

So many tourists now use the cross-Channel car-ferry service from Stranraer to Larne that we must spend some time in Wigtownshire and try to piece together the story behind that passage to Ireland.

The story does not begin with Stranraer. It takes us first over the Rhinns of Galloway to a quiet resort hemmed in by tall cliffs. This is Port Patrick, so named because St. Patrick once took in his stride the twenty-one-mile crossing from Donaghadee in Ireland to this little Scottish haven amongst the rocks. Later, scores of Patricks were to come over by that same route—but *they* had to use the ferry service that had developed from misty beginnings and subsequently carried the Royal Mail.

Not until 1790 was a lighthouse erected here. Before that time peat fires glowed by night from the rocks to ensure safe passage into the harbour. The early boats were flat-bottomed and on their arrival local people would wade into the water and help to drag the boats on to the beach.

Sir William Brereton left an entertaining account of this 'short sea route' in his *Travels* (1634-5). To follow him, even by proxy, is to draw upon all one's courage.

July 4 . . . We hired a boat [at Port Patrick] of about ten ton for five horses of ours, and for five Yorkshiremen and horses; for this we paid £1 and conditioned that no more horses should come aboard, save two or three of an Irish laird's, who then stayed for a passage, and carried his wife and three horses . . .

It is a most craggy, filthy passage, and very dangerous for horses . . . when any horses land here, they are thrown into the sea, and [they] swim out . . .

After a few remarks about the boat itself, and its inadequate crew, Brereton states, ominously, 'She took in four horses more than we covenanted . . .' Some time elapsed before they could draw clear of the rocks. The horses would have no stalls or boxes to keep them steady and quiet: that task was apparently left to the respective owners. It is a relief to read of the fairly speedy passage they made, once free of the shore. Suddenly, however, the wind drops and they start drifting. Just when passengers and crew are getting restive with inaction, a strong wind blows up again, accompanied by heavy rain. Even the sailors are bewildered by the boat's shuttlecock antics.

Perhaps Sir William and the Irish laird now took counsel together. We are not told that they did but in view of the emergency it seems probable . . .

Even in recent times, with well-designed modern ferry-boats, accidents have occurred on this very passage. It was as calm as the proverbial mill-pond when I crossed, on board the *Caledonian Princess*, with my friend's car safely stowed below deck among dozens of other vehicles. And if the wind had raged and rain fallen in torrents, we could have sat comfortably in the saloon of this mechanically stabilized vessel.

But aboard their flimsy sailing craft, Brereton, the laird, and those name-less Yorkshiremen had many horses, which could stampede. Mercifully, their worst fears were not realized. The storm abated sufficiently for the boat to make a very protracted landfall, not at Donaghadee, but twelve miles off route, near Carrickfergus. Brereton is worth hearing, on that final hazard: '. . . the ship came as near as she durst, and all the horses were thrown into the sea, and did swim to land and climb a great steep rock.'

Two others who used this ferry service, during its hey-day a hundred and fifty years later, were Sarah Siddons and her husband. Romney, Reynolds and Sir Thomas Lawrence were to paint the great actress's portrait, but the people of Port Patrick got a very different impression of her. She had arrived overnight by coach, intending to catch the ferry next morning so as to keep a theatre engagement in Belfast. A local man described the scene, just before Sarah and William went aboard: 'The packet was drawn out into deep water in the bay, ready to sail, when the husband and wife came down to the beach to be taken out in a small boat to the packet.' Sarah was so entranced by her immediate surround-ings that she stopped, struck her best stage manner, and began to declaim aloud from one of her favourite plays:

> Methinks I stand upon some rugged beach,
> Sighing to the winds, and to the waves complaining,
> While afar off the vessel sails away,
> On which my fortune and my hope's embarked.

A few people from neighbouring houses rushed out to see what was afoot. But Sarah's husband was equal to the occasion. Gripping her by the arm, he said, 'Egad, my dear, if we don't hurry, the vessel will be gone absolutely!'

The harbour-side houses are as quietly attractive today as when Sarah Siddons passed by. And one of them has a history of its own, for it served as the 'marriage house' when Port Patrick was Ireland's 'Gretna Green'. The ferry put twenty miles of water between the runaway couples and whoever might be in pursuit.

Port Patrick's decline, as the Scottish ferry terminal on this passage, makes rather dismal reading. Harbourage had always been a problem here, and residents cannot have been greatly surprised when the packet service was withdrawn, in 1849, and the mails transferred to the Clyde.

Attempts had been made, earlier, to improve Port Patrick harbour by providing deep water and safer approaches. Even as late as 1905 a local man could express himself thus in *The Gallovidian* magazine: 'The Government now are almost willing to spend many millions in driving a tunnel . . . under the bed of the North Channel, a few miles north of Port Patrick', but he swiftly adds, 'nothing would ever induce me to go through it so long as there was even an open fishing boat as an alternative.'

John Hannay, the writer of that article, loved the old ferry associations, and who—having seen Port Patrick—can blame him!

But the tide of official opinion was against those who had hoped to see Port Patrick brought up to date as a ferry terminal. In 1849 Captain Hawes, R.N., had described his efforts to introduce an effective, all-weather ferry service here. He often mentioned M' Cook's Craig, the large rock which protects the small harbour to seaward, and the steam ferry-boats as they came and went. Here is one of his terse remarks: 'In stormy mornings I took my station on the north pier, drenched at times, my old coxswain [at hand] to pass the word. The packet hung with check-rope to M' Cook's Craig; at the first lull, the order to start was given, and the question was, would she reach the next coming sea with sufficient steerage way on her to go well over it? Many mornings we had to wait till break of day.'

Other official reports made for the Board of Trade show that by 1884 the two piers were in a ruinous state, through neglect, and the outer lighthouse had disappeared. The lighthouse had in fact been dismantled in 1871 and re-erected—in *Ceylon*.

Meanwhile the Government had been experimenting over there in Loch Ryan, that great sea inlet sandwiched between the hammer-headed Galloway peninsula and the mainland. Stranraer, safely pocketed at the inner end of Loch Ryan, saw its first ferry-boat depart for Larne in 1862. Ten years later the service begun so tentatively, was restored with an iron paddle steamer, the *Princess Louise*. From then on Port Patrick was doomed. In 1874 its harbour was finally abandoned (save for small craft) and the following year Stranraer folk could pat themselves on the back, for a satisfied Government was now entrusting this new ferry service with the Irish mails.

Stranraer has been nurtured on its cross-Channel service. It has little beauty of its own. There is no Gothic cathedral, no baronial castle to draw visitors. What does draw them is the sight of a spruce-looking vessel making its way along the beautiful Loch Ryan, with Ireland over the horizon.

And what fine vessels they are today! Just before the *Caledonian*

Princess made its maiden voyage to Larne, in December 1961, the boat was 'opened to the public'. What the visiting mayors and provosts and other celebrities said, on looking the boat over, can perhaps be imagined, but one newspaper reporter 'listened in' to the schoolchildren as they swarmed over this turbine steamer with its sleeping berths, shower baths, dining saloons, and 'floating garage' capable of taking over a hundred cars. The crew were bombarded with eager questions, about the boat's dimensions, its height above water, its speed, and so on. 'One bright youngster made a quick drawing of the boat and proudly presented it to the Captain.' It was left to a small girl, however, to transpose the luxurious accommodation for passengers and their cars into canine terms. 'Where,' she begged, 'can *dogs* go for their rest?'

Before my friend could drive his Vauxhall out of the same 'floating garage', on returning from Ireland a few years later, there was a motley assemblage to be cleared: every imaginable make of car, plus caravans and trailers, lorries and bread-vans, with two or three pantechnicons to follow. But no *horses*. To get the savour of them, as ferry passengers, we had to go back—as we did gladly—to the pretty little place that had pioneered the 'short sea passage' to Ireland. A brief salute seemed the least we could offer to Port Patrick, just then. So we drove the seven or eight miles over the Rhinns and woke, next morning, to see *King Fergus*, an Irish fishing boat, moored in the harbour where it had proved so difficult to ship Brereton's horses.

We clambered about on M' Cook's Craig, talked to the fishermen, and bought ice-cream at the place where so many Kellys and O'Briens and Finnigans had been united after fleeing over the water in an obliging ferry.

Stranraer now has its *Antrim Princess*, fitted with every conceivable device for passengers' comfort and convenience, including a hydraulically operated 'visor bow door' to admit vehicles. Splendid! No sane person would have it otherwise. But I wonder how Sarah Siddons would have reacted! With a dramatic gesture, I think she would have sighed for her 'rugged beach'.

There is something peculiarly of the artistic fitness of things that . . . when our road comes to an end, we reach a ferry where a boat and a silent boatman meet us and we are carried over to a new land. The beat of the oar soothes us; we have ceased to trouble and to do. We lie like a helpless child whilst the water laps around us; the clouds behind come down shutting off what is past; we approach a new shore where there are white houses and green hills, and an outstretched hand to help us from the boat. So it was on that immortal day of ferries.

I wish there was room to quote Ramsay MacDonald's essay on ferries in its entirety. His feeling for their poetry was mentioned earlier; here we have his remarks on their place in the 'artistic fitness of things'.

In the 1920s, while he and his companions were exploring the Grampians, it would be natural to talk of 'bearded Charons pulling hard at their oars' and of certain outlandish spots where the intending passengers had first to bellow hard, and repeatedly, to summon old Charon from his slumbers.

Today, we shall probably have used several modernized ferries while travelling north from Port Patrick. Almost certainly we shall have sidetracked Glasgow by crossing the Clyde at Erskine Ferry, or at the Renfrew–Yoker passage. Indeed, the district proliferates with ferries. But after striking north from the Clyde and the Kyles of Bute, smart steamers and floating bridges may well give place to something simpler, something almost timeless, like one ferry Ramsay MacDonald describes, most evocatively, though without naming it!

Standing on the loch shore, in the rain, his companions took turns at blowing the ferry trumpet to call the boat from across the water:

The first shivering soul who tried the summons could not produce a note . . . The trumpet went round. Then at last something happened that appalled us. An unearthly sound came like the braying of a thousand herds of asses in pain, like the rending and riving of mountains, like the key-note of an orchestra of madmen in pandemonium. It wandered up and down, across and back, and in echo returned again and again. Dogs fled howling with drooping tails, infants wailed, doors opened and curious people peeped out to see the earth dissolve, anxious eyes were turned to the churchyard, the infuriated rain poured faster . . .

After another long wait, the boat and its owner emerged from the mist. The trumpet dropped back into silence. Peace and tranquillity returned, and the essayist could rhapsodize about 'the hidden land beyond' and a 'miraculous landing'.

I should like to find that ferry and blow that amazing trumpet. But where to look? In Parliament, Ramsay MacDonald could sometimes hold everybody spellbound with his oratory. Here we seem to have a literary example of his powers! But one must remember that in Scotland, as in Ireland, the man who can tell a good story and sprinkle it liberally with imagination is always welcome. Some stories that one hears from ferrymen come with the tang of the sea and beg to be memorized and perhaps elaborated.

Once when I was crossing from Oban to Mull the ferryman, whose craggy face shone like quartz, recalled a recent lady passenger who had sat throughout this most romantic of voyages *reading a newspaper*, only looking up to wave her poodle's paw at the seals as the boat passed Seal Island. She was clearly akin to the two ladies whose conversation I once overheard after they had returned from a ferry trip to Skye. But that incident must wait. Meanwhile there are David MacBrayne's ferry services to consider. They will take us to other magical places in this area. For years they have opened up the Hebrides and leave everybody restless and unsatisfied until Iona has been visited, and Harris, North Uist and Skye.

It is good to learn that some of MacBrayne's vessels steamed away from these waters, during the last war, to join the 'little ships' which helped to rescue British troops from Dunkirk. The epic account of that magnificent piece of rescue work is *The Snow Goose*, by Paul Gallico. This tells of a small, wildfowler's boat which left the Essex marshes to swell the mercy flotilla. But this flotilla also included ferry-boats from various places, as well as some of these steamships from the Western Isles. One of MacBrayne's ferry steamers also played its part in the Normandy D-day landings.

How all this would have astonished old David MacBrayne, who lived through the early years of the Company when the *Cygnet*, *Lapwing*, *Dolphin*, and *Iona* formed part of the firm's 'swift fleet'.

One of the services advertised in a MacBrayne sailing bill dated 1855 operated from Oban 'to Ballachulish, for Glencoe'. Ballachulish has its own (privately owned) ferry, but to it—on the north side—MacBrayne's started running a bus service in 1906–7. When I used this road service from Fort William, in 1930, the original rack-driven Daimler had vanished into limbo, along with a fourteen-seater Albion. My friends and I were bound for Alltshellach, the Holiday Fellowship Guest House. The bus which took us there, along the eastern shore of Loch Linnhe, aroused no particular interest. What did appeal to us was the fact that the Alltshellach grounds adjoined the historic Ballachulish Ferry. And for the next fortnight we were to use that ferry repeatedly. It was our only feasible approach to places like Port Appin, the Twin Peaks of Ben Vair, and Glencoe itself.

How well I remember those early morning ferry trips! Stepping along to the slipway, with the mountains all round and a rucksack on one's back, was just heaven. The raft-like boat could then take only two cars at most, leaving plenty of space for our vociferous party and plenty of opportunity to peer over the rails into the vasty deeps of this tidal loch.

The distance across the water is not great, but tidal currents caused the ferryman to tack, quite considerably at times. Meanwhile, some of us would lean over the edge again and try to count the jellyfish that swirled by. It seemed an odd setting for these repulsive creatures, and I mentioned them recently when writing to Commander I. T. Clark of the Ballachulish Ferry Company. 'They still float here in their thousands,' he confirmed, 'but they no longer cause the ferry to stop, as we have gratings over the circulating water-intakes so that the jellyfish cannot enter or foul the pipe.'

Mrs. Yvonne Clark's contribution to this correspondence followed other channels, historic ones, and having since made some study of the Ballachulish Ferry, I am inclined to echo her remark that it 'has been here pretty well for ever'.

First I was referred to the Vikings who sailed forty galleys into the narrows at Ballachulish, where the ferry runs. I then heard about *An Duine Mor*, the Big Man whose ghostly form haunts the ferry-side whenever disaster lies ahead. How ancient this tradition might be, there is no knowing. But men claimed to have seen *An Duine Mor* by Loch Leven on Friday, 12 February 1692—the eve of the Glencoe massacre.

The whole shameful business has lately been set forth afresh by John Prebble in *The Story of the Massacre*. He shows how Ballachulish Ferry, being a vital 'gateway' to Glencoe at that time, was in effect one of the chief *dramatis personae* . . .

The last few days for the clans to take the oath of allegiance to William III are fast running out. From his homeland beside the ferry, Cameron of Lochiel sniffs the oppressive air and hurries over the Loch Leven passage, probably to bestir Macdonald of Glencoe, twelfth chief of the clan, out of his dour reluctance. When Macdonald does move, he has to negotiate three ferries: Ballachulish (for he first goes by mistake to Fort William); Loch Creran, beyond Appin; then, after a night in captivity, Bonawe Ferry—with a snowstorm between him and the all-important register at Inveraray Castle. He arrives three days late. His signature is taken, under protest, but there is mischief brewing.

Once again, Ballachulish Ferry plays its part. On 1 February 1692, it brings the Campbells over, with orders to seek the hospitality of the Macdonalds in Glencoe Pass, away there beyond the Loch. Another command, given secretly, has a different accent and purpose. Major Duncanson of the Earl of Argyll's Regiment of Foot receives this message: 'Please to order a guard to secure the [Ballachulish] ferry and the boats there; and the boats must be all on this [north] side of the ferry after your men are over.'

The implication is clear. When Duncanson has ferried his three hundred men to the Appin (south) shore, and the boats have all been sent back, there will be one escape avenue the less!

The actual betrayal and massacre are entrusted to Captain Robert Campbell of Glenlyon. His final instructions are 'to put all to the sword under seventy . . . You are to secure all the avenues that no man escape . . .' As we have seen, Ballachulish Ferry is already 'secured'. To their lasting shame, at the given signal the guests fall upon their hosts . . .

We need not follow the story further, but in Loch Leven there is an island where some of the Macdonald victims lay buried. I used to row up there on an evening. Only after death did these Macdonalds get within range of the Ballachulish Ferry.

In *Kidnapped* R.L.S. wrote this of the neighbourhood: 'There was a good deal of ferrying . . . the sea in all this part running deep into the mountains and winding about their roots. It makes the country strong to hold and difficult to travel, but full of prodigious, wild and dreadful prospects.' That was written a century ago, but it gave Stevenson the right atmosphere for his romanticized account of the Appin Murder. Once again, Ballachulish Ferry was to be an accessory, in this strange affair which still puzzles many.

On that dolorous afternoon of 14 May 1752, one of the Campbells known as Red Fox crossed the ferry in the company of a sheriff's officer, a young Edinburgh lawyer and a servant. Red Fox was hated locally as a traitor to his countrymen. During the Forty-Five Rebellion he had sided with the English and now collected rents from Jacobites. While on the ferry-boat that day he must have been thinking of those families he was about to evict from their homes to make room for more Campbells. Soon after stepping ashore he was shot dead.

James Stewart, or James of the Glen, a local man who had fought with Bonnie Prince Charlie at Culloden, got the blame. After protesting his innocence, and reciting the Thirty-Fifth Psalm, he was summarily hanged on a knoll overlooking the ferry.

But even today, over two hundred years later, people around Balla-chulish still ask themselves, 'Who killed Red Fox?' Not James of the Glen, they are certain. Who, then? The ferry-boat will cross and recross Loch Leven many times before the mystery is solved to everybody's satisfaction.

Highland poesy has numerous lilting references to ferries and ferrymen.

> A Chieftain to the Highlands bound
> Cries 'Boatman do not tarry!
> And I'll give thee a silver pound
> To row us o'er the ferry.'

Thomas Campbell puts those words on the tongue of Lord Ullin's daughter.

Then there is the haunting Jacobite song:

> 'Come, boat me o'er,
> Come, row me o'er,
> Come, boat me o'er to Charlie;
> I'll gie John Ross another bawbee
> To ferry me o'er to Charlie.'

I cannot imagine Dr. Samuel Johnson humming either of these songs when he crossed over to Skye, but the traveller I once met on the train from Edinburgh to Fort William was a very different customer. Dr. Johnson was in one of his surly moods, which did not lift very much even after crossing from Glenelg and being welcomed to the MacDonald home at Armadale.

Now this train companion of mine was a *native* of Skye. After spending most of his life sheep-farming in Australia he was coming 'home'. All the way from Edinburgh he sat on the edge of the seat, humming little tunes to himself and gazing out of the carriage window with a beatific look on his rugged face. He told me he could hardly wait to change trains for Mallaig and there leap on to the Skye Ferry.

A few days later I, too, travelled along that wonderful 'Road to the Isles' and went over to Skye. This was one of MacBrayne's steamer trips to Lock Scavaig. In still, glorious weather we were then ferried over to the lonely shores of Loch Coruisk, there to bask for a time beneath the spell of the Black Cuillins.

Afterwards, two ladies of our party were asked if they had enjoyed the outing. 'Not much,' they replied; 'when we landed there we couldn't find any *shops!*'

As Otta F. Swire points out in her fascinating book, *Skye, The Island and its Legends,* few historically famous visitors used the now so popular ferry (for man, beast, and car) over the Kyle of Lochalsh. The Glenelg–Kylerhea crossing, owned by Lord MacDonald, took some of them, and other visitors made the longer, sea voyage to Portree or Dunvegan.

The Glenelg Ferry was probably the one used by the Yorkshire branch of the Macdonalds when, in the eighteenth century, the whole family would mount their private coach at Thorpe Hall, Rudston, near Bridlington, and eventually dismount at Armadale, near Kylerhea, on Skye. It was the late Sir Godfrey Bosville Macdonald who gleefully told me of those wayfaring adventures. How the Skye ferry-boat manœuvred the coach across, on that last stage of the journey, can best be imagined by recalling what happened within living memory when one of the early cars presented itself at the Kyleakin row-boat ferry. First, the car had to be run on to a couple of planks placed carefully over the thwarts. Ropes were then laced among the wheel spokes, and —given a kind wind and a favourable tide—the precarious journey could begin.

Many other ferries serve Scotland's famous island groups. Mull I have mentioned; Iona too—St. Columba's landfall after crossing from Ireland with his companions in a coracle. A wonderful holiday could be made by just using the various Hebridean ferries, one after another, day after day. A friend and I planned to do something of this sort thirty years ago. After visiting Muck, Eigg and Rhum, we would cross the Minch to the Outer Hebrides—that island group which, on the map, curiously resembles the vertebrae of some fabulous marine monster. My friend knew practically every ferryman in this tangled area; he knew most of the islands, too; but his premature death brought our ambitious scheme to nought. The Second World War came soon after, shattering the dream completely.

But the islands are still there, and the ferries are better equipped and rather more numerous. While I was motoring recently along the Mull of Kintyre, something of the old urge returned, for we could see the ferry that crosses from Tayinloan to Ardminish on the small, inner island of Gigha. And then, in the farther distance, Islay and Jura— which seem to be one long, mountainous island—stepped slightly apart to reveal a narrow sound. Across this sound a ferry operates between

Feolin, and Port Askaig on Islay. As long ago as the early 1800s, vast herds of island cattle crossed from Islay by this route; it was the first stage of their passage to the mainland.

If ferrying is second nature to Hebridean folk, what of the Orcadians and Shetlanders who inhabit that fascinating archipelago which plumes the northernmost point of Scotland! I have on my desk a list of the ferries that operate from Scalloway alone; they cover fifty miles of inland waters and link together—for purposes of culture, religion, trade and tourism—over twenty islands of the Shetland group.

Some idea of the islanders' dependence on their ferries is conveyed in a letter I received not long ago from the Reverend J. Christopher Ledgard, Methodist minister at Whiteness. His manse overlooks Whiteness Voe. On Sundays he or a colleague may have to be ferried over to Burra Isle to take a service there. Christ and his disciples ministering to people from a boat on the Lake of Galilee is a picture that comes readily to mind, in these waters, for the Lerwick and North Isles Methodist Circuit hires this ferry-boat regularly for the conveyance of its preachers.

And then Mr. Ledgard remarked, 'The daughter of one of my colleagues went on this boat last summer with her father and had sat on the seat in her new red coat before being told that on its last trip it had carried *coal*. You can imagine what happened!'

The Gospel, house-fuel, holiday-makers, fish—all come alike to those who man the Scalloway motor-boat ferries. And if you want further variety you can cross Bressay Sound to the island of Noss by first whistling for the shepherd who lives there. If you whistle loud enough he will leave his sheep and come for you in his rowing-boat.

In his evocative book, *Orkney and Shetland*, Eric Linklater mentions having crossed from Mainland to Papa Stour, a small island in St. Magnus Bay, by the local ferry-boat, 'a Shetland model with a sufficient engine and a boatman of superlative skill'. Superlative skill would seem to be the prime qualification for ferrymen in these chancy waters, where human beings, unless of the old Norwegian stock, could well regard themselves as intruders. Foula, served from Scalloway by the motor-boat ferry *Hirta*, houses only thirty people, mostly crofters. Its chief population—and the great attraction for most visitors—is the myriads of sea-birds, including Great Skuas, Puffins, Guillemots, and Fulmars, and the Atlantic Grey Seals which give Man a vacant stare as though he simply doesn't count around here.

The Shetlanders pay tribute to one of their sea-birds, the oyster catcher, by applying its colloquial name, Shalder, to the Yell ferry-boat. In fact, as though to placate this prolific bird, its portrait is also painted on the bows. In Shetland, to say that you have voyaged on the *Shalder* is tantamount to saying that you have just patronized the Over-land Service, and collected much local news *en route*. This service is operated alternately by buses and ferries, from Lerwick in the south, then via Yell Sound to Unst in the north: a kind of relay service, carefully timed at every stage.

Another service to the North Isles is operated by the *Earl of Zetland*, and if anybody remains deaf to the sea symphony of this route, which covers the ports of Symbister (Whalsey), Mid Yell, Cullivoe (Yell), Uyaesound and Baltasound (Unst), Brough Lodge and Hubie (Fetlar), and Out Skerries, he should be dumped in the middle of the Sahara.

Even now we have not exhausted the exciting possibilities of ferry-ing amongst the Shetlands. The ferrymen of Fair Isle run a converted fishing boat called the *Good Shepherd* to and from Mainland; as Fair Isle lies aloof in the barren ocean, twenty-four miles to the south of Sumburgh Head, the boat's name seems well chosen.

An inter-island air service is envisaged, up here, in the far north, but many of the ferries are likely to remain as indigenous as the birds and the seals and the rock lichens.

My tail-piece must be this story I heard not long ago concerning the Skye Ferry from Mallaig. It epitomizes the essential job of the ferryman.

An English tourist was waiting on the pier for the ferry-boat to take him 'over the sea to Skye'. The ferry was much delayed by stormy winds, but at last, out of the gathering darkness, the tiny boat (as it would seem) heaved into sight, tossed like a cork on the swirling waters. The Englishman approached the pier-master. 'Surely,' he gasped, 'it isn't safe to attempt to reach Skye tonight in a cockleshell like that!'

Mustering a tone that mingled reproach with assurance, the pier-master replied, 'Ye'll get to Skye tonight—*if nothing happens to Skye!*'

INDEX

Aber Ferry, Caern., 102
Aberdovey, Merioneth, 94, 96
Acland, James, 19-20
Adams, Henry, 61, 62
Addingham Ferry, Yorks., 4
Aire, River, 1, 2
Alec-Smith, Alexander, 16
Alec-Smith, Rupert, 15
Alexander I, of Scotland, 140
Allan, John, 57
Anglesey, Isle of, 103
Appledore-Instow Ferry, Devon, 84
Appleton Ferry, Yorks, 5-6
Arran, Earl of, 142
Arun, River, 54
Askew, John, 112-13
Atherton, James, 113
Atkinson, George, 10-11
Augustine, St., 52, 85
Aust-Beachley ferry-boat, 88
Aust Ferry, Glos., 85-6
Austen, Jane, 60
Avon, River, Bristol, 88
Avon, River, Hants., 63
Axholme, Isle of, Lincs., 24

Bablock Hythe Ferry, Oxon, 49
Baldwin, Archbishop, 104
Ballachulish Ferry, Argyll., 150-53
Bangor Ferry, Caern., 103, 105
Bardney Ferry, Lincs., 26
Barmouth, Merioneth, 96-7
Barnack quarries, Northants., 28, 29
Barrow-in-Furness, Lancs., 116, 117
Barry, Bert, 48
Barton Ferry, Lincs., 18-20
Bawdsey Ferry, Suffolk, 37-8
Beale, John, 37
Beaulieu, Hants., 61
Beaulieu River, 61, 62
Beaumaris, Anglesey, 98, 99
Bell, John, 96
Bell, Thomas, 43
Bertram, Robert, 132
Berwick-upon-Tweed, Nthb., 139
Best, James, 7
Beverley Ferry, Yorks., 14-15
Birkenhead Ferry, Cheshire, 110-12, 114
Birkett, Herbert, 124
Bishop's Ferry (or Garth Passage), near
    Bangor, 102
Blackwater, River, Essex, 41
Blackwater Ferry, Hants., 64
Blake, Peter, 72-3

Bodinnick, Cornwall, 76, 77
Bolton, James, 3
Bolton Priory, Yorks., 4
Booth, Laurence, Bishop of Durham, 132
Booth Ferry, Yorks., 13
Boston, Lincs., 27-8
Bottom Boat Ferry, Yorks., 2
Brede, River, 53
Bredwardine, Heref.: Trap House Ferry,
    90
Brereton, Sir William, *Travels*, 145-6
Brewer, Donald, 16
Bridges, Robert, 50
Bristol Channel, 84-5
Brockweir Ferry, Glos., 88
Brownsea Island, Dorset, 66
Buckingham, Duke of, 42
Buckler's Hard, Hants., 61-2
Bure, River, 33, 35
Burgh Island, Devon, 70-1
Burney, Fanny, 31, 32, 69
Burnham Ferry, Essex, 41, 42
Burton, Decimus, 115
Bury Ferry, Sussex, 54
Bury St. Edmunds, Suffolk, 29
Butler, Rodney, *The History of Kirkstall
    Forge*, 1
Butler, Thomas, 102-3
Byng, Hon. John, 98-100

Caernarvon-Abermenai Ferry, 100-1
Calstock Ferry, Cornwall, 75
Camel, River, 83
Campbell, Captain Robert, 152
Campbell, Thomas, 153
Canterbury, 51-2, 97
Cantley Ferry, Norfolk, 33
Canute the Dane, 29
Carroll, Lewis, 133-4
Catchpole, Margaret, 38-9
Catherall, John, 107
Catherine of Braganza, 99, 120
Cawood Ferry, Yorks., 11-12
Cawsand, Cornwall, 74
Charles I, 14, 42, 50, 85-6
Charles II, 120
Charles V, Emperor, 45
Chaucer, Geoffrey, 51, 68, 104
Chepstow, Mon., 88
Chester, 107-8
Chesters Ferry, Nthb., 134
Chiang Yee, 122
Chichester Harbour, Sussex, 55
Christchurch Priory, Hants., 63, 64

157

Clapham, Mrs. Blanche, 76
Clarence, Thomas, Duke of, 32
Clark, Daniel, 34
Clark, Commander I. T., 151
Clark, Mrs. Yvonne, 151
Clark, John and Joseph, 26
Clarke Hall, Yorks., 2, 3
Clifton Ferry, Yorks., 6
Coldham Hall Ferry, Norfolk, 33
Cole, T. J., 76
Coleridge, S. T.., 88
Collings, John, 73
Colne, River, 41
Columba, St., 154
Constable, John, 26, 41
Conway, Caern., 99–100, 104; Ferry, 105–6
Conway, River, 97, 98
Coquet, River, 138
Coracles, 83–4, 91, 92
Cornwall, Barry (Bryan Waller Procter), 19
Cornwall, Earls of, 70, 74, 75
Cory, Robert, 35
Creeksea Ferry, Essex, 41
Cremyll Ferry, Cornwall, 71–4
Crocker, Tom, 71
Cromarty, 'Booner', 138
Crouch, River, 41, 42

Dart, River, 68
Dartmouth-Kingswear Ferry, Devon, 67–8
Davies, Henry Rees, 98
Dawson, Sir Benjamin and Lady, 5, 6
Deben, River, 36–8
Dee, River, 107–9
Defoe, Daniel, 18, 20, 36, 71, 84
Deganwy Ferry, Caern., 104
Derwent, River, Nthb., 134
Derwent, River, Yorks., 13
Derwentwater Ferry, Cumb., 122–4
Dickens, Charles, 48, 51, 102
Dittisham Ferry, Devon, 69
Dogdyke Ferry, Lincs., 27
Doggett, Thomas, 48
Doughty, Peter, 115
Douglas, Hugh, *Crossing the Forth*, 140
Dovey estuary, 94–6, 104
Dovey Ferry, Wales, 95–6
Doyle, Miss Camilla, 35
Drake, Gilbert, 69
Duckham, Baron F., *The Yorkshire Ouse*, 6
Dunfermline, Fife, 143
Dunham Ferry, Notts., 26
Dunster Castle, Somerset 68
Durham, 131

Eccleston Ferry, Cheshire, 108
Edgcumbe family and estate, 72–4
Edmund, St., 29
Edric, legend of, 48–9
Edward the Elder, 85
Edward the Confessor, 24
Edward I, 104, 108, 139
Edward III, 53, 110
Egremont Ferry, Mersey, 112–13
Eliot, George, *The Mill on the Floss*, 25
Elizabeth I, 42, 45–7, 60, 66
Elwell, Fred, 14–15
Ennion, Dr. E. A. R., 29
Erskine Ferry, Scotland, 149
Exmouth-Starcross Ferry, Devon, 69

Fairfax, General Thomas, 6
Fal, River, 80
Fambridge Ferry, Essex, 42
Farndon Ferry, Notts., 25
Felixstowe, Suffolk, 39
Fenwick, Colonel George, 132
Feolin-Port Askaig Ferry, Scotland, 155
Ferres, Thomas, 20–1
Ferry-boats
  Antrim Princess, 148
  Armadillo, 74
  Border Chief, 139
  Border Pride, 139
  Caledonian Princess, 145, 147–8
  Cambria, 110
  Carrier, 75
  Cleddau King, 92
  Cygnet, 150
  Despatch, 87
  Dolphin, 150
  Drake, 122
  Duke of Lancaster, 118
  Earl of Zetland, 156
  Etna, 114
  Fairy, 114
  Forester, 61
  Good Shepherd, 156
  Guarantee, 116
  Harry Glasper, 114
  Helvellyn, 116
  Hirta, 155
  Iona, 150
  Iris, 124
  Jane, 87
  Jemima, 74
  King Fergus, 148
  Lady Beatrice, 38
  Lady Quilter, 38
  Lapwing, 150
  Lincoln Castle, 20
  Magna Carta, 20
  Mary Queen of Scots, 142

Ferry-boats (*continued*)
 May Queen, 122
 Mercury, 137
 Patriot, 18n.
 Pelham, 23–4
 Planet, 137
 Playfair, 116
 Prince Albert, 59
 Princess Louise, 147
 Princess of Wales, 59
 Public Opinion, 19
 Queen Margaret, 142
 Robert the Bruce, 142
 Royal Charter, 19
 Royal George, 1–2
 Shalder, 156
 Shuttlecock, 74
 Sovereign, 23–4
 Star, 137
 Tattershall Castle, 20
 Thomas Wilson, 114
 Venus, 137
 Viking, 66, 116
 Waterlily, 114
 Wingfield Castle, 20
Ferryside-Llanstephan Ferry, Carm., 91
Fiennes, Celia, 63, 73, 112
FitzGerald, Edward, 37–8
Flambard, Rannulf, 131
Fleetwood, Sir Peter Hesketh, 115
Fleetwood Ferry, Lancs., 115–17
Forth Bridge, 141–2
Foster, Miss F., 36
Foster, Gilbert, 4
Fowey, Cornwall, 76–7
Framilode Ferry, Glos., 88

Gallico, Paul, *The Snow Goose*, 150
Galsworthy, John, 54
Garth-Port Dinorwic Ferry, Menai Straits, 103
George I, 48
George IV, 114
Ghostly Crier of Claife, 121–2
Gilbert, Sir Humphrey, 67, 69
Gill, Dick, 124–5
Gilpin, William, 86–7
Giraldus Cambrensis, 91, 94, 104
Glencoe, massacre of, 151–2
Glenelg Ferry, Inv., 154
Glover, William, 124
Goodrich Castle, Heref., 89
Goodrich-Kerne Ferry, Heref., 90
Granton-Burntisland Ferry, Midlothian, 141
Great Ouse, 31–2
Great Yarmouth, Norfolk, 35
Green, Harold, 48

Green, Walter, 11
Grimsby-Hull Ferry, 23
Gunwade Ferry, at Milton, Northants., 28–9

Haldane, H. C., 2
Haldingham, Richard de, 90, 91
Halton Ferry, Cornwall, 75
Hampton Load Ferry, Shropshire, 93
Hamworthy Ferry, Dorset, 65–6
Handel, G. F., 48
Hannay, John, 147
Harold, King, 25
Harwich-Zeebrugge Train Ferry, 40
Hastings, Sussex, 54
Hatfield, Bishop, 132
Hatton, Admiral Sir Christopher, 65
Hawes, Captain, 147
Hawthorne, Nathaniel, 114, 115
Hayle Ferry, Cornwall, 83
Hayling Island, Hants., 55
Heath, Charles, 89
Helford Ferry, Cornwall, 76
Henbury, John, 65–6
Henderson, Charles, 71, 79, 81
Hengistbury Head, Hants., 64
Henry III, 33
Henry IV, 44, 89–90
Henry V, 44, 89
Henry VI, 44, 79–80, 132
Henry VIII, 42, 45, 79, 85
Herbert, St., 123–5
Hereford, 90
Hereward the Wake, 29
Herringfleet Ferry, Suffolk, 35
Hoby, Lady Margaret, 18
Hodgson, Victor, 122, 123
Hogg, T. J., 105
Hoggart, Thomas, 'Lament', 120–1
Hooe Ferry, Cornwall, 75
Horning Ferry, Norfolk, 33, 34
Horsey Ferry, Hunts., 29
Howden Dyke Ferry, Yorks., 14
Hudson, George, 8
Hull, Peter, 72
Hullbridge Ferry, Essex, 42
Humber, River: Humber Ferry, 1, 17–18, 22–3; Stoneferry, 16; Maison Dieu, 16; proposed bridge, 16, 22; Barton Ferry, 18–19; Thomas Ferres of Hull, 20–1; Grimsby-Hull Ferry, 23–4
Hunderton Ferry, Heref., 90
Hungus (Pictish king), 140
Hythe Ferry, Hants., 60–1

Iona, Argyll., 154
Itchen Ferry, Hants., 60

Jack-y-Garth, 102
James VI, of Scotland, 140
Jarrow-Howden Ferry, Co. Durham, 136, 137
Johnson, Dr. Samuel, 87, 105, 153

Ken, Meredith ap, 98
Kent, River, 118–20
Kerne Bridge, Heref., 89
King Harry Ferry, Cornwall, 76, 79–80
King's Lynn, Norfolk, 31–5
Kingsley, Charles, 67; *Westward Ho!*, 84
Kinnard Ferry, Lincs., 24–5
Kirkstall Abbey, Yorks., 1
Kirkstall Forge, Yorks., 1
Knox, John, 143
Kyleakin Ferry, Skye, 154

Lambton Ferry, Co. Durham, 131
Lancaster, Edmund, Earl of, 111
Landguard-Harwich Ferry, Harwich Harbour, 39
Laneham Ferry, Lincs., 25
Langrick Ferry, Lincs., 27
Laud, Stephen, 39
Laud, Will, 38–9
Laugharne, Carm., 91–2
Ledgard, Rev. J. Christopher, 155
Leland, John, 65
Lenche, William, 72
Lepe Ferry, Hants., 61
Lincoln, 26
Lindisfarne (Holy Island) Nthb., 138
Linklater, Eric, *Orkney and Shetland*, 155
Little Ouse, 33
Littleborough Ferry, Lincs., 25
Liverpool Ferry, 110–13, 115
Longcroft, Charles J., 55
Looe Ferry, Cornwall, 75
Lucy, Sir Eustace de, 113
Lund, Tommy, 12
Luttrell, Lt.-Col. Walter, 68
Lymington, Hants., 62
Lynher River, 75

MacBrayne's ferry services, 150, 153
Macdonald, Sir Godfrey Bosville, 154
MacDonald, J. Ramsey, 140, 142, 149–50
McIntyre, G. S., 132
Maison Dieu (now the Charterhouse), Yorks., 16
Malmesbury, Earl of, 64
Margaret, Queen, 140, 142
Marvell, Rev. Andrew, 19
Marvell, Andrew, 6
Mary Stuart, 143
Medway, River, 51

Menai ferries, Wales, 98–101
Mersey, River, 109–10; Birkenhead Ferry, 110–11; Liverpool-Birkenhead rivalries, 111–12; other ferries, 112–15
Miller, Eli, 64
Mitchell, Richard, 124, 125
Mollet, Cecil, 34
Montagu, John Duke of, 61, 62
Montagu, Lord, 62
Morden Robert, 108, 109
Morecambe Bay, Lancs., 116, 118–19
Morgan, D. W., *Brief Glory*, 96
Morris, William, *News from Nowhere*, 49
Mount Edgcumbe. *See* Edgcumbe family and estate
Mudeford Ferry, Hants., 64
Mull Ferry, Argyll., 150, 154
Murdac, Henry, Archbishop of York, 15

Naburn Ferry, Yorks., 10
Nene, River, 28
Nennius, 16–17
Nevern, River, 93
New Brighton, Cheshire, 110, 113, 114
New Holland, Lincs., 23
Newby, N. M., 126
Newby Hall, Yorks., 9
Newcastle-upon-Tyne, Nthb., 135–7
Newnham Ferry, Glos., 88
Newport Ferry, Pemb., 93
Newson, Thomas, 37
Newton, John, 6
Nichol End Ferry, Cumb., 124–6
Noel-Buxton, Lord, 17
Norfolk, Dukes of, 54, 55
North Shields Ferry, Nthb., 136, 137
Norwich, Norfolk, 34
Nun Appleton Hall, Yorks., 5–6
Nun Monkton, Yorks., 6

Oare Church, Somerset, 84
Orwell, River, 39
Osborne, I. o. W., 59
Ouse, River, Sussex, 54
Ouse, River, Yorks., 6–14

Padstow, Cornwall, 83
Par Ferry, Cornwall, 76, 79
Parry, Grace, 102
Passiful, Ablett, 38
Patrick, St., 118, 144
Peel, J. H. B., *Portrait of the Thames*, 50
Pegwell Bay, Kent, 52
Pelham Steam Company, 23
Pepys, Samuel, 45–6, 60
Peterborough, 28
Piel Island, Lancs., 127

Pill Ferry, Somerset, 88
Pitt, Govenor, 76
Pole, Michael de la, 16
Poole Harbour, Dorset, 65-7
Poppleton Ferry, Yorks., 6
Port Patrick Ferry, Wig., 144-8
Porthaethwy (Bangor) Ferry, Caern., 101
Portington Hall, Yorks., 14
Prebble, John, *The Story of the Massacre* 151
Press Gang, 3, 39
Pretty, Mrs. E. M., 37
Pritchard, Dr. Arthur, 106
Pull, John, 34

Queensferry, West Lothian, 140-3
Quiller-Couch, Sir Arthur, 75-8
Quiller-Couch, Miss Foy, 77, 78
Quilter, Sir Cuthbert, 38

Raleigh, Sir Walter, 69, 84
Ramsey Abbey, Hunts., 29
Rawnsley, Rev. H. D., 125
Red Fox, 152-3
Redbrook Ferry, Mon., 89
Redhill Ferry, Hants., 65
Redstone, the Misses G. and L., 37
Regan, Captain J. L., 112, 113
Renfrew-Yoker Ferry, Scotland, 149
Ribble, River, 80
Richard II, 108
Riddlesford, Hants., 65
Roa Island Ferry, Lancs., 116, 127
Roach, River, 41
Roberts, Thomas, 26
Rock Ferry, Cheshire, 112-14
Rockliffe Castle, Cumb., 127
Roger le Ferman, 55
Roscoe, Thomas, 57-8
Rustyngton Ferry, Sussex, 54
Ryan, Loch, Wig., 147
Ryde, I.o.W., 56, 58-9
Rye Ferry, Sussex, 52-3
Ryther Ferry, Yorks., 5
Ryton Ferry, Nthb., 135

Sadler, Sir Ralph, 12
St. Benet's Abbey, Norfolk, 33
St. Herbert's Island, Cumb., 123, 124
St. Ives, Cornwall, 83
St. Just, Cornwall, 80
St. Mawes Ferry, Cornwall, 80
St. Michael's Mount, Cornwall, 81-2
Salcombe-Portlemouth Ferry, Devon, 70
Saltash Ferry, Cornwall, 71, 74
Saltney Ferry, Cheshire, 108-9

Salvin, Thomas, 96
Sandling, Germaine, 34
Sandside Ferry, Lancs., 119-20
Saracen's Head Ferry, Heref., 89
Savage, Charlie, 88
Saxton, Christopher, 60
Scalloway Ferry, Shetland, 155
Scott, Peter, *The Eye of the Wind*, 119
Scott, Sir Walter, 120, 127, 130, 144
Segelocum, 25
Selby Ferry, Yorks., 12-13
Severn, River; the Old and the New Passages, 85-8; the Tunnel, English Stones, other ferries, 88
Shamble, Mary, 56
Sheffield, Sir John, 14
Sherborne Abbey, Dorset, 69-70
Short, Bernard C., 67
Siddons, Sarah, 146, 148
Skiddaw, Cumb., 123
Skirlaugh, Walter, Bishop of Durham, 13-14
Skye, Inv., 153-4, 156
Slingsby, Sir Charles, 10
Slingsby, Sir Henry, 18
Smeaton, John, 13
Snodland Ferry, Kent, 51
Solway Firth, 127
South Shields, Nthb., 137
Southampton, 59-61
Southwold-Walberswick Ferry, Suffolk, 35-6
Spittal, Robert, 144
Spittal Ferry, Nthb., 139
Stanground Ferry, Hunts., 29
Stanley Ferry, Yorks., 2-3
Stephenson, Robert, 87
Stevenson, R. L., 67, 142, 143, 152
Stewart-Brown, R., 112
Stixwold Ferry, Lincs., 26-7
Stockton-on-Tees, Co. Durham: Bishop's Ferry, 130
Stoke Bardolph Ferry, Notts., 25
Stoke Ferry, Norfolk, 33
Stoneferry, Yorks., 16
Stoniewath, Cumb., 127
Stour, River, Hants., 63-5
Stour, River, Kent, 51-2
Stour, River, Suffolk, 41
Stow, John, *Survey of London*, 44-6
Stranraer Ferry, Wig., 144, 147-9
Stukeley, William, *Itinerarium Curiosum*, 17-18
Sunderland Ferry, Co. Durham, 131-4
Surlingham Ferry, Norfolk, 33
Sutton Hoo Ship Burial, Suffolk, 37
Swanage, Dorset, 67
Sweine Estrithson, 17
Swire, Otta F., 154
Symonds Yat, Heref., 89

Tal-y-Cafn Ferry, Caern., 106
Tamar, River, 71, 72
Tattershall Bridge, Lincs., 27
Taylor, John, 20, 47, 50, 53-4
Teifi, River, 91
Teign, River, 70
Teignmouth-Shaldon Ferry, Devon, 70
Teith, River, 144
Telford, Thomas, 87, 103, 105
Ten Mile Bank Ferry, Norfolk, 33
Tenby-Caldy Island Ferry, Pembr., 92
Terrington St. Clement, Norfolk, 29
Thames, River: Tilbury, 42-4; the Long
  Ferry, 44; processions etc., 44-6, 48;
  the watermen, 46-8; Doggett's Coat
  and Badge, 48; legend of Edric, 48-9;
  ferries on the upper reaches, 49-50
Thanet, Isle of, 52
Thomas, Anne, 104-5
Thomas, Dylan, 91
Thorney Abbey, Cambs., 29
Thurne Ferry, Norfolk, 33
Tilbury, William de, 44
Tilbury: Gravesend-Tilbury Ferry (Cross
  Ferry), 42-4; the Fort, 42; World's
  End Inn, 43
Tillingham, River, 53-4
Tintern Abbey, Mon., 88
Tolverne Ferry, Cornwall, 81
Torpoint Ferry, Cornwall, 71, 73-5
Towing Path Act (1809), 90
Towy, River, 91
Tranmere Ferry, Cheshire, 114, 115
Trent, River, 24-6
Tressilian River, 81
Trevelyan, Lady Mary, 81
Tryon-Wilson, Brigadier, 119-20
Tuck, Rev. Julian, 36
Turner, J. M. W., 48, 54, 88
Tweed, River, 130, 139
Twickenham Ferry, 48
Tyne, River, 130, 135-6

Ure, River, 9-10

Vantini, Zenon, 116
Victoria, Queen, 59, 130

Wagtaile Ferry, Suffolk, 39
Walberswick, Suffolk, 35
Wall, S. D., 39
Wallasey, Cheshire: Seacombe Ferry,
  112, 114

Walmsley, Leo, 77
Walney Island, Lancs., 126-7
Walpole, Hugh, 122, 123
Walton, Suffolk: Ferry Boat Inn, 39
Warkworth, Nthb., 138
Warner, Richard, 105
Washingborough Ferry, Lincs., 26
Watermen and Lightermen, Company of,
  46, 48
Waters, Brian, 91
Waveney, River, 35
Wawne Ferry, Yorks., 15-16
Wear, River, 130-3
Wearmouth, Co. Durham, 131-2
Wesley, John, 14, 24, 73-4, 101
West Kinnard Ferry, Lincs., 24
West Wittering-Hayling Island Ferry,
  Hants., 55
Westminster Abbey, 49
Wilberforce-Bell, Sir Harold, 14
Wharfe, River, 3-6
Whitgift Ferry, Yorks., 14, 24
Whorlton Ferry, Co. Durham, 130
Wick Ferry, Hants., 63
Wiggenhall St. Germans Church, Nor-
  folk, 30
Wight, Isle of, 63; ferries, 56-9
Will the Boatman, 128-9
William the Conqueror, 25, 29
William of Orange, 26
Williams, Hugh, 100-1
Windermere Ferry, Westm., 120-2
Wissey, River, 33
Witham, River, 26-7
Wolsey, Cardinal, 11, 44-5
Wombwell, Sir George, 10
Wood, Donald, 4
Woodbridge, Suffolk, 36-7
Woodruffe-Peacock, E. B., 23
Woodside Ferry, Cheshire, 112, 114-15
Wordsworth, Dorothy, 88-9, 143-4
Wordsworth, William, 88-9, 109, 120
Wright, Leonard C., 11
Wye, River, 88-90
Wyre, River, 115, 116

Yarborough Hotel, Lincs., 23
Yare, River, 33
Yarmouth, I.o.W., ferry packets, 62
Yell Ferry, Shetland, 156
York Ferries, 6-9
York and Ainsty Hunt, 10
Younghusband, Rev. Edward, 26